Missing Persons

Missing Persons

JACK OLSEN

New York 1981 ATHENEUM

NOTE: *The city in this work is a creation of the author's imagination, as is every character. The massacre of Monte Sole is a historical fact, however, and the references to it are based on interviews with the few survivors.*

Library of Congress Cataloging in Publication Data

Olsen, Jack.
    Missing persons.

    I. Title.
PS3565.L77M5   1981   813'.54   80–69375
ISBN 0–689–11133–9

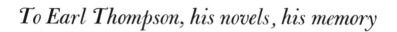

To Earl Thompson, his novels, his memory

I Tuesday, August 12

1

Early on the night his wife disappeared, Gamble spotted the dirty black clouds of a squall approaching from the bay. He congratulated himself on his timing. They would be under cover before the storm hit, and when the movie was over, they would exit into a laundered night: the hollow sky dotted with stars and a new breeze off the water and their faithful old car beaded with rain.

He glanced at Margot, sitting alongside him in the open TR-3. Her narrow thighs were splayed like a schoolgirl's, her tanned face tilted back in the windstream, her eyes shut. She could relax in seconds—anywhere. He wished he could.

As they bumped across the tracks at Bayshore, he noticed a light salty sea-smell, as though someone in the distance had opened a single clam. Port cities pleased his senses; he enjoyed the moist air and the waterfront bedlam and the way the old neighborhoods perched on scalloped hills over the bay. The early settlers must have been drawn to the water the way the eye is drawn to a point or a line or a splotch of color in a fine painting. Nearly a million people lived here now, and yet it seemed to Gamble that the city retained its authenticity and its grace.

The sharpening wind was off the fir and cedar forests across the bay, and the only pollution came from open-front stalls where shrimp and oysters and fish were browned into carboniferous husks in hot oil. He liked to come down here with his big Strathmore pad and Niji pens and sketch auklets and herring gulls preening the water for snacks, harbor seals broaching in the ferry wakes, killer whales flashing their black and white flanks in the sun. He couldn't resist another deep sniff.

"What're *you* smiling about?" Margot asked, raising her dark eyes toward him. He hadn't smiled, but she had sensed his pleasure. She was always surprising him that way: reading his mood, anticipating.

"The air," he said. "I was just kind of . . . breathing."

"That smelly *smell?*" Her thin retroussé nose crinkled, and she reminded him, as she often did, of all the classic portraits waiting to be done. *Margot Seated in TR-3, after Modigliani.*

"Yeah," he said. "Low slack tide. Rotting seaweed, eelgrass, old bait, the whole mix. Smells *good* to me. I ever tell you that, hon?"

"Yes, Severn. About a hundred times. This year."

She giggled, and his face warmed. Was he becoming repetitious? Senile at twenty-nine? God, what would she be saying on their golden anniversary? *Severn, you're been telling that same story for fifty years. . . .*

"We all repeat ourselves once in a while," he said, feeling suddenly dull—six feet five inches of insufficiency—the way he'd always seen himself before he'd discovered palette knives and pigments and point chisels.

She leaned across and kissed his ginger beard, and a few loose strands of her long black hair tickled his nose. "You always sound new to me, angel," she said.

They sped past a ruined forest of masts—seiners, crab boats, long-liners, gill-netters, drag boats, trollers, and a disheveled old whaler taking on provisions. Rusty stains mottled her plates like tobacco juice. He craned his neck to see the registry: Yokohama. Why were whalers always so soiled? From shame? His artist's eye spotted an imbalance: The vessel sat at an angle, stern submerged to the Plimsoll, bow rising. Whoever painted that picture, he said to himself, will have to repeat the course.

The Triumph's balding tires whirred over the metal grid of the East Canal bridge, and he had a fleeting view across five miles of bay. The squall was approaching fast, pressuring the water into agitated ripples. Anchored freighters swung their prows into the stiffening breeze and rode deeper on their chains. Huddling gulls and ducks turned suddenly neckless, their feathers blowing the wrong way in wisps. The sky changed from the rose tint of early evening to a deep Prussian blue as a screen of clouds streamed across at a slant, parting briefly to reveal lighter and darker layers moving along in different planes.

A skewed sky, Gamble mused. If he could only catch all that motion and energy on canvas . . . Would the faculty board's eight old anachronisms call the painting unnatural, "lacking balance and restraint," the way they had the last time? But nature itself could be unbalanced and unnatural, he argued in his head, where he won all debates to tumultuous applause. Nature itself could be as gaudy as a Mexican painting on black velvet. Just the evening before, he had watched the setting sun bathe the sky in a flamingo wash. Not red, not purple, not coral, but flamingo as loud as a Vegas marquee. Gamble had shouted for his wife to quit typing and look, and with arms entwined they had drunk in the gaudy sight till an unexpected squirt of viridian green had marked the close of day.

"Who'd believe a flamingo sunset?" Margot had said. She'd pulled him close and asked in her throaty voice, "Anyway, what would you mix to make flamingo?"

"Two flamingos?" Gamble had answered, and she'd rewarded him with a giggle and a kiss. Ever since his one-man show had failed, she'd been the perfectly adoring, perfectly supportive, perfectly perfect artist's wife, ready to argue with anyone that his paintings were bolder than

Pollock's, more subtle than Manet's, and at least as imaginative as Picasso's, except that poor Picasso lacked Gamble's splash technique. She *embarrassed* him with support.

Then how could Ciel have happened? Of all the rotten things to do to a woman like Margot . . .

As they approached downtown, she leaned across the seat to rest against his shoulder and pat his cheek. "What a nice birthday," she said softly.

The Slow sign came up like a diamond-format Mondrian, and he rammed through the intersection. "It won't be such a nice birthday if we don't beat the storm," he said. "You and your party dress." It was her new summer shift, ounces of nylon in blue so dark it was almost black.

"And my party feet!" she added, curling her long legs up to reveal the thonged sandals from Ecuador. "Oh, Severn, you have the nicest taste. Who else would have thought of these?"

Anyone else going broke, Gamble said to himself. The shoes had cost $7.45 at Pier Imports, and in her size, too. Not a store in town stocked 7AAA. Such fine, slender feet, supporting such an . . . *economical* body. The body of a store model, her first job. His own feet were 13C and shod in a ratty pair of Saucony Hornets that once were tan before successive layers of oil paint had spattered them into surreal objects of art. I ought to offer them at Sotheby's, he told himself, chortling under his beard. My shoes'll be a commercial success before my paintings. . . .

"*Now* what're you smirking about?"

"Huh?" He yanked the leather-wrapped steering wheel, and the Triumph spurted around a city bus that smelled as though it were running on urine. "Oh . . . nothing."

They had reached the old part of the waterfront where the Justice Building and the Unicorn Art Theater stood a few blocks from each other, and a lucky juxtaposition, too, Gamble told himself, since they were going to both places. It wouldn't be much of a birthday observance;

they'd already seen *Le Jour s'élève* twice.

"You gonna be in there long?" he asked as the bulk of the J-Building loomed in its rime of sooty black.

"A minute, that's all. He said he'd leave the work with the janitor."

"With *who*?" An air cover of fat gulls flapped nervously above the car and wheeled out of sight.

"The janitor—I mean the maintenance man."

"The building engineer," he corrected her. "Janitor's a cuss word, like *broad*. The whole world's turning into a euphemism."

"And you're turning into a grouch," she said, touching the tip of his nose. "I'll be in and out fast. So be patient . . . this once."

Well, at least it wouldn't happen again. Ciel had phoned today—hinting?—and he had cut her short. . . .

"Look," he said as the main entrance came into view with its faded American flag. "Officer Friendly." A police van was parked in front.

"The latest in the war on crime," Margot said. "No stopping in front of the J-Building till after seven."

"Not even to drop somebody off?"

"Nope. Pull around the corner. It's only a few steps."

He made the turn and stopped. "See ya 'round," she said. The last he saw of his wife was the flash of her ankle sliding from the car.

He squeezed the Triumph into a parking place between two Detroit ore carriers and took another deep gulp of the waterfront air; it smelled less saline now as the storm approached. When a raindrop hit him in the eye, he buttoned up the convertible and began an impatient tapping against the bare-metal pedals.

They had just enough time if she didn't dawdle. He'd rather not arrive half-drowned. He looked at his steel-rimmed watch: 6:49. She'd been gone . . . four minutes. High above the little car, the wind was coming to life in whoops and whines. The bottom half of the J-Building had been made of polished black-veined marble slabs, the upper half of umber-colored textured brick, as though the money had run out. At the roofline, a member of the Viennese school of marzipan design had fashioned a busy edging of scrolls and curls that caught the wind and sheltered birds. Well, at least the guy tried, Gamble reminded himself. At least he produced something more imaginative than the giant-sized box of Cap'n Crunch that's going up to replace it.

He tried to pinpoint the source of his grumpiness and knew it was the same old thing: the fact that his wife took in typing. It wasn't much different from taking in wash. As the rain began to peck at the windshield, he thought of all the nights and weekends she banged away at her secondhand Selectric, transcribing tapes or deciphering handwritten notes while every clink of the old type-writer's bell reproached him for his failures. He yearned for the day when his shows wouldn't fail and they could start making kids together and there'd be no more cheap piecework for a bunch of new lawyers who couldn't afford secretaries. And no more kissing the ass of the faculty board either. "Artist in Residence." Another euphemism. Fancy name for a bum. Were welfare cases "workers in residence"?

He wondered what was keeping her. Was she searching room by room for the janitor? Correction: building engineer. No, *building engineer in residence;* that was it. He didn't like the idea of Margot's going inside to pick up a package from a stranger.

He almost laughed out loud at himself. Christ, he was turning paranoid. This was the Justice Building! What a joke. Soon the wreckers would flatten it. Whole floors were already abandoned; slabs of steel sealed off all the basement windows, but the old beldam was still head-quarters of the city police and the county sheriff and the few courts that hadn't moved to the cereal box. Even now, just before seven o'clock on a stormy Tuesday evening, there were bound to be cops and deputies inside, prosecutors, bailiffs, jailers, maybe a few judges working late. Some danger!

In a marriage as close as ours, Gamble thought as he leaned back and closed his eyes, a hell of a lot of mental energy is wasted worrying about each other. Sometimes the relationship seems as much parental as marital. Is that love? Of course it is.

An image of Ciel popped into his mind, and he felt like a hypocrite. Ciel hadn't represented love. Stupidity, lust, selfishness, yes. But not love . . .

He opened his eyes and sighed. The first raindrops lifted puffs of dust from the sidewalk. The cold green digits on his ten-dollar watch blinked a warning that the movie started in . . . six minutes. A single sheet of newspaper fluttered up the street. The summer sky had darkened to something between violet and indigo, the last two colors of the visible spectrum. They could still beat the storm; a little rain wouldn't drown their evening. And once they were in the lobby, let it come down! A free car wash. Two bucks saved . . .

The wind picked up. The color drained from the sky. She couldn't possibly take much longer. His fingers brushed back the sleeve of his best Levi shirt, and he watched the ghostly numbers blink into view on his watch: 6:58.

Now they *would* be late. And wet. The rain began to beat across the windshield at a slant. A few dead leaves spiraled through the air. Any second, the deluge. It seemed so degrading to subject themselves to a drenching just to pick up eight or ten dollars' worth of free-lance typing. Couldn't it have waited? Why not *after* the movie? But she'd said she would feel more comfortable if she made the pickup first; she wanted to give her full attention to her birthday movie.

At exactly seven o'clock he squeezed his long body from under the wheel of the Triumph and locked both doors. Margot had already spent fifteen minutes on a two-minute chore. Probably prowling the building looking for the damned maintenance man. Well, he'd go in and help find the guy, and they'd rush to the Unicorn and maybe miss only the previews.

The police van was still parked in front as he passed in his long stride. One of the cops was behind the wheel, face in shadow, and the other was closing the rear doors. Gamble took the wide granite staircase three steps at a time, muscled through the bronze entranceway, and dried his lenses on a paint-stained handkerchief. When he shoved the glasses back on his nose, the shadowy lobby came into view.

High above, a reticulated dome of bottle green glass had been stained almost black by the years and the pigeons. A weak lemony light leaked from a gap-toothed chandelier thirty feet above the floor. Sandstone gargoyles stood in a wide semicircle, guarding shallow niches. Faded murals looked as though they had been scrubbed every day for a hundred years; the thin light made them even harder to see and therefore not as unsettling as they had seemed when Gamble had first visited the lobby as an art student and gawked at the cut-rate Orozco: radial-engined airplanes and a puffy blimp and triple-stacked ocean liners and steam locomotives crisscrossing each other's trajectories.

There I go again, he admonished himself, knocking some poor sucker's work, comforting myself with the silly syllogism of the unrecognized artist: *My efforts don't pay off, and my efforts are honest and good; therefore, all efforts that do pay off must be dishonest and lousy.* Well, all other efforts weren't lousy. Just this one . . .

No one attended the heavy metal reception desk, but something was centered atop the scratched surface. The manila envelope appeared to glow in the strange light, as though a single ray had been aimed on it from the old chandelier. Over an indecipherable signature, he read: "MARGOT GAMBLE Hold for Pickup. Tnx!"

He frowned. In fifteen minutes she hadn't even reached this desk?

He jerked his head around. The cavernous hall was hushed. He whispered, "Margot?" without thinking, then *"Margot?"* again, louder. There was no answer.

2

Johnny Boon ripped a "Wanted For" off the teletype and stared through a cloud of smoke at the latest in the endless parade of fools and assassins who cluttered his life. For a second the words seemed blurred, and he moved the message a half inch closer to his face. That police surgeon *can't* be right, he said to himself. I do *not* need glasses. What's he think I am, a goddamn fingerprint clerk? Does a guy that can drill twenty out of twenty bobbing targets need glasses? How many would I hit if I wore glasses? *Twenty-one* out of twenty, for Chrisakes . . . ?

He brushed the canary-colored hairs from his eyes, fired several short salvos from his Swisher Sweet miniature cigar, and dumped the "Wanted For" in the trash. If the police department of Pascagoula, Mississippi, wished his assistance in locating Forest W. ("Booger") Johnson, they'd have to write something more inspiring than "wanted for suspicion of burglary." In Boon's file, burglary was a petty offense.

The alerter produced its raucous squawk. He lowered

his Thom McAn aviator boots from the desk, took three steps in his loose-hipped shamble, and picked up the phone.

"Boonhomicide," he said. He halfway hoped for a run. Anything would be an improvement on two hours of staring at the want books and reading arrest reports and wondering if the French Foreign Legion would accept a thirty-four-year-old dick with ulcers.

"Foot of Sunset, Sarge," the night dispatcher's voice squawked. Men in Nam had shouted "incoming" more soothingly. "One DB. White male. Elderly. Parked car. See the officer."

"Dead body? A traffic stiff? Why me?" Bored or not, he couldn't leave the office for a milk run.

"Supposed to be a hole in the victim's head."

"What size?"

"About twenty-two."

"A suicide, huh? Why the hell—"

"Something's—"

"—send me?"

"—missing, Sarge."

"Huh? What's missing?"

"A gun."

He grabbed his short gabardine jacket, cinched up his brass-tipped lariat tie in its silver bolo ring, and hit the hallway at a trot.

In the elevator he stepped behind a judge—Betty Jane Holder, the cop hater—and blew a burst of smoke at the back of her short gray hair. Years ago she'd bawled him out for smoking in the jury box during recess. Her Holiness was flanked by a couple of lawyer types in dark raincoats and shined shoes. The queen and her court . . .

The lobby was empty except for a tall bearded freak standing by the desk. Boon slowed when he passed close and looked up at the man's face. There was fear and panic there—the same puzzled squinty look that fighters get when they're decked by a left hook the other guy doesn't have.

He couldn't stop. If the dude needed help, he was in the right building. Time to find out how this DB blew himself away. Without a gun . . .

3

Gamble felt stupid for not approaching the elevator occupants and asking if they had seen Margot. But the heavy woman in the sensible shoes had hurried out the front door with the two men in her wake, and the broken-nosed man in the cowboy tie had disappeared into a door marked Police Garage.

He heard the sound of feet shuffling around the corner and turned to find the building engineer approaching on the bias, like a crab fighting the tide. "Uh, sir?" the artist said, feeling self-conscious. The thin, short man unlocked a closet at the far end of the elevator bank and pulled out a wheeled cart of tools and equipment.

"My wife," Gamble said, talking louder. "She was, uh, she was supposed to pick up this envelope."

The little man turned, his face as benign as a Botticelli *cherubino* hanging in space. When he saw Gamble, he smiled apologetically and held out his hands, palms up, as though the statement had been difficult to comprehend. Or was he deaf?

"Did you see her?"

The maintenance man mumbled and grinned, showing yellowing niblet teeth with a few missing. He had a pasty complexion like a newborn mouse, as though he never left the building.

"Excuse me, I didn't hear you," the artist said.

"No." The word seemed extruded with effort from the region of the belt buckle.

"You didn't see her at all?" His voice broke like an adolescent's. "You *must* have. I just let her out. At the corner."

The janitor shook his head and began pushing his cart down the hall on its squeaky rollers.

Gamble caught up in a few strides. "She was coming in here to pick up this envelope. See? She does—typing." He shaped his big hands over an imaginary keyboard. "Margot Gamble? Tall? Black hair? Kind of, uh, slender?"

The man peered intently at one of Gamble's slightly walled eyes, then at the other, then at the domed ceiling. "Nobody come. No lady. Nobody." His manner said he hoped he would be forgiven if the answer was unacceptable.

"A woman didn't walk in here in the last fifteen minutes?"

"Nobody." The janitor exposed a slit of pale tangerine gumline on one side of his mouth; it appeared to be intended as a reassuring smile. Maybe there was a language barrier. Gamble thought he'd detected an accent. Maybe the guy was a retard, a war victim. God knew what poor souls they were hiring these days for custodial jobs. Half the newsvendors were blind.

He touched the man on the arm and felt the stringy muscles contract. "I let my wife out around the corner awhile ago," he said, trying not to sound like a hysteric. "She was coming in here to pick up this package. From *you.*"

The man pulled away, the smile fading from his gray eyes. "*Nessuno.* No see nobody."

Gamble spun around. "Margot!" he called. His voice came back in a hollow echo. "I can't believe it," he said as the janitor hurried away. "I can't be*lieve* it!" Of all the crazy stunts—where the hell *is* she?

Settle down, he ordered himself. *Cool it.* You're acting like a jerk. There's a logical explanation; there has to be.

She could have come in a side door and bumped into somebody she knew—a client, a judge maybe, a big shot, somebody she couldn't ignore—and they're still gabbing away, and pretty soon she'll come rushing in and grab the package, full of apologies.

But that would be totally unlike Margot. She would never make them late for her favorite French movie. Besides, there was no side door. There was only one main entrance—and she hadn't come through it.

Or had she come through and then walked back to the car and somehow, in the rain and confusion, passed him on the way?

That was it! They'd both walked with their heads down, trying to keep their faces out of the rain. Talk about weird . . . But hadn't he already told himself there had to be a simple explanation?

He turned and started toward the exit almost at a run and stopped so fast he skidded into the door and braked himself with both hands. If she was on her way back to the car, why was the package still on the desk?

Is it possible she had never come through the door in the first place? Is it possible that somebody . . . ?

The thought made him blink in the dim light.

Oh, Jesus, somebody grabbed her!

But . . . who? *Why?*

The cops! Were they still parked in front? They'd have noticed.

The heavy door eased shut as he returned to the pelting rain.

The green and white police van was just pulling away from the curb when he ran up, his long arms flailing the air. "Hey!" he shouted into gusts of spray. He thought he saw one of the cops turn and look back over his shoulder, but the van accelerated and disappeared toward Bayshore, its roof light spinning.

He took a few steps and heard the squish-squush of his worn joggers, then backed into a signpost and leaned while he wiped his glasses. He looked up: NO STOPPING 7 AM 7 PM. Yes, of course. That was why he'd had to park around the corner.

He heard the receding wail of a siren. The police van? He was sure one of the cops had seen him. Why hadn't they stopped? The whining sound mocked him.

He tried to look everywhere at once as the rain mingled with the sweat on his face. He didn't want to call her name aloud, but the impulse was too strong.

"Margot!" he cried, then "MARGOT!" in the opposite direction, toward their car. The storm drove into his eyes, up his nose, spat into his mouth as he shouted, dripped down his face and neck and under the collar of his sopping Levi shirt.

A black Mercedes pulled to the curb; a white-haired man with rimless glasses frowned and stared. Gamble waved him away. "Go—on!" he shouted, running at the car. Damned gawker. I must look crazy, he thought. Well, the whole thing's farcical, ridiculous. She's probably sitting in the TR-3 right now, wondering where the hell *I* went.

I swear to God, I'll never let her out of my sight. . . .

He ran through the rain and turned the corner with his long arms outstretched for balance like a Keystone Kop.

The Triumph was still in its parking place. He clenched his fists and looked inside.

Empty.

He covered his mouth with his hands and raised his face to the glaucous sky. A gray swirl of water blew off a ledge and spattered his glasses.

He turned and took a few steps one way, then a few the other. Where should I look? Oh, Margot, oh, honey, you can't do this. You can't just . . . disappear. IT'S YOUR BIRTHDAY, HONEY. YOU CAN'T DO THIS ON YOUR BIRTHDAY. . . .

He didn't know if he had spoken the words or thought them.

She got sick. *She got sick, that's it.* Thank God. An attack or something. She's in the ladies' room, doubled over. She needs help. . . .

He ran toward the entrance. The half-lit hall was empty. He passed the lunchroom where they sometimes had coffee. The place was dark behind metal grates; he kicked them spasmodically and called her name and looked around in embarrassment, afraid he'd been seen. But the halls were empty.

One elevator was midway between the first and second floors; as he watched, the arrow indicator rotated upward in jerks. He rammed open a scarred wooden door marked LADIES and called into the darkened room, "Hello? Anybody in here?"

His paint-stained nails scraped the wall till he found the light switch. The room flared into relief. No one was at the washbasins. The doors to the three booths were all open. "Margot!" he said. *"Margot?"* The compartments were empty; the toilets smelled faintly of ammonia and cologne.

The men's room was dark and empty. He rushed back into the rain and stood at the top of the wide granite staircase, trying to see through the watery shrouds.

She's playing a prank, he told himself. A silly, thoughtless, cruel prank.

But they didn't play pranks, least of all on each other. Did they? *Ciel. Was Ciel . . . a prank?*

He had to stay calm. Something—had happened—to his wife. . . . On the street. It must have happened a few feet from where he'd parked. But Margot would *never* get into a stranger's car.

She'd have to be forced. She'd have to be hit or shot or strangled or doped. She'd fight like a wild animal; she was surprisingly strong for her size. Wouldn't he have heard the struggle, sitting around the corner in his car?

No. The Triumph had been sealed against the storm; he remembered snapping down the lid when the rain began. She could have used a PA system, and he wouldn't have heard.

He felt wet within and without; his sweat and the rainwater met at his boxer shorts. To the east a fork of lightning split the sky. Without thinking, he pushed blindly through the heavy doors and back into the old building.

The No. 1 elevator was between the first floor and the basement; the other two looked shut down for the night. The package lay untouched on the reception desk.

"MARGOT GAMBLE Hold for Pickup. Tnx!"

Water seeped from his shoes as he clasped a hand to his forehead and forced himself to admit out loud: "They've taken Margot."

4

That big hairy guy in the hall really looked wasted, Boon thought as he shifted into second on his way out of the police garage. Nice-looking dude except for all that fuzz. Looked ready to bawl. I should've told him about Anna; then he'd know he's not the only guy with problems. . . .

The force of the storm caught him by surprise as he gunned the Charger across the pavement into the street. Sitting in the office, he had mistaken the sudden darkness for the approach of night. He flicked his wipers on and forced a laugh as he hit the wailer and watched the traffic peel away. A forced laugh was about the most he could manage these days. But then he'd never laughed a lot; wasn't that one of Anna's beefs? Maybe he could work on it, learn from some of the animals in the detective bureau. Simple souls, they'd laugh at their mothers' drownings. Well, it was another way to cope. . . .

He rammed the black sedan into a power drift and jiggled the wheel when the rear tires slid a few inches wide on the slick pavement. He looked at his dash clock. The call had come three minutes ago, and he wasn't halfway to the scene. He'd have to do better. The fool could be at the city limits by now. . . . .

He drove through the old dock area in spurts and skids, his tires hissing like tape being ripped from its roll. He watched his hands turn from eerie blue to sickly yellow as the unmarked police car passed under mercury arc-lights and sodium floods. Flashes burst from a dry dock: welders in metal hats working through the downpour. He passed one of the towering orange cranes that rode on their own tracks and frisked out cargo like the quarter machines in the arcade where he could never get the claws to grab the camera.

Traffic thinned as he neared the beach, and he killed the siren and turned up the classical station. Kabalevsky's *Romeo and Juliet,* second movement. He swerved around a kid on a bicycle and thought of all the hours he'd spent listening to Shostakovich's Fifth and Prokofiev's *Scythian Suite* and Khachaturian's Piano Concerto and so many other works by the modern Russians. In one of the last foster homes of his childhood, the director had been a pop-eyed sissy with a collection of Melodiya records which he'd permitted Boon to enjoy while he trembled and sweated and stared at the boy's face till that final night when Boon had had to fight him off with fists and feet and make a run for it, his little brother Richard at the end of his outstretched arm.

He dropped the Charger into second as the wind vane atop the public toilet came into sight. Whatever had happened tonight between the dead man and the killer, he would lay eight to five it had started in one of the stalls inside. The gays congregated in four or five of these "tearooms" around town, but this was the most notorious. A few ambitious watch commanders assigned peep cops to the crawl space in the ceiling and made arrests by the carloads: businessmen in eye shadow, iron pumpers, rough trade, now and then a minor celebrity from out of town. Boon remembered the half-pint TV actor "just passing through," his mouth pressed to the glory hole between the booths. Strange people. Most cops hated gays; Boon was too busy hating genuine fools and assassins. A few of his snitches were gays who ratted out on killers and slashers to protect themselves. There were worse types. . . .

The DB sat upright in the driver's seat of an angle-parked Chrysler New Yorker, ivory, four-door, so new its clear plastic factory polish was unscratched. The man's thin, veiny hands rested at his sides. His balding head leaned back against the headrest as though he had dozed off. His glazed yellow brown eyes stared wide at the rivulets running down the windshield.

Boon felt his usual spasm of rage at life cut short at a fool's whim. *Dirty son of a bitch!* He took two hot drags on his Swisher Sweet and stuck his dampened head inside the open front passenger window.

The victim's upper plate had slipped, making him appear to be grinning. Not only had a fool killed the poor old guy, but he'd left him on public display, advertising his false teeth.

A beach "C" bus pounded by in the rain, its big tires sending out plumes of spray. The victim's narrow head jiggled lightly, and Boon saw where the bullet had entered: a red-rimmed hole, geometrically perfect, just below the squared hairline at the right temple. He couldn't see an exit wound. Blood had dribbled down the man's bony cheek and over his fresh shave. A few drops had spattered the shoulder of his loose yellow sport shirt with the bright floral design: just the outfit for dying.

Boon knew that the flow couldn't have lasted long. Blood pressure fell to zero seconds after death, and the brain didn't hold much blood to begin with.

He reached across the seat and brushed the man's cheek with his knuckles. The skin was warm, soft, the muscles barely beginning to tense. This killing wasn't an hour old.

The fool who'd done it couldn't be far.

5

The framed directory in the lobby informed Gamble that the police department's patrol office was on 4, but all he could see after riding in the creaky elevator were long hallways that faded to black. He turned left and walked fast, trying to compose his face. He had an idea how a bunch of hard-ass cops would react to the sight of a bearded giant going to pieces because he couldn't find his wife.

The air smelled like mildew, as though the storm had seeped into the files. He passed door after door, dark and sealed, padlocked reminders that the building was going out of business. Stark block letters leaped at him: FORENSICS, BUNCO, CRIMES SPECIFIC—as strange as the names of the moons of Saturn.

At the dead end of the hall, he spun and began to retrace his steps. Someone stood as still as a statue in front of the elevators; the form was backlighted, the face a blank. It began to move toward him in a familiar stiff-legged walk. The building engineer.

"Where can I find a cop?" Gamble called out.

The frail-looking man indicated a corridor with a smile and a turn of his head. A short distance down the hall

Gamble pulled up in front of a counter where a young red-haired policeman sipped at a cobalt blue pipe and talked politely into the phone: "Yes, sir. . . . Certainly. . . . Will do. . . ."

Gamble raised his hand for attention, felt silly but kept wagging it till the cop said, "Hold the line a second, sir," and stared across the scarred composition counter. "Help ya?"

"My wife. She . . . she's gone." He hated putting it so baldly.

The young deskman nodded as though he'd been expecting the news. After a few more minutes on the phone he hung up and turned to Gamble. "Mislaid his cat," he said, jerking his thumb toward the telephone. "He—"

"My wife disappeared!"

"Your wife?"

"Disappeared, right!" His head bobbed, and he made an effort to slow himself down. He owed Margot his total self-control. "Just before the rain," he went on. "She was, uh, coming inside to pick up . . . uh, coming in here, she was—"

"*Whoa!*" The stumpy young cop raised his hand as though directing traffic. "Slow down, sir, please! This . . . just happened?"

"A few minutes ago."

"Oh, gee. Then it's too soon."

"*Too soon*? For what?"

"For the wife to be handled as a missing person."

There was a commotion down the hall, and a pair of cops in visored helmets and knee-length boots stomped into sight, dragging a bare-skulled black of about fifteen. "Lighten up, peeg," the boy said. "You be cuttin' me!"

"You gonna be nice?" one of the policemen asked. "Huh? *Huh?*" Each time he said, "Huh?" he yanked up on the cuffs that held the prisoner's hand behind his back. The three figures moved around the corner.

Too soon? Had the deskman actually said that? Margot

was missing, for God's sake. How could it be too soon to hunt for a woman who was missing?

"See, sir," the deskman went on, "a subject can't be classified as missing for twenty-four hours. Unless there's evidence of foul play. That's procedure. I can't even take a report. I mean—"

"Procedure? Whose procedure?"

"The police department's. It's SOP, sir. Like I said, unless there's extenuating—"

"There are, there are!" Gamble broke in. He could feel his ears reddening with aggravation. He hadn't expected an argument; he'd expected whirling sirens and flashing lights and a door-to-door search: dogs, helicopters, command cars. Just like TV.

"Look, I told you," he said, gripping the front edge of the counter. "She was coming in here to pick up a package. But she didn't make it. *She didn't make it, man!*"

"I appreciate that, sir. Absolutely. I can see why you're upset. I *do* understand." Now the damned cop was trying to humor him. "But I have to go by procedure. It's—"

"God's sake, man, something's *happened* to her. *Happening* to her. Right now! My wife. Out on the street. Alone—"

"Sir—"

"—and helpless. There's gotta be something you can do."

"I'm sorry. I don't make the rules."

He felt as though there had been a tidal wave, and of all the people in the world, it had hit only him. "They took her."

"Who took her?"

For an instant his breathing and his talking conflicted and he couldn't utter a word. "I . . . I . . . I . . ."

"You think she was snatched? Uh—kidnapped? In front of police headquarters?"

Gamble closed his eyes and clutched the edge of the counter. He had a vision:

Margot is naked. Three men are beating her, raping her. Blood mats her long black hair. She tries to open her mouth to scream, but it's taped shut. . . .

Underneath his thoughts his mind kept repeating itself: Where where *where* WHERE?

He would risk his life to help her, but—*where to start?* His body convulsed as though he had touched a live wire, and then, as though standing away from himself, he heard his own voice speaking in measured tones: "I don't know she was kidnapped. But I do know she wouldn't leave on her own. Not my wife."

"Answer a few questions, will ya?" the young cop said, touching him on the arm.

Gamble nodded.

"She have any enemies?"

"None."

"You?"

"Me what?"

"Any enemies. What's your occupation?"

"I'm, uh . . . an artist."

The deskman frowned. "Like a . . . recording artist?"

"A sculptor, a painter. No. No enemies."

"You make your living painting?"

"Uh, yeah." It was a small lie.

"What makes you think anybody'd kidnap your wife?"

He felt like a man running in sand. "All I said is she went off to do a one-minute errand, and that's half an hour ago. She's gone. That's it. She's *gone!*"

"No chance she slipped back home ahead of you?"

"No chance. It was . . ." His eyes welled up. For God's sake, he couldn't bawl in front of a cop. Was it unrealistic of him to feel so scared? So . . . panicked? *What difference did it make how he looked?* It was Margot who mattered now. Only Margot. He bit hard on his lower lip. "We were on our way to the movies."

"You have a fight?"

"We don't fight."

"Here." The cop slid the phone across the counter. "Call home."

"I told you. She's not home."

"Give it a try. It's procedure."

The great god procedure again. He began to dial, but his index finger slipped, and he started over, holding his right wrist with his left hand to steady it.

"What's your number?" the cop asked, pulling the phone back. He dialed with sure strokes as Gamble stammered the numbers. After a long wait the deskman hung up and said, "Nobody's home."

"I know. Look, Officer"—he squinted to read the nameplate—"uh, Officer Pierson, I have to talk to somebody in Missing Persons. Right now."

"Missing Persons is part of, uh—Homicide." The cop looked sorry he'd had to use the word. "The homicide detectives, they take missing person cases in rotation. Depends on who's catching."

"Who's catching tonight?"

"Johnny Boon. Sergeant Boon." The cop paused, as though waiting for a reaction, but the name meant nothing. "He's on a run. Dead man at the beach. Sir, listen." He lowered his voice. "Go get a good night's rest. These things happen, know what I mean? If she's not back this time tomorrow, gimme a call. We'll file a report, get to work."

"You . . . don't . . . understand," Gamble said. He was sick of being jollied along. He turned away, swallowed spitless into the dry hole of his throat, then stared for a few seconds at the chipped green wall. When he spoke again, his voice was steady. "Imagine if this were your wife."

The deskman took a deep pull on his blue-metal pipe and said, "I understand. Hey, I understand."

"Then call your detective. He's wasting time on a dead man. My wife's . . . alive."

"Answer me this: Has she ever walked out on you before?"

"She's never walked out on me, period. She didn't walk out on me tonight. She wouldn't."

What if she found out about Ciel? Would she walk out then?

The deskman interrupted the thought. "No chance she's, uh, fooling around?" The round, stupid face retained its opacity; the man didn't even have the grace to look embarrassed at asking a question like that. Gamble's fingers tightened. Where did they get these cookie-cutter cops with their prefab questions, acting as though every case were the same, as though the only conceivable reason a wife could disappear was the inadequacy of her husband? Were they trained to look for the tackiest explanation? Can't the dumb son of a bitch see? *Margot and I are* tight. *She couldn't have left on her own. Can't he see that?*

The cop stared out of cloudy blue eyes, his gray shirt pressed into two thin ridges down the front, his shield glittering, his face the inane blank of the bureaucrat. *Don't make waves. Cover your ass. Follow procedure.* No wonder the guy was behind a desk instead of on the street where cops belonged.

"There is *no* chance she's been fooling around," Gamble said slowly. "None."

"Neither one of you? Look, Mr. Gamble, I gotta ask these questions. Okay?"

"Procedure again?" The cop nodded, and Gamble forced himself to unclench his fists. "We don't, uh, fool around. Neither one of us." Another small lie. The smallest. Ciel was an accident, a mistake that would never be repeated.

"The missus, was she by any chance in her, uh, change of life? A lotta women, when they reach—"

"She was twenty-seven today."

Pierson nodded. "History of mental disorders?"

"None."

"You?"

"None." Gamble almost added, "Till now." Holding onto this counter to support his knees and feeling like strangling a cop—maybe he *was* temporarily nuts. Or the cop was. Or the system . . .

"Where were you going tonight?" Pierson's questions were coming faster, as though he had something else to do.

"We were on our way to see *Le Jour s'élève.*" The cop looked puzzled. "A movie."

"And she came in here to pick up . . . a package you said?"

"An envelope. She does typing. Mostly for lawyers."

The cop put two fingers to his lips and flicked a sideways glance. "She came here to meet . . . a lawyer?"

"*No!*" God, he wasn't even listening. "Not to *meet* a lawyer. To pick up a package *left* by a lawyer. On the reception desk. Downstairs. She never got there."

"So she musta disappeared—"

"Outside. In the rain. In front."

The cop fished a form out of a desk drawer and began a whole new set of questions, scribbling rapidly as Gamble answered.

"How was she dressed?"

"A lightweight shift. Nylon. Deep indigo."

"Deep *what?*"

"Just put black. . . ."

When the last question had been asked and answered, Pierson knocked the ashes from his metal pipe in three slow, deliberate raps against an oversized glass ashtray, as though hesitant to act. Then he sat in front of a pale lime machine with a flat keyboard and began typing. When he was finished, he unrolled a sheet of paper and slid it across the counter. "Here," he said, "check this before I send the tape."

Gamble read:

MISSING PERSON 9-1-80 1945 HOURS
CASE NO. PENDING

MARGOT WILLIS GAMBLE
8743 STINSON AV. N.E.
446-9210

SEVERN H. GAMBLE
HUSBAND
SAME

MISSING PERSON REPORT
MISSING FROM FORDING & FULTON SINCE
1900 HOURS DATE. MARGOT W. GAMBLE
WF 27 5-8 110. BRN EYES. LONG BLK
HR. FAIR COMP. UNK REASON FOR
LEAVING. GOOD PERSONAL HABITS. GOOD
MENTAL & PHYSICAL COND. BLACK
DRESS THONG SANDALS NO HOT NO
JEWELERY.

LAST SEEN BY SEVERN H. GAMBLE 446-9210.

"Hat, not hot," Gamble corrected. He started to point out "jewelery" but realized it didn't matter. "Why does it say 'Case Number Pending'?"

"I told you, Mr. Gamble," Pierson said slowly, as though dealing with a slow learner. "I can't make an official report for twenty-four hours, and Communications won't assign us a case number without a report. It's all—"

"Procedure."

The cop nodded and pushed a button. The machine began to chatter. "I'm sending this in the meantime. It's a judgment call."

"But that's not enough!" Gamble insisted, pounding the counter with a closed fist. "Don't you understand? That's just paper work. *She missing right now!* It's gonna take men—manpower. You're shuffling papers!"

"Sir, uh, look. This teletype's going to every precinct

station right now. The county's getting a copy, the state. Watch commanders'll be reading it in a few minutes, sector sergeants. It'll—"

"But—"

"—be clipped on every board in every car. It'll be read at roll calls till we take it off the hot sheet, and a thousand officers'll be hunting for"—he glanced at the teletype copy—"for Margot." The phone made a buzzing sound, and he picked it up.

Look at that, Gamble said to himself. Just *look* at that. He's got to peek to see what her name is. That's the extent of his interest, his concern. The other cops'll be the same. Nobody'll really be looking for Margot, not the way I'd be looking for her if I could only clone a thousand of myself and beat the streets and the back alleys till she turns up . . . alive.

A prayer ran through his mind:

God, please God, let her be alive. . . . And God . . . let her not be in pain. . . .

6

The young beat cop made a concise report, the kind Boon liked: "Chrysler's registered to a Hayden W. Harrier. No wants or warrants, no record. I already called the ME and the lab." Thank God for small favors, Boon said to himself; for once somebody else gets to notify the next of kin. Personally he preferred root canal work.

The cop introduced a shaken young couple and explained that they'd strolled up to the window of the ivory car to ask directions. The girl, shocked, wet-haired, was sniffling into an embroidered handkerchief. Boon wondered why she was so upset, then reminded himself that everybody wasn't a rhino-skinned homicide dick. Some people retained a natural sense of sadness and awe in the presence of death. A form of respect. A nice *human* way to be. He wished he could recover that state of innocence, to be able to approach a killing in sorrow instead of rage, to view it simply as a tragedy instead of a personal affront to Det. Sgt. John Doe Boon. But weeping and wailing didn't get the job done. Even at a wake some poor sucker had to dress the stiff.

He noticed that the four-door New Yorker was immaculate inside, as though the old man had known he had a final date with the photographers. He encoded the victim in his head for future reference: "W-M, gray, brn, approx. 5-10, 60–70, no dist. fac. marks." The man's feet rested against the pedals as though he intended to drive away any second, and his tasseled brown loafers wore a high gleam. He wondered if the elderly ever went shopping and realized they might be buying the clothes they'd be found in. How spooky it must be to get old and know you could kick off any second. He hoped he never found out.

Something caught his eye. Male sex organs weren't high on his list of art objects, but the one protruding from the man's lap put him in mind of a ripe apricot. He knew a couple of candy-assed patrol cops who would have tucked it back in "for the family," but a good cop didn't take liberties with murder scenes. Any minute now the evidence examiners would arrive with their Junior G-man fingerprint kits and benzene and alcohol and No. 15 Chemcraft sets, and they would futzle around with the car and the body and then report that Hayden W. Harrier was sure as hell dead.

In a way Boon was relieved to find that the killing was sex-related; now he had means, motive, and opportunity. The killer must have joined the man in his car, promised him instant relief, and whacked him out while the horny old guy was arranging his jewels. Iced for a few bucks.

What a world. "Any signs of a wallet?" Boon asked the beat man.

"On the floorboards. Empty."

A sharp gust of wind lifted Boon's collar, and a fresh new cloudburst filled his ear like water from a cup. The others rushed toward the shelter of a green and white patrol car; Boon slipped into the back seat of the Chrysler, touching the door handles at the tips so he wouldn't spoil any latents. He wiped his face with the sleeve of his jacket, lit a Swisher Sweet, and began scribbling in his spiral notebook. The odometer read 124, mileage more typical of a suicide vehicle. A lot of suicide candidates bought dreamwagons in desperation, and when the great American toy didn't improve their lives—*bang.*

A boy came skateboarding by in sine waves, his brown, curly hair dripping. He sideslipped to a stop and gaped at the DB. "Hey, Josh!" he yelled. "C'mere 'n' look. It's neat!"

Neat, Boon thought as he waved the kid away. Yeah, we're a real neat sight, me and my friend here: three hundred pounds of flesh, half of it alive, keeping dry. It's cases like this make people call cops garbagemen.

What a crock! But he had to admit there were a few minor resemblances, especially on days when you saw so much blood and gore your brain went numb. No matter how bloody the day, you were expected to turn into an instant daddy that night: kiss the wife and praise the TV dinner and read "Mrs. Tittlemouse" to the kids. Some of the guys claimed they could make the adjustment; Boon couldn't. The cop's worst mistake: taking the job home.

The rain hit the roof like pebbles on a snare drum. He figured he might as well stay put; the technicians would arrive any second, and he couldn't do much till they'd finished their dusting and poking around. He glanced again at his grinning companion, still dead, shook his head in pity and anger, and remembered something his field training officer had told him ten years before: "Cops and football coaches, John. They gotta be smart enough to do their jobs and dumb enough to think it matters. Well, it don't."

Funny how often that comes back to me, Boon said to himself as the water sluiced down the windows. Maybe because I'm still trying to prove him wrong. Maybe because I *am* dumb enough to think it matters. He hoped he wasn't turning into another bleeding-heart idealist. Idealism wasn't on the curriculum where he'd grown up. Toughness was. Adaptability. But mainly vengefulness: You gave back double what you got. Nail the fools before they nail you. Look at brother Richie; the kid let his guard down only once. . . .

Boon knew what he had learned as a child; it was what he hadn't learned that bothered him. He shook his head. Six institutions—no, seven—hadn't prepared him for married life. How to drop your guard and trust somebody. How to love and show it. He had to admit that group homes and orphanages didn't produce the best husbands. God damn it, Anna, he said under his breath, *let's get back together!* Give the docs and me another chance. You don't have to drink yourself to death just because we—*I* —screwed up. . . .

He hoped she was safe. Well, she must be, he told himself; she *must* be. It's not as if this were the first time she'd left her new apartment for a few days. Christ, two dead marriages and I'm thirty-four years old. Never again.

Was it all my fault? Both times? A guy can't be sure of a damn thing anymore. Her landlord said he hadn't seen her in two, three days. Well, she disappeared a week the last time. Phoned her sister long-distance when her money ran out, and I drove to that cinder-block motel on my siren and found her sprawled across the bed in her panties, feet flecked with red, a bottle of Polish vodka busted on the bathroom floor. . . .

The wind shook the soft-sprung sedan so that the driver's head bobbed against the headrest the way it had when the bus passed. He marveled at the human body's resilience, even in death. Given half a chance . . .

He imagined the scene of his brother's execution, the body barely recognizable when they'd untied him from the chain-link fence. And me in a rice paddy eight thousand miles away, fighting a stupid war. The unfairness. I couldn't help my own brother. Oh, those bastards. Ramming him with a car till he was . . . pulp.

He bit hard on his little cigar. His stomach boiled, and a twist of pain made him jerk forward on the car seat.

The dark green portable crime lab slid alongside, but nobody got out. He understood the reluctance: one burst of rain across the front seat of the Chrysler, and they'd never get a clean lift. He stuck his head through the window and asked, "What took you guys?"

"Andy forgot his evidence case," a kid in a squared-off cap called out. "We had to double back to headquarters."

Boon nodded and rolled the window up against the side-spitting rain. All this case needed was an evidence examiner without an evidence kit. "Andy" was probably like the rest of the young cops nowadays: there was room in their heads for about three things at a time, and two of them were poon.

He leaned back against the smooth new nap of the seat and tried to visualize the kind of human being that could dump a skinny old man with one slug in the temple, cold and final. He was always surprised when he collared a killer and found himself looking at a person instead of a carnival freak. The worst fools came camouflaged in ordinariness. He thought of Speck, Starkweather, Gacy, Corll: colorless creeps. If you sat at a bar and talked to them, you'd die of boredom. Losers and misfits with runny noses and bad teeth. Pissed their shorts when you collared them . . .

The department shrink's warning came back. *You can't*

*keep taking your job personally, Sergeant. Back off, get
a little perspective. You'll wind up on a disability retirement.*

Tell it to the fools, Boon thought. You try putting me
on a disability retirement, you better send a Swat team
and some dogs.

Ribbons of foam curled off the bay, but a patch of pale
blue had opened in the west. The rain fell straighter now,
past the steamy windows of the car.

He opened the back door and stepped outside. The two
evidence examiners sat in their van in silhouette, watching the sky. Let 'em wait, he thought; they got their time-
table, and I got mine.

He sucked so hard on his cigar that the insides of his
cheeks almost touched. He waved his hand at the living
and the dead and strode toward the public baths. Someone
might be hiding inside, waiting for a sea change. It was
a start.

7

The red-headed desk cop finally finished his long telephone conversation and said, "Another peeper. Must be
a full moon." While he'd been on the phone, Gamble had
looked around and studied the place for the first time.
Everything was dull and barren. How could the mind
function in such a void? He couldn't believe that he was
trapped in this setting, that a seamy police office had
become crucial to his life. He had always tried to solve
his own problems, and now he was as dependent as a
newborn bird.

"What next?" he asked the cop.

"Huh?" Pierson cocked his head as though surprised

by the question. "Oh, uh—we did all we can do, buddy. Hey, relax! You look like you're gonna pass out. That wouldn't help the missus, would it?"

"But what do we do now?" Gamble insisted, afraid of the answer.

"I don't know about you," the cop said. "Me, I got a ton of filing. Some of these guys don't even write up misdemeanors till they're a day or two old. Why, I had—"

"*No!*" He didn't want to hear any more. "I mean, what about my wife?"

"I told ya, we'll take it from here. You just go home and—"

Gamble reached across the counter with his long arms and grabbed the cop by the epaulets. "God damn it, don't humor me!" he yelled.

He yanked with all his strength, and the deskman popped up like a piece of toast. Gamble spoke into the expressionless face: "My wife . . . she—"

Something cold and hard pulled tight against his voice box and jerked him backward. He lost his grip on the desk cop and toppled to the floor, clawing to keep from being strangled.

He turned on his side and tried to yell, but only a squawk came out. He kicked at the counter and shoved himself a few feet across the wooden floor, but someone rolled on his back and rode him like a bucking horse.

His Adam's apple was being crushed. "Don't make me hurt you," a voice said. *Jesus, was it a woman?*

Red disks whirled in front of his eyes. "Be nice!" the high-pitched voice said from miles away. *"Be nice, mister!"*

The red disks turned to black, and the black disks congealed into night. He fell and fell, his long body tumbling in space.

He awoke on the floor of the police office. "Oh, God," he croaked as the chokehold slowly loosened. "I'm sorry. I didn't mean . . . My wife . . . She's—"

"Back off, Tally!" a male voice called out. "The man just got a little upset there."

Gamble swallowed and sucked air. He tried to stand, fell backward against a wall, and slithered to a bench. His tormentor swam slowly into focus: a trim uniformed woman with the slender legs of a dancer. She was peering at him distrustfully from wide-set green eyes while she tried to blow back a loose curl of light brown hair.

"You gonna be nice?" she asked, holding a long black flashlight in front of her like a crusader's cross. She leaned so close he could read her plastic name tag: "T. WICKHAM."

"He's okay," the desk cop repeated cheerfully as Gamble sat bewildered. "I'll take care of it, Tally. No problem."

"Assaulting an officer? That's no problem?" The woman talked so fast her words sounded jumbled. Or had his hearing been affected by her attack? "What's it take to rile you, Billy? Set you on fire?" Pierson laughed.

"Good thing I was here," the woman went on, shoving her flashlight into a ringholder with a clack. "You need me for charges or anything?"

"Oh, gosh, no," the deskman said. "Me and Severen here, we're okay now. Huh, Severen?"

Gamble was too weak to do anything but nod. He'd been steadily patronized ever since he got off the elevator, floored by a female who looked like a flower girl, and now he was being forced to sit helplessly and listen to his name being mispronounced. And Margot was still gone. He lowered his head.

"I'm on a call, Bill," the policewoman said, disappearing behind some lockers.

"I didn't hear anything."

"A missing boy. It wasn't on the air."

"What's it about?"

"Probably a false alarm," she called back. "He's a friend, sorta. I'll feel better if I check it out."

"Female intuition?" the desk cop said, rearranging his shirt.

"Come on, Billy. I had enough of that garbage at roll call." Seconds later her face reappeared. "The, uh, individual?" she said, nodding toward Gamble. "You're sure?"

"I'm sure," Pierson said, his blank bureaucratic face reconstituted. "Hey, what happened at roll call?"

"The usual. The lieutenant says, 'Officer Wickham? A message from the clinic. The rabbit died.'"

"Funny!"

"If he could do impressions, I'd rate him with the Ayatollah."

Gamble tapped his fingers against the wooden bench. He couldn't believe they were exchanging wisecracks while Margot was lost. He thought of Robert Burns, wondering how the birds could sing when he had lost his love.

The policewoman said, "Hey, I'm late," and vanished through the door.

"Okay now, Severen," the deskman said, leaning over Gamble as though he were an afterthought. "How about we call it a night?" He motioned toward the doorway. "Go home and relax." He lowered his voice. "You can't help her this way."

"Will you—?"

"We'll be looking all night. Now listen. You got it together, don't ya?"

"Y-yes," Gamble said, accepting the outstretched hand. "I'm sorry. I . . . I . . ." The deskman pulled him to his feet and slapped him on the back.

"Anything develops, I'll call you," Pierson said. "That's a promise, pardner. Me personally. And I'll tip the next watch to keep an eye out."

"Thanks. I'm sorry."

The cop smiled. "Quit saying you're sorry."

"I'm . . . sorry." Gamble turned and walked down the hall.

The elevator door opened, and he caught a whiff of his wife: her own ineffable essence of mint soap and fennel toothpaste, herbal lotion and apple-blossom shampoo. I wonder how long I'll keep on imagining things like that, he asked himself. As he stepped in, he heard a final message of chccr from the deskman around the corner:

"Don't worry, Severen, she'll turn up. They always do. Usually . . ."

The doors shut.

8

_____

As Tally Wickham turned the wheel to park in the darkened alley, a familiar pain stabbed her arm. "Oo-*ooh!*" she said, grabbing herself just below the elbow. A year ago she'd strained the arm in a volleyball game and spent months nursing tendinitis, and now it was back, like an unwanted guest, and all because that damned Billy Pierson had an underdeveloped command presence. Imagine letting a confrontation reach the point where a citizen would have the nerve—*the nerve!*—to jump an officer at headquarters.

The moon made its first appearance of the evening as the remains of the storm streamed off in shreds. If she knew Pierson, he probably wouldn't bother to make a report. Peace at any price; that's our deskman. Lordie Lord, if my arm's wrecked again . . . Without something in writing, how can I claim it's job-connected? Diathermy, whirlpool, X ray . . . stuff like that *costs*.

She locked her brick red Honda and hurried up the wooden steps to the rear porch of the fourth-floor tenement. There were still a fcw of these leaky firetraps left in the blocks behind the waterfront, and they always made her feel guilty, as though her own full life were partly financed by the poverty inside.

The first time she'd stood on this unsteady landing it had been to call on Samuel Schulte, a retarded child in a protective white hard hat. His liquid brown eyes had swum behind oversize horn-rimmed glasses held in place by a strap. The boy had lifted a box of lipsticks from a dime store on the instructions of a nine-year-old Fagin. "He didn't know it was wrong," the mother had said, shielding the frightened child with her body. "God in heaven, do you have to take him in?" Of course not. For some, life was punishment enough.

The next time she visited the tenement, Sammy had treated her like a relative, hugging her skirts and trying to say her name over and over: "Offa Wiggum, Offa Wiggum!" They'd wound up playing checkers—throwing checkers was more like it—and he'd squeezed her when she'd said good-bye.

She started to knock, but as she raised her fist, the pain chewed into her forearm again. Maybe I overdid it, she admitted to herself. Well, how was I supposed to know what was happening? That big guy could have *killed* Pierson. Lucky I didn't crack the poor guy's hyoid bone. Imagine the headline: LADY COP STRANGLES CITIZEN AT HEADQUARTERS.

She dictated a short description of the tenement into her Minitex pocket tape recorder and knocked.

"Oh, it's you. I thought it might be . . . him." Betty Schulte stood in a wedge of light from a light bulb hanging from the kitchen ceiling by a wire. She didn't look much like the sweet-faced woman with hennaed hair and starkly defined Frosty Cool lipstick who checked Tally's groceries. Her face was drained, her usually overdone eyes naked and rimmed with red.

"Come in," she said. She managed a wan smile with lips that looked as though they'd been chewed by a mouse. "Place is a mess—"

"You should see mine," Tally said.

"This here's, uh, Uncle George."

A balding man in a sweaty undershirt and café au lait skin stared at her through liver-colored eyes. "Listen," he said, "this is no false alarm." He spoke as though he expected an argument. "No way Sammy woulda—"

"George?" Betty Schulte interrupted, touching him on the arm. Tally wondered if he was an uncle or an "uncle."

The woman weaved as she led the way to a living room slightly bigger than a packing crate. She motioned her guest to an easy chair with cottony stuffing leaking through a slash in its side. The floors were covered with bare linoleum in a pattern of ruined squares. A twenty-four-inch TV sent flickers against the bare walls; every so often a muffled shriek would come from a turned-down quiz show, like someone crying for help from far away.

"I love these," Tally said, lifting a water glass that held a few fresh daffodils.

"The manager lets 'er take 'em home," George said quickly. Tally remembered dollar bunches at the Safeway. She was sure the family ate leftover food, too. People from this neighborhood haunted the throwaway bins at the big markets. She'd always thought stories like that were exaggerated till she started her field research as a cop, working toward her Ph.D. in public administration. One month to go. If she made it.

"No way he run off," Uncle George resumed, thumping a spatulate finger on a card table. "I know that kid."

"Ten hours now," Betty Schulte said in a voice that Tally had to strain to hear. The woman perched precariously on the front edge of a wooden chair that looked like part of a broken kitchen set. She had gone to the trouble of putting on a thin two-piece summer suit in lightweight linen, still showing its hanger marks. Pity the poor; they had so little to dress for. Weddings. Funerals. And special occasions like when their children ran away. Tally felt guilty again.

"Did you phone the precinct?" she asked. The woman nodded, her face drawn down as though a hand pulled at her chin. "What'd they tell you?"

"Said to call later."

"Whatta they care?" George said.

"We *do* care!" Tally said, and wished she hadn't. People in pain weren't themselves; a police officer, even an imitation one, should know that. "Would I be here?" she added gently.

"I meant the cops," he said. "The *men*."

Betty Schulte rose from her wooden chair and lurched like a sleepwalker toward a mauve settee so frayed and flattened its fern design looked like an old tracing. As Tally watched, the woman arranged herself in a sitting position. She seemed to force a half smile; then her eyes rolled up, and she began to topple forward.

George broke her fall and lifted her to the couch. Tally felt her fluttery pulse and pulled back an eyelid; the pupils almost filled the cornea. "Shock," she said. "Get something warm."

She arranged a cushion under the woman's feet and rubbed brisk circles against the clammy wrists. The man came back with a pair of blankets and a rag throw rug covered with animal hairs. A few seconds after Tally finished the wrapping job, Betty Schulte began to moan.

'Here," George said. He held a shot glass to her lips.

The woman made a face and sipped slowly. She lifted herself into a sitting position, shedding coverings as she rose, and looked across the room with the wide eyes of someone confronting a knife. "Samuel's been . . . run over," she said in a whispered monotone. "I feel it. We never should of—"

"He *hasn't* been run over," Tally said before the woman could work herself up again. "I checked before I left headquarters."

"Sure you did," George put in.

Tally looked again at the mottled pigmentation in the

man's face, the brownish yellow skin with the oversize freckles, the two colors fighting for dominance. Poor Uncle George, trapped between races; he must have had a hellish life. "We do things by computer these days," she said gently. "In seconds. There hasn't been a juvenile hurt in traffic in two weeks."

Betty Schulte stood up unsteadily, George at her elbow. "You . . . still think he . . . he run away . . . from home, huh?" She pushed the words through her gnawed lips like someone just in from bitter cold. She looked fifty and sounded eighty, but Tally seemed to remember she was thirty-four. "I called down at headquarters today six, seven times," the woman went on. "They gimme the same answer every time. 'He probably run off, he probably run off.' My boy did *not* run off."

"How can you be sure?" Tally asked.

"Because yesterday morning we picked up his—" Her voice faltered.

"His new bike," the man said. "A Sears ten-speed. We saved up. Tips and stuff. He works as a boxboy, so him and Betty can . . . keep an eye on each other."

"Is his bike—?"

"Gone, yeah. Irish green metallic paint with gold flakes. Two mirrors. A big tall Day-Glo flag so he wouldn't get hit. A speedometer, a—"

"He missed work today," Betty Schulte mumbled, more to herself than anyone. "He never misses work." A gray cat with half a tail sauntered into the room and stared at Tally, slowly swishing its stump. She had a momentary feeling of being surrounded, distrusted, hated. The normal paranoia of a cop in the house of the poor. Well, that was what she had joined the force to study: public attitudes toward policemen. *Hatred* wasn't quite accurate. But they certainly weren't loved.

She couldn't see any significance to the news about the bike. A new ten-speed might inspire a boy to stay home, and it might inspire him to take off. But why argue the point? These two needed to believe the worst. People in crisis always did. It was as though they were accepting their pain before it was due, establishing credit.

"There's other things," the mother said as George helped her up to the settee. "His puppy."

"His salamander's here," George put in.

"He didn't take his coin bank or the dollar bill you give him for his birthday," the mother said. "God in heaven, would he run away without money?"

"Does he, uh, understand about money?" Tally asked.

"*All* about it," the woman said emphatically, as though surprised to be asked. "He's got a brain, ya know. Some ways he's as normal as you and me." She pulled a handkerchief from a pocket of her suit and poked at her eyes.

Tally wished there was something encouraging to say. The boy was only twelve; he was impaired; he had dropped from sight for ten hours: enough to terrify any parent. She had handled runaway cases before, and she felt the mothers' desolation. But she knew that cops weren't supposed to empathize. Cops were supposed to be inured to the pain of others. That was the only way they could function day in, day out.

She knelt in front of the settee. "Betty, I . . . I'm sorry. I mean, I'm really sorry." Empty words. You got tired of saying you were sorry; there had to be something more.

She tried to think. Maybe if I just checked around the neighborhood, asked a few questions, put out the word. It does seem odd that a runaway would leave his money behind. Even a retard . . .

She put her hands on the mother's quivering shoulders and said, "Betty, I'll do what I can. Okay? I'll try to get a detective over here, and if I can't, I'll check around. But I need to know *everything*. Family fights. Where he goes when he's not home. Who he plays with. People he might have run off to visit. Don't hold anything back."

Betty Schulte smiled gratefully and made her feel like

crying. She knew how little she could do, how little the whole department could do. She wondered how a hard-nosed old harness bull like her father would have handled this case, and how she managed to get so emotionally involved, and where on earth she would find the time, and whether she might get in trouble for jumping calls in somebody else's district. . . .

But then she told herself that it wasn't really a case of right or wrong or jumping calls or finding time. It all came down to a very simple truth:

Anyone's child had a right to be found.

9

Boon stepped from the public bathroom into the salty air. The rain had slowed to spits, but everything was still darkened by the wet. He decided to let the evidence examiners do the stall-by-stall research; he was satisfied that no one was hiding inside. The regular tearoom guests must have shagged ass when they heard the shot.

He was walking toward his Charger when one of the technicians leaned from the window of the police van and said, "Sarge? Dispatcher called your number. I told 'em you were nine-three-four for a few minutes."

934. Out of car. How helpful. "You couldn't come in and get me?"

The technician stretched the palm of his hand out the window and let a few drops fall on it, as though in answer. Boon turned away to conceal his annoyance. I ought to be used to that kind of lazy crap by now, he said to himself. There's cops that'll walk through a boxcar of snakes for you, and there's jerk-offs that don't want to lose the crease in their pants.

He wiped the back of his hand across his forehead, climbed in his car, and fired up a fresh cigar. He lifted the mike from its slot and mashed the button and growled his call sign into the microphone: "Two-Two Henry."

"Uh, Two-Two Hen*ry*," a female dispatcher's voice answered in a singsong lilt. "Can you give me a six-one right back? Desk two?"

"Received." Boon's heart thumped. Anna must have phoned in; the dispatcher couldn't put personal messages on the air.

He hurried to the coin phone at the end of the tearoom and asked for desk two. "That was quick," the voice said, not so official-sounding now. "Uh, Sergeant, I know you're on a call, but is there any chance you could make a run on a missing person? Before you come in? The officer says it doesn't look good—"

A goddamn missing person. What a jerk he'd been to get his hopes up. "Who's missing, for Chrisakes? The mayor? The governor?"

"A twelve-year-old boy. Retarded. The officer's very, uh, concerned. She says—"

"*She?*"

"Wickham, Juvenile. She's working out of the First Precinct for a while." Must be that new one, the rook that Jerry Fordyce swore he was gonna fuck or go blind. Most females worked meters or desks; the ones on patrol were tokens for the feminists. Boon could never understand why women fought for the right to be shot at and abused. It was different with men. . . .

"What's bothering her?" he asked. There were lady cops who cried at card tricks.

"She suspects kidnapping."

"What's she got to go on?"

"Who knows?" The dispatcher sounded tired. "Make the run for me, will you? When you get a few minutes?"

"When I get a few minutes from what? I'm working a hot call. Course it's only a homicide."

"I know. But—"

"You haven't got anybody else," Boon said.

"I'm sorry, Sergeant." Her voice was full of phony sympathy. "I guess you're just indispensable."

"Okay, *okay*," Boon said as her giggle filled his ear. He wouldn't crack back; all calls were recorded on the same multichannel Sony that taped incoming complaints and radio traffic. You never knew when Internal Affairs would summon you for a word about your telephone manners or climb your ass for swearing over the air. He didn't need another beef. "What's the location?" he asked.

"One-six-six-eight Ranker, fourth floor in the rear. Meet the officer."

Well, this wasn't the worst time to blow an hour. The technicians would be busy with the murder car: dusting for prints, vacuuming, emptying the ashtrays into sealed plastic bags, arranging for the body to be posted. It would be tomorrow morning before the medical examiner's protocol and the technicians' report appeared on his desk.

But . . . a missing persons call? A twelve-year-old kid? Nobody got excited about missing juveniles anymore. Christ, half the country was unaccounted for. His own wife . . .

This case must look real bad, he said to himself as he tucked into Ranker at the 1200 block. Must be a show of blood or a kidnap note or something; otherwise, we'd never waste time on a lost kid. Might as well get involved. He only had fifty-one cases in his active file; fifty-two was a nice round number. He wondered how many cases the TV detectives were handling at the moment. One at a time, he'd bet on that. A nice leisurely pace, summer breezes blowing, pretty girls begging to help out, and half-naked corpses with thirty-eight-inch bustlines heaving at the camera in death. Me, I got Hayden W. Harrier and his upper plate and a thorough search of the shithouse, and I can't even give that my undivided attention.

A moon the color of blue cheese played its light on a

rickety flight of bleached gray stairs. He could imagine
the place in the daytime. Yowling cats and panting dogs.
Wash flapping in the breeze from the bay. And deals going
down on every landing.

"*Psssst!* Up here." A mellow female voice. He climbed
the way he walked, with no feeling of effort, his aviator
boots keeping to the outside of the stairs to avoid making
the risers squeak. The storm had chased the fools off the
streets, let them do their mischief inside for a change.
The second-floor apartment was cooking cabbage or boil-
ing socks. The third-floor apartment was frying cowflop
or smoking grass. A woman stood on the fourth-floor landing.

"Boonhomicide," he said, offering his hand.

"Wickham, Juvenile," she said, stepping out of the
shadows. "Tally Wickham."

He felt ill-at-ease: his standard reflex on meeting
women.

'Sergeant," the woman said, "before we go in"—her
firm hand gripped him by the elbow and steered him away
from the half-open back door—"there's a few—touchy
things."

"There is?" he said dumbly as the light from the window
revealed Ptn. Tally Wickham. Yeah, it was the rook
Fordyce said he'd kill for. The one with the build. She
had brown hair about a foot longer than regulation and a
small turned-up nose and blue or green eyes that looked
dark in these shadows. As she moved into the light, he
saw that her hair was pulled back from her face and a
yellow daisy peeked from in front of each ear. A new
uniform of the day, but a hell of a job of packaging; no
wonder Fordyce was taking cold showers. Well, J. Boon
was no Fordyce. This ginch was a cop. He'd treat her like
one.

". . . Last seen this morning," she was saying. "Rode
away on his new bike. Nothing since."

Jesus. A kid took off on his new bike. Call the marines.

"That's all you got to go on?" he asked.

"No. I've got—it's just—well, I talked to the mother and the, uh, uncle, and I . . . I've got a feeling. Things they said. They're convincing. You'll see. This is the last kid in the world that'd run away." How little she knew. *Every* kid was the last kid in the world that would run away. Just ask the parents.

"You got a feeling, huh?" Boon stared into the darkness toward the cannery next door. He understood; he'd been a rookie himself a thousand years ago. This Tally What's-her-face must be all of twenty-two years old. "Listen, kid," he said, "you gotta—"

"Wickham. Tally Wickham. Juvenile Division."

"Okay, Tally, now—"

"Why don't you just call me Wickham?"

Boon had absorbed his maximum safe dosage of lip. "Listen, lady," he said as he headed for the steps, "you know what I was doing when you called for a detective?"

"What?"

"Working a homicide."

"Why didn't they send somebody else?" Her voice had softened a little.

"Because I'm catching. Two guys are sick, and I'm covering for a friend."

"You double-shifted?"

"Since eight this morning." He was three steps below her on the stairs. "Tell ya what. You gimme a call they find the body. Boon. J. Boon."

She skipped down the stairs and blocked his descent. "If you want to make a fool out of me," she said, talking to his belt buckle, "there's lots better ways."

"Name six," he said, trying to keep his voice down. A light went on in the dump below.

"Just come in for a few minutes," she said, motioning him upward. "Don't decide before you start. What're you gonna tell the dispatch office?"

"False alarm," he said. "They'll understand."

"False alarm? A retarded child's been gone all day and half the night? A boy who never leaves his mother? And her a basket case with fright? *A false alarm?*" She sounded so upset that she could have been talking about her own family. She was concerned, that was for sure. Not a bad quality, if it didn't kill you.

"Sergeant," she implored. "*Please.*" She grabbed him by the sleeve of his shorty jacket and began pulling. "Just for a few minutes?"

Oh, Christ. Why was he such a pushover?

An hour later they were headed back down the stairs, Boon in the lead, walking faster than usual. He hoped the policewoman would take the hint, but when he reached his car, she was already opening the door on the passenger's side. "What're you doing?" he asked.

"Don't you want to talk it over?" she asked, climbing in.

Boon sat down and grabbed his microphone. "Two-Two Henry returning," he said.

"Returning?" The rookie sounded surprised. "What're you—?"

"Look, I feel just as sorry for those people as you do, but if you start falling to pieces every time a kid runs away, you're gonna be spread so thin you'll be invisible."

"Not even if he's been . . . kidnapped or murdered or God knows what?" In the moonlight, golden specks reflected off her widely opened eyes.

He ripped open a new package of Swisher Sweets, started to light one, but stopped out of animal instinct. This dizzy rook might bring him up on charges: smoking on duty, smoking out of season, some fool thing. "And besides," she was saying, an edge in her voice, "I've been off for hours. So what business is it of yours what I—?"

"You interrupted my investiga—"

"I *didn't* interrupt your investigation. The dispatch office did. This boy's—valuable."

"He's a runaway."

"He's a missing child! Somebody's flesh and blood. He's . . . *loved!* But you, you wouldn't understand." She stretched a long leg out of the car. "Cops like you make me sick. So—so cold. I guess I haven't turned cynical yet. Thank God." She slammed the door.

The self-righteous speech irked Boon. Too many judgments had been passed on him in the imitation homes of his childhood; he was rubbed raw on the subject of his own deficiencies. Besides, this snotty Wickham didn't know him well enough to call him—what was it? Cold! She was a horseshit student of human behavior. "You got me classified already, huh, Wickham?" he called out. "A cynical old dick, right? Look, I couldn't feel sorrier for that poor woman. Nothing I'd rather do than find her kid. Even if he *is* just a runaway." He told himself not to get excited. He was the sergeant here; he was the one with the ten years. Besides, she wasn't trying to get out of work; she was looking for more, and on her off time. He had to admire that. "Would you believe it?" he said, trying to be sociable. "Police used to chase runaways? Ran 'em on the hot sheet? It's different nowadays. Nowadays—"

"I just *love* cops that keep up on current events," she said through his open window. "I bet you know all about the women's suffrage movement, don't you? Should we join the League of Nations?"

He felt his face redden. "If you paid attention at the academy, you'd've learned a few things," he said, trying to keep his temper. "Number one, the time you waste on a runaway you're gonna be missing six rapes, a dozen burglaries, a couple of stickups, and maybe a homicide. It's a question of priorities, is all."

"My free time's my—"

"Right, right. Your free time, you wanna spend it spinning your wheels, that's your business. I'm just trying to smarten you up." She shot him a look: insolent and superior and judgmental all at once. "But then there's types that don't learn easy," he couldn't resist saying. "They're just . . . slow."

She poked her small nose inside the car window till it almost touched his. "Save your opinion and save your advice," she said evenly. "I've studied *your* type. In abnormal psychology."

"Which school of flower arranging did you attend?"

"Stanford. Police science and public administration. You might look up my master's thesis. Can you read?"

"*Back off!*" Boon said, annoyed at himself for losing control. "What is it with you college women? Anybody disagrees with you, he's dumb. Anybody questions you, he's sexist. Hey, there's certain things men can do better, certain things women—"

"Can do better," she finished for him. "Ironing, that's one, eh? Dishes, right? Women are *terrific* at doing dishes! It's in the genes, wouldn't you say? Mopping, sweeping—"

"Bitching," Boon said, turning the ignition key so hard it bent. "That's in the genes, too."

"I can't be*lieve* I'm having this conversation," she said over the grinding of the hemi-head engine. "You're left over from the sixties. An artifact! You're—you're *a troglodyte!*"

He left her in a cloud of exhaust. Just before he turned out of the alley, he glanced in the mirror. She looked a hundred percent better. Her mouth was shut.

10

Gamble had just completed another circumnavigation of the Justice Building, poking into corners, shaking doorknobs, when he noticed the moon squatting atop the domed stadium. He slumped to a concrete bench and watched the storm swirl away to the east as though sucked down a drain. A flight of night birds wheeled overhead, turning and twisting like shutters, their shade changing from light to dark and back again.

It was V minutes before IX by the old clock on top of the building. He had been walking the periphery of the dark hulk for over an hour, and the exercise had helped him pass out of the panicky stage. Now he was only scared.

Where was Margot?

Amnesia. Could it strike a person with no previous history of mental problems? He thought he had read that somewhere. He *hoped* he had. Amnesia was better than . . . the other possibilities.

If she'd suffered an attack of amnesia, she would have wandered off, not knowing where she lived or who she was. She would still be wandering, confused and chilled and wet in her new sandals and her thin dress. He headed down Fulton, zigzagging back and forth across the rain-washed street to inspect alleys and doors and call her name. After a block he stopped at a staircase that descended to a doorway below street level. He shuddered as he read the familiar sign:

CITY BELOW THE CITY
Underground Tour Starts Here

Could she have. . . ? Without stopping to think, he ran down the steps and yanked at the door.

Padlocked.

Something touched the small of his back and made him whirl. No one was in sight. As usual, the place was giving him the creeps. Last summer they had taken Margot's parents on the tour, and an attack of claustrophobia had dried his mouth and shortened his breath. This part of the city had been built atop stone caissons and landfill, and

some of the rubble had settled beneath the streets, opening underground chambers that had been linked together.
The guide had led them down dark corridors, past storefronts and through abandoned rooms that once had
swarmed with life, and the tour hadn't ended fast enough
for any of them.

He ran up the steps to the sidewalk. Margot wasn't lost
in the underground; he was wasting his time. *Her* time.
The daily tours had ended hours ago. She was walking
somewhere, lost, alone . . . calling his name . . . if
she still remembered it. . . .

He hurried back up the hill, feeling tightness in legs
more accustomed to standing in front of eas ls. He loped
across Fording Street toward the J-building entrance.
Something iridescent caught his eye behind a low orna-
mental hedge. He parted the branches and saw a cadmium green bike with chrome yellow flecks impregnated
in the finish. A cyclist must be working late. Funny place
to park . . .

A sound like a grunt came from deeper in the patch
of green. "Uh, hello?" Gamble whispered.

He heard a low groan and stepped over the bike. A
body lay huddled against the wall. He squatted for a
better look and saw a man in the fetal position, breathing
in snorts and gasps. A sharp smell like semen mingled
with the stench of vomit and wine.

He touched the man's torn jacket. "You need help?"

"Git fucked!" A belligerent old derelict sleeping it off.
He wondered how anyone that drunk could ride a bike.

A fat cop had replaced Pierson at the front desk. "Any
word?" Gamble said, digging at his eyes.

"Pertaining to what?" the cop answered without turning away from a locker. Gamble explained, and the cop
said, "We got your phone number, don't we?"

Was this his punishment for Ciel? "If you hear anything, you'll call?" he asked.

The cop turned around for the first time. There was no sign of concern on his broad face. "We'll call," he said. "We'll *call*."

Gamble felt unaccountably ashamed. He turned away, then turned back. "It was her birthday," he explained.

"Right, right."

As he drove the TR-3 up the hills toward the university district, his eyes seemed sensitive and sore. He realized that he was straining to see into every passing car. A fantasy formed in his mind: he would arrive at their brightly lighted little house and hear the clack-clack of the Selectric and Margot would smile at him and say—

What would she say? April Fool? In August? They didn't play jokes.

She would explain that she'd—she'd rushed home to finish a job. She never *dreamed* he'd be so worried. She hadn't known. If only—

Pipe dreams.

The word that he had fought to suppress all night reeled through his mind in a Möbius strip: KIDNAP KIDNAP KIDNAP . . .

He stopped in front of their bungalow with a squeal of brakes. He almost fell as he ran up the shaky front stairs.

No light shone within or without. The moon had slipped behind a black balloon of cloud.

He could hear the faint ringing of the phone as he poked at the keyhole. Just as he stumbled through the door, it stopped.

II

A soprano voice answered from an inner office of the Starlight Motel, "We're full. Try another place."

"Police," Boon called out, reaching for his tin and his ID card. "I want to see your register." He was in no mood for discussion.

"Forget it," the high voice said from behind the half-closed door.

Boon sniffed a few times and tried to remember the exact ruling at his last departmental trial. Then he stepped around the counter and walked into a small back room.

A circus fat man sat behind a small desk. Except for his girth and his chirpy voice, he appeared to be the stock midnight-to-eight cinder-block motel night clerk, straight from Central Casting. To Boon in his present mood the face looked sculpted from gray bread dough with a handful of sparks thrown at it for acne. Skin the color of a bled-out chihuahua. Right hand out of sight in his lap, left squeezing a magazine. "The register," Boon said abruptly.

"You . . . Vice?" Boon's trained ears caught a note of fear.

"Homicide."

"Forget it," the man repeated. Apparently only the Vice Squad scared him, suggesting that nobody was committing murders or assaults or robberies on the premises, but that pimps and whores and johns were probably running in and out on double shifts. "Not without—"

"Authorization?" Boon asked.

The man nodded once and resumed his reading.

Boon was still aggravated by his meeting with the

policewoman, but he bit his tongue and began leafing through the register. "Hey!" the clerk called, slowly struggling to his feet. "I said—"

"Siddown, asshole," Boon said.

The clerk grabbed the heavy register and hugged it to his chest like a chubby brat protecting a toy. "I said *no!*" he repeated in his strange high voice.

Boon grabbed the man by the shirtfront and walked him fast into the rear wall. A print of an autumn farm scene clattered to the floor.

"Was there any further authorization you needed?" Boon asked, straddling the wreckage. The clerk sniffled and rotated his neck from his vantage point on the floor. "Make yourself comfortable," Boon advised. "I gotta check a few names."

There was no Anna Boon or Annaliese Boon or Anna Kuretz or A. Kuretz or anything resembling his wife's married or maiden name. He wasn't surprised. Why would she come to a sleazy joint like this? Her little apartment wasn't the Holiday Inn, but at least it was clean and private. Still, he'd feel better if he checked. Alkies tended to repeat themselves, and she had holed up here before.

"Stand," Boon said, offering his hand. It was like lifting Jell-O. "Let's run down these names. Ruth Adamson— you know her?"

"No. The day man musta checked her in."

"When?"

"Dunno. Five, six days ago."

"Sure?"

"Positive. Hey, you hurt my neck, man."

"How about—Esther Tannenbaum?"

"She's permanent. You got plenty balls, man. You know you twisted—?"

"Mrs. P. Ross?"

"Uh, she come in last night." The clerk was rotating his shoulders. Boon knew what was going through that pea brain: if he couldn't make a whiplash stick, he'd try the pinched nerve route. A buck was a buck. . . .

"What's Mrs. P. Ross look like?"

"Black. Fat—"

"Okay." Wrong on two counts.

The last female name on the register was the No. 2 alias of a well-known aging whore who performed special tricks for twenty dollars and down. Dealt a little, too, but only to her johns; the herpes simplex was free. "Nice little clientele you got here," he said. The clerk kneaded his blubber. "Maybe I'll have to call in the Vice. Maybe not. It depends."

"On what?"

Boon flipped his wallet to a full-face picture of Annaliese. "Seen this lady?"

The clerk looked grudgingly at the wide face and the short, frizzy hairdo and the hollow, staring eyes. "I—no. *Unh-unh.*"

"She stayed here four, five months ago. You here then?"

"No."

"She hasn't been around the last coupla days?"

"No."

"You sure?" Boon stepped closer.

"Uh, yeah. Positive."

"Okay. She comes in, ring me." He pulled out his business card and scribbled his apartment phone number on the back. "Home or office, night or day. Even if you see her on the street."

"You must want her bad. What's the charge?"

Boon headed for the door. "Suspicion of—" He was stumped. What *was* the charge? "Uh, suspicion of . . . desertion."

The clerk arched his back in a sensuous fat man's stretch and squealed his pain in G above high H. "You hassled me for—*desertion*? That a big fucking deal now?"

"It is to me."

12

Gamble paced his front room like a prisoner. Against his better judgment, he dialed headquarters and asked if someone had just called him at home. "Definitely not," the new deskman said, still sounding harried. *Then who had?*

"What can I do to help find my wife?" he asked, embarrassed by his tremor.

"You really wanna know? You can quit bugging us."

He turned on the radio for the 1:00 A.M. news; maybe the station knew something the cops didn't. But the news was flat and boring and political. He thought of phoning . . .

Who?

Margot's parents were five hundred miles away; a wake-up call at one in the morning would scare them half to death, and what was the point? So he could have someone to commiserate with? Another self-indulgence. Tomorrow would be soon enough.

A sense of solitary impotence pressed down on him. By himself he couldn't make her come back, couldn't make the phone ring, couldn't even collect his thoughts. His starting point was his ending point: *Margot was gone.* Somewhere under the dark summer sky . . .

He dialed Brooks and slammed the phone down before the first ring. What if Ciel answered? He'd barely seen her since . . . that night. He'd had one drink with Brooks in the faculty lounge, staring steadfastly at the bridge of his friend's nose to keep from giving away his shame; that was the only time they'd been face to face in two weeks. He'd asked Brooks half-seriously if an artist had to be phobic and neurotic, and Brooks had laughed and produced the expected answer: "No, but it helps."

Now Gamble desperately needed to talk. He picked up the phone and put it down again. His mind was mush; he couldn't decide. He realized that indecision was an early sign of mental disorder. *Has Margot disappeared, or am I imagining all this?* Was it just a case of altered perception?

He walked to the bedroom. He wished he knew what to look for. Nothing was disturbed. Her jeans and tank top hung on the chair—the outfit she had worn all day. A sheet of legal-sized paper stuck out of the Selectric. He leaned over and read what she had typed: " . . . and in his counterclaim respondent further prays for immediate relief. . . ."

Immediate relief. There was a half bottle of Sauza Gold in the cabinet, the same treacherous booze he had drunk with Ciel, and there were a few capsules of Seconal in the bathroom. Tequila and sleeping pills; that would make him crash, all right. But what if the phone rang and she needed help? Or the cops needed some information?

Any pain was preferable to letting her down—again.

He tried to relax by breathing deeply and striding from room to room. Don't panic; *think!* She's alive, I know that much. How do I know? Because . . . what's that German thing? *Was muss man, das tut man;* what one must, one does. Margot has to be alive, because . . . she *must.*

Reciting familiar words had always comforted him; it was like clutching a talisman, a charm. Classic works of art calmed him the same way. The great painters had always seemed to talk to him through their work. "I suffered, yes, everyone suffers, but I survived, and I produced . . . *this.*"

He gazed at Fiorentino's *Descent from the Cross*, hanging in faded repro from the wall, glanced at a few other paintings, and felt the presence of friends. He turned and looked out the front window. The storm had blown the night air clean. The city lights were captured on the surface of the bay; whole buildings lay on their sides, as though held with fixative.

Somehow reassured, he decided to call Brooks. He picked up the phone and dialed and this time let it ring till a sleepy voice said, "Hello?"

Ciel.

He started to disconnect but pulled his hand back. *Was muss man, das tut man.* His own unease was beside the point.

"Ciel? Severn."

"S-Severn?" Her voice was weak. "What, uh, what *time* is it?"

"Late. Uh, Ciel, something's . . ."

"You're calling *me*?" She sounded as though a dentist had packed her mouth.

"I'm calling Brooks."

"He isn't here, Severn." She had finally found her ex-cheerleader's voice. "He's at the Surfside. In Ocean Beach. Tolliver threatened suicide. Brooks'll be back, uh, late tomorrow."

"Tolliver?"

"*You* know. His manic-depressive?" She sounded surprised that he didn't know. It was so like her; she always presumed that the entire world was involved in her personal mythology, that names important to her must be important to everyone.

"What's *happened*, Severn?" she asked. She sounded wistful, vulnerable, but he would never again make the mistake of taking her at face value. Hearing her voice, he saw the appalling act committed before his eyes and accepted again that the fault was as much his as hers. Maybe more. What a thing to do to Margot. And to Brooks. Friend from childhood, brother in every way but biological. *Is that what this disappearance is all about?* Some bizarre kind of retribution?

"Severn? You there?"

"Oh." He gulped. "Uh, Ciel, Margot's . . ." Her name stuck in his throat.

"Sev, whatever is the matter?"

He struggled to keep control. He didn't want to sound like someone sucking around for sympathy.

"Margot, she's . . . gone away."

"She *left you?*" The little-girl voice skittered almost out of range.

"No!" he said. Why did everyone want to believe she'd left him? Was the thought so pleasing? He tried to speak, but the words stuck again. If he told Ciel what happened, then for some strange unfathomable reason Margot would be gone for sure. It wasn't like that stupid game of cops and robbers down at headquarters; Ciel and Brooks were *real*. With effort, he said, "Margot, uh, she went, we went . . ." He took a deep breath and shut his eyes hard. Lack of self-control was unmanly. When he was five, he would hold back the tears till it felt as though an ice cube were stuck in his throat. Now the ice cube was back.

"Severn?" Ciel's voice had softened; she was into her motherly role now. Once he had loved her like a sister.

"I'll call Brooks later," he said.

"Sev, did it have anything to do . . . with *us?*"

He wanted to say, *Ciel, there is no "us" and never was,* but this wasn't the time. "No," he said.

"She *couldn't* have left you. She loved you—*loves* you, I mean. Severn, come over right now. We'll brew up a pot. You mustn't be alone. Brooks'll be here soon. He'll have ideas, we'll make plans. We'll . . . get her back!" Jumping from mood to mood in her childlike way, she was beginning to take on the tones of a subteen planning a play, but then her voice dropped again. "No one could leave you for good. Oh, Severn, I've—we've missed you. Come over. I just want to help you."

Two weeks before, she had used the same expression. Then it had meant sex as analgesic, sex as tranquilizer. What did it mean tonight? He couldn't believe that she was trying to take advantage of Margot's disappearance. Even for Ciel, that would have been crass. Or did she just feel guilty?

"I have to look for her," he said evenly. "I have to stay by the phone."

"How can you stay by the phone and look for Margot? You're not making sense."

She was right. It was one of the little impracticalities that arise when a wife drops off the face of the earth. If he left the house, the police might call, Margot herself might call. She could have been the one who tried to reach him earlier when he'd rushed into the house one ring too late. The phone had sat silent ever since. Suppose she'd been abducted; how could the kidnappers contact him? By letter? He was locked in his house by the circumstances.

"Ciel, thanks. I'll, uh, talk to you later."

"Are you coming—?"

"I'm sorry. No. I mean—uh, thanks."

He put down the phone and walked to the window. In another hour dawn would begin in muted red, tinged at the edges with pink, its summertime color till it changed in the fall with the leaves. Sleep was out of the question. If only—

The phone rang.

He crossed the room in two leaps and almost shouted into the phone, "YES?"

"Severn, *please*—"

"Ciel, I can't." He hung up.

He dropped to the recliner, his long legs hanging over the end, and tried to work through the problem logically. It was a waste of time. What could explain the way she vanished? A flying saucer? A gang? What would they demand for ransom? Paintings and sculptures he could hardly give away?

He realized he was hungry. The familiar sensation disturbed him. Was it fair to be thinking of his stomach when Margot was missing?

He broke two farm eggs in a buttered pan and watched them bubble and brown. The pungency of sautéed puffballs still hung in the air; they had picked them together in the woods behind the arboretum and gorged at her birthday dinner, tête-à-tête, a few hours before. Stacking the dishes afterward, she had tapped him on the shoulder with a serving fork and proclaimed, "I dub thee—*healed!*" At last. He had worked night and day for three months getting ready for his one-man show, and when the show had collapsed, he had gone into a depression so profound that his friend Brooks had talked of having him hospitalized. But tonight he had been pronounced healthy again, by wifely proclamation. And now she was gone. . . .

When he tried to lift the fried eggs, they stuck to the bottom of the skillet. How unreal, he told himself. She's gone, and I'm frying eggs. *Burning* eggs. "Oh, honey," he said out loud in the empty kitchen, "I'm sorry, I'm so sorry." His appetite was gone; he dumped the pan in the sink.

He needed something to do, something to keep him from gorging on memory, on guilt. He couldn't just sit by the phone and leave everything to a bunch of uninvolved cops. But what could he do that would help?

Paint . . . ?

The police would need a good picture of Margot. Why hadn't they asked for one? Pure carelessness. How could they hunt for someone they'd never seen? He would find a good likeness and have it copied and paper the town.

He opened his wallet to the color shot from their honeymoon. At nineteen, she'd been bony from her modeling diet and blistered from the sun; nobody would recognize the mature Margot from that picture. And anyway, he'd have to tack up a hundred copies at least, and copying machines turned photographs into blobs. He needed something stark and black that the machines could reproduce.

A line drawing.

He slid his charcoals from their place on the shelf. He slapped fresh paper under the easel clips and laid down the long curve of her head from the scalp to the neck in a single sweep. He sketched in her narrow nose, her full lips, her high cheekbones, her gently sloping eyes. The flow stopped only once, when he had to rub out the line of her chin with his shirt sleeve and replace it with a stronger one. He finished with hundreds of fine strands of coal black hair that looked real enough to stroke.

For the first time all night, he felt pleased with himself. The picture defined Margot better than any photograph, and it would copy as well as a typewritten page. He stood back like Gossaert or Gilbert Stuart after weeks of posing a subject. *Margot from Memory* . . .

He thought again of Brooks. He wanted to talk to his best friend, no matter what unspoken shame hung between them. Brooks knew human problems; every day he worked with people *in extremis,* like—what was his name? Tolliver?

"Operator," he said, "I need the number of the Surfside Motel. Ocean Beach."

A few minutes later he was asking a sleepy-voiced man with ruined vocal cords to connect him with Mr. Tolliver's room. Brooks might as well treat two patients tonight. Just hearing his voice would be a help—

"Not here," the clerk said.

"Huh?" The answer caught him by surprise. "Checked out?"

"Never checked in. Name like Tolliver, I'd remember."

"How about Asbury? Dr. Brooks Asbury?"

"Hold on." This time the pause was shorter. "You got the wrong place, mister."

"I . . . thanks."

Why had Brooks lied to Ciel? He didn't play around. *Did he?*

There would be a simple explanation. As the new man at the clinic Brooks caught the wildest patients, the ones who were always threatening to kill themselves or others, running afoul of the law, waking the doctor at 3:00 A.M. to air their grievances. Tolliver probably disappeared down the beach waving a butcher knife, trying to escape the poor M.D. who was trying to calm him. And Brooks was probably on his way home to store up some sleep for the next crisis. . . .

He couldn't picture an unfaithful Brooks. But when this night had begun, he hadn't been able to picture a missing Margot. He looked out the front window. Far down the slope of the sleepy streets, the surface of the bay was beginning to glow. A red Martian dawn had arrived without her.

II *Wednesday, August 13*

13

Tally Wickham awoke feeling troubled. Was it the hot dreams? No, they brought relief of a sort, and they'd never make her pregnant. Still, the real thing wouldn't hurt now and then. Without thinking, she flopped an arm across her Japanese futon bed and hit . . . no one. Half-asleep, she tried to remember how long it had been. Occasional abstinence was good for the soul, but three months? Wasn't that bad for the pancreas or something?

She disconnected her Abyssinian cat, Jerome, from her neck and tried to remember the last time. Gwillin, of course. Now he was halfway around the world at a Save the Whales seminar, but she didn't miss him as much as she'd expected. So much technique and so little warmth. Not that she minded occasional innovation, imaginative strainings toward perfection, but the Me Tarzan You Jane number was getting old. Maybe on his trip he'd connect with someone more compatible. An acrobat, say, or a contortionist. They could start their own act. . . .

She opened one eye and saw her revolver, empty as usual, hanging over the nearest chair in its holster. Damn. She should have hidden the thing so it wouldn't assault her eyeballs the first thing in the morning.

She looked across her studio apartment at the table with the white-on-white tablecloth and the miniature Wedgwood vase of primroses centered as though she were expecting company. Maybe that's what was bothering her: the lack of same. Not that there wasn't a surplus of availables: doctors and lawyers and the geologist from the Heights and the broker from Shearson and the young traffic judge and *platoons* of fellow officers, except that she'd made it a rule never to date a cop. One of her term papers at Stanford had stated her position quite nicely, she thought: "The role of policewoman is not the ideal vantage point from which to observe the basic civility of the American male. The typical female police officer lives in a state of siege."

Besides, she said to herself as she started to roll up the futon, cops were the world's worst lovers; everybody said so.

She was waking up the way she always woke up: mind crackling, body responding like an enervated sloth. She slid the bedroll behind her tattersall-checked sofa and stretched her newly tender arm an inch at a time. She felt only a touch of pain, rubbed the elbow briskly, and then hauled herself to her feet and aimed her naked body across the polished parquet floor toward the kitchen. On the way, she passed her Mach I weight machine in front of the mirror and noticed that her breasts seemed to be jiggling more than usual, each in its own direction and out of sync with the other. Funny she'd never noticed so much movement. Was that normal? It couldn't be. Breasts didn't start to droop at twenty-three. *Did they?* God, the mysteries of female construction.

She stepped closer to the mirror and did a lazy hip-flip and noticed that her left breast seemed to shake a split second longer than her right. Maybe it would be better if they were a size or two smaller. Certainly would simplify things on the job. Those leering cops. Had her father been that way? She doubted it. There was a new generation of lawmen now: tough, dedicated, and blunt. Mostly blunt. Not that she couldn't handle them, at least for the four more weeks till she went back to Palo Alto and began her dissertation. She had become accustomed to the passes and the cracks and the double entendres; standard everyday work hazards. She wasn't the least surprised when she'd read about the two deputies who'd cornered a meter maid and exposed themselves; it struck her as a classic example of police courtship ritual. Women had been working as cops for a hundred years; wouldn't you think they'd be accepted as equals instead of peculiarly equipped oddities by now?

"*Unh*-unh," she answered herself aloud. Not if you knew cops.

She remembered what the lieutenant had told her after she helped nail the mugger. "Lady, you really got balls." The *ne plus ultra* of police compliments. Was *that* what was troubling her mind this morning? Police sexism?

She blew at her origami birds and set them to swinging and dipping like swallows while Jerome circled her slim ankles and purred for his breakfast. This was her day off, and she had better things to do than sit around bemoaning male chauvinism. First a little shopping; she'd finally saved enough to replace that ratty lamp behind the sofa. And this afternoon: *akido.* She'd throw that smug black belt teacher if it took six more years. Oh, *no,* not today. The damned tendinitis. Wonder how long it'll last this time . . . ?

Her sleepy hands needed four tries to fit the blender jar on its base. She measured the ingredients, spilled some on her polyurethane countertop, plopped in a banana for flavor, and watched as dolomite, brewer's yeast, wheat germ, safflower oil, yogurt, and assorted vitamins and minerals swirled and bounced into a gritty, chalky blend which she downed in one long swallow. This day was beginning to show promise. For once she'd remembered to peel the banana.

The boy!

Lordie Lord, that was it. . . .

She sat naked in the lotus position on a corduroy pillow

and flung open the phone book. Schafer, Schell, Schockley —there it was: "Schulte, B." The number rang once, and a male voice muttered, "Yeah?" as though accepting a challenge.

"This is Tally Wickham." She tried to keep her voice light.

"Who?"

"Uh, Officer Wickham? Juvenile?"

"*You found Sammy?*" The voice shook with joy. Uncle George was human after all.

"No. I mean . . . I don't know. Anything at your end?"

"Not a goddamn word." He was himself again. "We set by the phone all night." He sounded as if it were the PD's fault.

"I'm sorry. Is Betty—?"

"Went to work. Didn't sleep two minutes."

"Tell her not to worry. We'll find him."

"Sure," he said, and hung up.

She thought about the terrific emotional support she'd been getting from males lately. Surly George and his charming manners. Her main squeeze, Gwillin, off on a long trip without even kissing her good-bye. The watch commander and his sexist cracks, and—

Oh, yes, Sgt. J. Boon. The wise old philosopher. *There's certain things men can do better.* So out of touch. Normal people didn't even *discuss* those things anymore. Well, the poor guy probably has a high school equivalency diploma and finished eighty-ninth in a class of ninety at the academy and wouldn't have been accepted in the first place if the corruption scandal hadn't caused so many retirements. Now he's Dick Tracy and Sherlock Holmes combined. If he were female, he'd still be writing meters. There's certain things men can do better. . . .

She pulled a tired bouquet of nasturtiums from a jar and put them in the refrigerator for salads. She'd have to pick more today. What if that Boon put her on report for calling him off a homicide? She watered the jade plant.

Was he a fink as well as a jerk?

The health drink was beginning to do its work. She looked at the oven clock: 7:40. Second watch roll call was in four hours and five minutes; she'd be on her fifth personal errand by then. She wondered if the sergeant would give her time to check out Sammy Schulte when she went back on duty tomorrow. Not a chance; there were too many warrants to serve, too many school crossings to check, too much paper work and protocol and procedure and the inflexibility that passed for intelligence: the same wrongheadedness that made the great Boon advise her not to turn every runaway into a big deal. . . .

The only answer to that kind of stupidity was to go out and prove them wrong. Jerome rubbed against her ankle and meowed in agreement. Or hunger. She opened a can of Hi-Pro cat food and decided not to shop today; she could buy the lamp anytime. She'd made a promise to Betty Schulte.

She left the apartment wearing a cream cotton seersucker dress and the flattest of flats in pale bone, the sort of summer outfit that wouldn't shriek "Fuzz!" where she was headed. She remembered something her father had said: "Patrol cops, we're nothing but a bunch of damn mules. We go out and beat on doors till our hands hurt, talk and listen and ask questions and hear everybody's troubles till all of a sudden—somebody gives something away. Then we tip the dicks. Every time you hear a big case's been solved, nine times out of ten your mules turned it." Capt. Andrew Simmons Wickham, the paradigmatic mule. If only he hadn't made that one mistake. If only the shame hadn't broken him . . .

This morning the residents of Sammy Schulte's sagging tenements weren't feeling especially friendly toward the police department or its mules, even the ones in cream cotton dresses. At ground-floor rear, a slammed door almost fractured one of her pattynails. On the second landing a boy who appeared to be about ten asked, "You the heat?" and when Tally nodded, he said, "Don't be comin' 'round here wit'out no warrant."

A painful conversation with a child who said he was named Ol' Mose developed nothing beyond the fact that Samuel Schulte had worn out his welcome by sitting on the family's velveteen sofa in wet overalls. "But he's *retarded*," Tally said, not quite sure why she was defending the boy.

"My mama say—kin I tell ya what my mama say?"

"Of course."

"Piss stink the same from a broken jar." The folk sayings of the deprived . . .

She was walking toward her Honda when she remembered Karen McCauthen, the nine-year-old female fence who once had put Samuel up to burglary. Her mother supported the family by hustling while the father served a nickel for breaking and entering. Not a very promising interview. But a mule wasn't supposed to make judgments in advance.

The back door opened a slit, and a small voice said, "Yep?" Tally recognized a pair of black eyes like polished coals. Hearing that tiny voice again, her mind flashed a readout of the girl's future: smoking grass at ten, into heavy dope at twelve, annual abortions starting at thirteen, on the street at sixteen, used and abused by pimps and johns till she wears out at twenty-one, and after that a trip or two to the joint, like her father, and oblivion. Looking into the gleaming round face, Tally refused to believe that every year a little of the glow would dissolve from those impossibly lustrous eyes till they turned flat, and dull, and dead.

"Hi, Karen," she said. "Remember me?"

The door widened to an inch. "Uh, yes, may-am."

"May I come in?"

"Uh, nobody here."

"Could you come out a second?"

"Sho."

The child stepped into the bright morning light that fell on the porch of the wooden tenement. "Oh," she said, taking a step backward. "It's *you*."

"It's me, honey," Tally said, trying to sound disarming. "It's about Sammy again."

"Sammy? Honest to God, Miz Wicken, whatever he's did, I din't do it. Miz Wicken, may-am, it's *different* now."

Tally squatted alongside the child and reached out a hand. To her surprise, Karen McCauthen took it and said, "Sammy okay? He din't, uh, git busted again, did he?"

"No, Karen. Nothing like that. Can I ask you a few questions?" The girl nodded. "When did you see him last?"

"Yesterday morning. Hey, I'm goin' over there in a while. He got him a new ten-speed. A *Sears*. Cool, huh?"

"You saw his bike?"

"*Rode* it! Yesterday morning. I'm the one tol' him git it licensed, the bloods from the projix'll steal it if he don't."

"The bloods from . . . the projects?"

"Yeah. If you don't git a license, they'll snatch it. If you register it, they still might snatch it, but at least there's a chance to git it back." Out of the mouths of babes . . .

"You told him that?"

"Yeah, and I took him over to the J-Building. Four blocks"—she pointed—"that way."

"Did he register the bike?"

"Reckon. I walked on home."

"With Sammy?"

"No, may-am. See, he got stuck in line or sumpin. He was in there like . . . *hours*. I couldn't wait. Hey, whyn't you ask him? He just live"—she pointed again—"right over there."

"So the last you saw him, he was—?"

"Walking into the building, yes, may-am."

"With his bike?"

"No, may-am. He *park* his bike. Behind the hedge in

front of them big doors. I guarded it for a while, but nobody'd take nothin' with all them cops around." She smiled ingenuously, as though she were enjoying their chat. Where was the tough little Fagin who had told Tally to go to hell a few months back?

"Thanks, Karen. You've been a big help." She walked toward her Honda, whispering into her tape recorder, and the child skipped alongside. Tally couldn't resist saying, "You're so changed, Karen. What happened?"

"You mean like rapping with you and all?"

"Well, yes. Remember how you were the last time?"

"Yeah. I 'member. You gotta realize . . ." Her small voice trailed off.

"Realize what?"

"I'm ten now."

Tally parted the dusty green hedges and found the green bike with the golden flecks. She wheeled it into the property room, signed four sets of receipts and evidence slips, and hurried upstairs to her locker. Sammy Schulte was no runaway. She couldn't wait to tell Boon.

14

Boon arrived at the homicide office like an incoming train, opening the swinging doors with his chest and spewing smoke across the open bull pen. His own twenty square feet were in a far corner and included a bludgeoned old desk with a missing drawer, a metal filing cabinet bulging with papers, a Royal typewriter with a missing cover, and a beige Touch-Tone phone that Annaliese had bought him to "soften things a little." Above on the stained wall hung a pinup calendar featuring Teri Astaire the Tassel Queen, courtesy Lou's Tire Hospital, Satisfaction Guaranteed, Dr. on Duty 24 Hours.

As usual, he was halfway to his desk before Francine Largent called out, "The *roster*," and as usual, he waved his hand behind him as though shooing off a Spitz. The harassed receptionist raised her substantial backside from a cushion pressed as thin as a slice of smoked salmon and took two steps to a blackboard with a list of names under the headings "Time Out" and "Expected." Boon remembered scribbling something under "Time Out" one day a few years ago, but no one had ever seen him write anything under "Expected." They could expect him when they saw him.

He plopped down in his bare wooden chair and tried not to watch as Francine chalked an oversize "IN" next to his name and crashed back into her own seat, popping Freedent and glaring at a point above and beyond his head. Boon avoided her glance. After last night he had no desire to confront any female except his missing wife. Tally Wickham's words still burned his ears. *Cops like you make me sick. . . .* He ought to make her eat his commendations one by one. Daisies in her hair, for Chrisakes. Probably hasn't fired a round since the academy . . .

It took two hands to lift the contents of his in box. Hours of boring paper work lay ahead, and his eyelids felt like lead weights. At three thirty in the morning he had clawed his way out of his standard nightmare: Richie tied to the fence, the car backing off to ram again, and his own screams and yells as he ran and ran without getting closer. In this production the car would speed off and Boon would finally reach the mashed remains of his brother. Sometimes Richie was silent; last night a few words had issued from the twisted hole of his mouth like cries from the bottom of a well: "John, why didn't you help me? *Why didn't you help me?*" When the dream took this form, Boon always woke up and snapped on the light; otherwise, the scene repeated itself for hours. He would read *Law and Order* or *The FBI Bulletin* or one of his gun magazines till the sun touched his curtains, and then he would encase his head in pillows and try to sleep fast before his alarm went off at seven.

He dumped the contents of his in box on the desk and riffled through:

A half dozen yellow "call-back" messages, two left over from yesterday. He would make the calls later, assuming he found time.

A memo from the medical examiner's office in the new building: Did Sergeant Boon wish to observe at the Hayden W. Harrier post-mortem this morning? Sergeant Boon did not.

A priority message from Wanda Marquez: Manuel was threatening to cut her again. Would Sergeant Boon mind. . . ? Not at all. He would drop around with his faithful slapjack, and peace would reign till Mano went on another tear.

A BOLF on a woman named Gamble. He tipped it in the wastebasket. He was too busy worrying about his own wife to "Be on Lookout For" somebody else's.

No call in three days now. Where the Christ *was* she? He consoled himself that she still had four days to go to beat her last disappearing act. No skin off my ass, she wants to fade away. I wish I really felt that way. . . .

He unwrapped a cream cheese and jelly sandwich, stoked up another cigar, and bent his scrawny bones over the desk, trying to make a match on a rapist who was giving the office fits. He didn't know which was more useless: the composite sketch he held in his hand or the blurry mug shots in his personal album of fools and assassins. His eyes narrowed to slits as smoke streamed from the side of his mouth and rose in levels of gray. Every few minutes he would rest his little cigar on the side of the desk and grope for the sandwich at arm's length. Staring at the album in front of him, he would eat and smoke and try to maintain his concentration.

He looked up and caught Francine's scowl. It put him in mind of another female who had frowned on the way he smoked while he ate, called him an animal one night a couple years ago. Funny how you remember those things. That was before Anna got so deep into vodka that he could have set her on fire and she wouldn't have noticed.

Captain Mondragon passed through with all the grace of a runaway elk just as Boon's eye fell on a possible. He leaned forward for a closer look at:

ADAM RAHMAN MUHAMMAD
Wanted, Detroit. Mich., homicide, assault.
Wanted, Cape Girardeau, Mo., manslaughter 1.
FBI: Dyer Act, Unlawful flight.
Note: Former girlfriend, Lola Saad Muhammad resided 4231½ South Manor late 1979. Both regarded armed, dangerous

For several minutes he looked for ID points, found a few that checked, but too many that didn't. He stretched his skinny arms till his dagger tattoo showed on one arm and his green beret on the other, mementos of a drunken three-day pass in Saigon. He slammed his fools' album shut and said, "Balls!" in a loud voice. Three detectives working at their desks declined comment. So did the receptionist.

In the back of his mind, he heard that annoying voice again. *He's a missing child! But* YOU *wouldn't understand.* . . . No, HE wouldn't understand; HE was too dumb. A couple weeks on patrol and she knows all the answers. Christ, she don't even know the questions yet.

He wrenched the cigar butt from his lips and fired it ten feet into one of the Justice Building's few remaining cuspidors. A short hiss confirmed a direct hit as he reached in the pocket of his crumpled Arrow shirt for another Swisher. They should hire women to do this tedious goddamn desk work, he said to himself as he scraped his nail across the head of a wooden match.

A loud ring interrupted the first pecks of a tack hammer headache over his left eye. "Boonhomicide," he answered, holding the phone an inch from his ear as though it had teeth.

"Candy." The name was spoken in the low tones of someone lurking behind a potted palm. *This is Candy,* it seemed to say. *Don't turn around.*

How the hell did *he* know I was looking for help? Boon asked himself as he listened to the heavy breathing. Candy was a female impersonator, a cokehead, and a licensed car booster, but most of all, he was a snitch. At Boon's behest the detective bureau indulged him in his car-pilfering habit because he would roll over on his own mother for a toot, and without a few gay informants the department's record on homicides would be even drearier than it was.

"I've, uh, got something prime for you," Candy began in his hoarse morning croak. Boon could feel the pain over the telephone wire. Old whores like Candy spent their evenings hustling dick, and if they scored big enough, they had a high old time all night, practicing their vice versa, but whether they scored or not, they paid a heavy price the morning after.

"Go ahead," Boon said.

"I'd rather tell you, uh, *you* know—face to face."

"Gimme a hint first."

"H. W. H. *H. W. H.* Oh, God, I'm so . . . *wrecked!* Tell me I'll live."

"You'll live, Candy. Wait! You mean Hayden W—"

"*Hush!*" For the first time there was life in the voice. "The walls have earsssss." Little did the poor fruit know; Boon had hit a button, and the conversation was being recorded. With snitches you had to get the information while they were in the mood. Otherwise, they might go diving in a lead suit and leave you empty.

"You can talk," Boon said. "This is confidential."

"Promise?"

"Who can you trust if you can't trust me?"

"Well, I think maybe I, uh, saw something." A cough, then silence.

"Candy, Chrissakes, come *on*, man!"

The voice became almost inaudible. "I think I saw . . . the guy that did it."

"No crap." Boon tried to sound unimpressed, as though snitches threw him killers every morning before break-fast.

"Yesterday afternoon I was just leaving the tearoom"—Boon pressed his ear against the phone—"and I clock this dude running away from a parked car like it tried to fuck him, ya know? Looked like a new Dodge, but I see in the paper it was a Chrysler."

"What time?"

"Five, five thirty. Just before the storm."

"What'd he look like?"

"Will you hold your *panties* on? Forty, fifty, sixty. An older type, ya know? And he was short and—oh, God, I'm so *ssstrung!*"

"That's a great help, Candy. With that description I can bust half the town."

"Listen, sweets, lighten up, will ya? I wasn't paying all that much attention, ya know? I'd just finished a little, uh, tearoom business, dig? The *last* thing I imagined was the guy was dirty. Then I pick up this morning's paper, and the time's right, the car's right, everything matches up. Listen, Sarge, this little stud's your man. I'd stake my reputation on it."

"You'd risk that much, huh? Okay, I'll need you to look at a mug shot laydown."

"Do you, uh, have a little something for me?"

"If you come across, yeah."

"I always come across. Be right down."

Boon was surprised. "You're coming here?"

"Yeah. Uh, Sarge, would it be okay if I wore . . . an outfit? I have an appointment, and they want me in something special. Is that like cool?"

Sometimes Boon felt like a germ talking to other germs in a language only germs could understand.

"What kind of outfit?" He dreaded the answer.

"Uh, religious drag? But . . . tasteful."

"Religious drag?"

"It's not really what you'd call drag. It's more, ya know, sort of a nun's outfit. You'll *love* it. A black cotton bonnet and a gathered black dress that covers my knees. Oh, yeah, and a rosary that wraps around my neck about six times. And—"

"Look, Candy, let me bring the pictures over your place. You're still in the Baltic, right? It'll just take a minute."

"No, *don't!* I've got—*you* know—business." He sounded slightly panicked at the prospect of a cop's visit. Boon didn't want to push too hard; Candy had been known to take long drives. For a month or two.

"How soon can you be at headquarters?"

"A half hour."

"I'll wait."

An hour later Boon's extension rang.

"Hi, sweets."

"Where *are* you?"

"Downstairs. In the lobby."

"Dressed as . . . a nun?"

"Don't worry, nobody's made me. I bought a paper, the newsdealer said, 'Thank you, ma'am.' "

"The newsdealer's legally blind."

"Be up in a minute."

Boon looked at his watch: 10:40. Thank heaven for little girls; at least he'd have something to work on. A forty- or fifty- or sixty-year-old killer . . . Well, it's better than nothing. The body hasn't even been posted; I barely started a file on Hayden W. Harrier, and already an eye-witness is waiting downstairs. If Candy isn't hustling me for a quick snort, I'll clean this one up fast.

He lit a Swisher Sweet from the old one, walked to the reception desk, and peered down the hall, trying to be the first lucky detective to spot a stout nun in black. What the hell was keeping him? Must've stopped for a pick-me-up. Or a primp . . .

He heard a female voice in the back of his mind. *I studied your type in college. In abnormal psychology.* That goddamn Wickham, her wisecracks repeated like a Mexican lunch. He'd spent the first ten minutes of his workday looking up the word *tragladite*, but it wasn't even in the dictionary. Just as well. If he told that little snip what he really thought of her, there'd be a departmental beef sure as hell.

At eleven fifteen he walked to the window and peered through a gray blue layer of haze at pawnships, bail bond offices, sandwich joints, the Paradise Billiards Parlor: same old view. Somebody said the detective bureau in the new building wouldn't have any windows. A definite improvement.

He cursed to himself. That crazy coke-sniffing snitch had phoned from the lobby twenty-five minutes ago. Damn, I at least had a start on the case, but now—

"Sergeant Boon?" the receptionist called from across the room. "A lady to see you."

He blew out a long, refreshing stream of smoke. Thank Christ for small favors.

He turned and saw Tally Wickham.

15

Gamble swilled down the last searing slurp of a double mug of instant Blue Mountain coffee and walked out to his TR-3 in front of the little house. The sky was a deep blue of absolute clarity; the air, clean and breezy. But the weather was no comfort.

He had slept for five minutes, sitting up; it had made him feel vaguely disloyal to Margot. He could remember other sleepless nights, but they were almost always caused by anticipation of happy events: big games, plays, ego trips like his one-man show. Sleeping had seemed like a maddening waste of time then, an obstacle that separated him from the next day. But last night it had seemed like an act of contempt.

He knew this was overdramatic, unfair to himself, but he also knew that he would be bounced around by his moods till she came back. The way he had grabbed that desk cop; God, how stupid! He had to control his impulsiveness. There would be plenty of time later for temper tantrums.

He turned the key and pulled the hand throttle to let the engine smooth out while he double-checked his list, scribbled in charcoal on a scrap of drawing paper. The first item was "bank."

The teller counted out $143.18 and asked him if he was closing the account. "I'm not sure," he answered.

"Will we hear from you?"

"Uh, yeah." He was already halfway to the door.

The second item on his list was "phone recorder." A sign in the window told him that Discount Radio opened at ten. He looked at his watch and felt annoyed that someone he didn't even know could make him wait at a time like this. He banged hard on the door, but no one answered.

Damn! He shouldn't be leaving his phone uncovered. Maybe Brooks would baby-sit the house for a while. No, it was too early. Brooks would still be . . . wherever he was.

A patrol car rolled slowly down the campus street, and a young cop with a handlebar mustache studied him. He realized he must look suspicious, peering into a locked store. He walked to the curb and bent down to talk through the opened window. "Uh, Officer," he said, "could you tell me . . . I mean, is there any word on the missing woman?"

"Missing woman?" The cop was about Gamble's own age; his eyes were bloodshot, as though he had stayed up all night. That makes two of us, Gamble said to himself.

"Her name's Margot Gamble," he said.

"We got something on a missing woman, Phil?" the cop asked his partner.

The driver said, "Hey, we're late now. . . ." The words dropped off.

"What'd you say the subject's name was?" the young cop asked.

"The *subject?*" Relax, he told himself. That's just cop talk. "Margot Gamble. G-A-M-B-L-E. She's a . . . she's a—legal secretary." Why hadn't he just said "typist"? What was it about cops that unnerved him?

"Lemme check," the young cop said lazily. He slid a clipboard from under the dash and perused two or three pages of small print.

"All those people're missing?" Gamble asked.

"This is mostly hot cars. The rest—yeah, here she is. Margot Willis Gamble. White female—"

"Does that mean she hasn't been found?"

"Yeah. How long ago'd she split on ya?"

He reined himself in again. "We got separated, uh, last night. She just—"

"You check the bars?"

Gamble had a sickening feeling of déjà vu. More cookie-cutter cops. Were they all like that? "Yeah," he said, "I checked the bars."

The car drove off. It was just as well. The last time he'd asked the law for help he'd wound up with a sore neck. These two guys would have jumped out and unleashed their clubs if he had spoken his mind. Every cop in town was supposed to be looking for Margot; wasn't that what the red-headed deskman had promised? But these two didn't even know she was gone till they looked it up. His missing wife: the joke of the year . . .

He cut through the trees to the quadrangle and bought two dozen uppers from a fresh-faced kid who looked like a candidate for the varsity chess team. He hadn't popped an amphetamine since his undergraduate days, but he didn't intend to sleep till Margot came back.

The cheapest telephone-answering device was eighty-eight dollars. He listened distractedly as the salesman showed him how to hook it up, then sped home and had to learn all over again from the instructions. He taped a short message and ran a test. When it was working, he went to the bathroom and splashed quarts of cold water over his head and his face. Then he left the house again.

He heard the shout just as he rammed the Triumph into second and started to turn the corner. "Severn! HEY, SEV!"

He stood on the brakes and looked in the mirror and saw the faded gray '57 Chevy pulling up in front of his house. He backed with a loud squeal of rubber. "Oh, Jesus, Sev, I just heard," Brooks called out as they both jumped from their cars. "What happened, man? *What happened?*"

"Let's go in," Gamble said. On the way up the wooden

stairs, Brooks took his arm as though supporting an old man. Inside, he paced back and forth as Gamble made more instant coffee. "Ciel and I, we'll do anything," he said. "I mean, jeez, Sev, *anything.*"

"I know, Brooks." He felt relieved, almost optimistic. His ordeal was in its second day, and finally, there was someone who would listen and . . . believe. Misery *did* love company; he remembered his father's comment that most truth was lodged in clichés.

Brooks heard the story with varying expressions of anxiety and incredulity. He had never been the typically cautious therapist; he worked closer to the bull, showing his own emotions and speaking out. His slightly soft features made him look gentle, almost motherly; his thick glasses and squinty brown eyes came across even to strangers as intensity of focus, deep personal involvement.

". . . So then I phoned you," Gamble said, nearly finished.

"I was working. Some poor guy threatened to cut his wrists."

"I know. I tried to get you at the Surfside."

"You *called?*"

"Around three in the morning."

Brooks's cup jiggled lightly on its saucer. "I was, uh— the guy never checked in," he said. "I talked him into going back to his wife. Then I drove home and heard the news."

Why the hesitations? The two of them were more like brothers than friends. Brothers should tell the truth. "Who was the patient this time?"

"A new one. Furst. Wilbur Furst."

Last night Ciel had said it was Tolliver. Had she screwed up the name? Unlikely. She was a bear on names.

Whatever Brooks was doing last night, Gamble realized, it's something he doesn't want Ciel to find out, and he's afraid to tell me because I might let it slip later. Well,

I've got a worse secret to keep from him. *Oh, what tangled webs we weave* . . . Another venerable cliché.

"Sev, how's your head?" Brooks asked, standing up. The last couple of weeks he'd spent a lot of time worrying about Gamble's head. Or was he trying to change the subject?

"Sort of addled." Wasn't it plain that if Brooks was lying, he was lying to deceive Ciel, not him? Besides, he had to take help where he could get it. "At first I flipped," he went on. "I told you, I actually jumped a cop. In uniform. At headquarters. Then I thought about living without Margot. I just couldn't *imagine* it. I figured I'd lay down and die, you know that feeling?" Brooks nodded. "And then for a while I was really pissed off. The whole thing seemed so, you know, so goddamn unjust. So that's how it went all night. Bouncing around from feeling to feeling."

"Mood swings. Not abnormal, considering. Must be a bitch of a trauma: now you see her, now you don't."

"And talking to cops who act like I misplaced my car keys or something."

"How you feeling right now?"

"Spacy. Kinda . . . wired. But I'll be okay if I don't stop to think. I made a list. Things to do. Occupational therapy. When the list runs out, then maybe I'll get crazy again."

Brooks walked over and grabbed his upper arm. "You name it, buddy, and I'll do it. Listen, what about Ciel?"

Gamble said, "Ciel?" too quickly; he hoped his friend hadn't picked up on the reaction.

"I mean what can she *do* for you, dummy? Whip up a quiche? Fold your underwear? Fluff your pillow? Hey, man, Ciel's a great little hand holder." Was there an edge in his voice? Did he know something?

"I'm okay. Thanks."

"Lean on us, Sev. When you get a break, give us a ring. Come over for a tub." Gamble blanched. *Oh God Brooks*

you don't know Oh Christ Brooks why did you have to get
called away the one night when Margot wasn't there
either . . . ?

"Ciel or me," Brooks was saying. "Anytime. If I'm on a
case, Ciel can come over, and if we're both tied up, I'll
beep for a replacement." His voice lowered. "You're our
number one priority, Sev. I was pretty worried about you
for a while—after the show, I mean. If you got through
that, you can get through this. Hang tough. Don't let yourself slip back into depression. Margot, she's . . ." He
paused. "She's somewhere."

Gamble walked to the window and looked at a cloudless
sky over a shimmering bay, the kind of view he and Margot used to watch together, arms entwined. "She taught
me how to love," he said without thinking. "Sounds corny,
doesn't it? 'Taught me how to love.' She'd always tell me,
'Whenever we say good-bye, you have to say you love me
because you never know if it'll be the last time.' Strange,
huh? She said one of us might step in front of a truck,
and she couldn't stand going through life without me,
unless . . ." He paused, and Brooks patted him on the
shoulder. "Unless she knew I'd loved her to the end.
Jesus, when I think about the time I wasted." He tasted
salt. "What I'd give to have just one of those days back."

"Sev, don't—"

"The funny thing is . . . last night? When she got
out of the car? She said, 'See ya 'round.' She didn't . . .
she didn't say, 'I love you.' "

"Sev, this isn't helping—"

"It is, Brooks, it is! Look at me. I'm not breaking up,
am I?" His eyes were wet, but he was in control. And he
would stay in control. It was a function of maturity.
Mourning was over; the Gamble family couldn't afford the
luxury.

His friend took him by the elbow and steered him to
the sofa and said firmly, "Let me just say one thing."

"Will it cost me a hundred an hour?"

Brooks smiled. "A hundred and fifty," he said. "I'm on overtime."

"Keep it short then." The banter made him feel a little less uncomfortable, a little less exposed.

"Stop thinking about it. Work on your list. There's an old rule, Sev: When you can't do anything—*do something!* Chop wood, organize your files, square the circle, anything but sit around and brood. It's like when your show went bust and you were ready to kill yourself. I told you to hump your ass on some new paintings, and it helped, didn't it? You see that?"

"I see it," Gamble said, standing up. Brooks struggled to his full five-eight and hugged him lightly. "Thanks," Gamble said, embarrassed again but comforted. "Thanks for . . . being here."

Brooks pulled away. "Don't worry," he said, "I'll bill Blue Cross," and Gamble managed a smile.

16

Tally was already kicking herself for approaching Johnny Boon. He was the meanest, stubbornest damn cop she'd ever seen. "I don't have time right now," he kept saying, spinning away in the detectives' bull pen as if she had rabies. "I'm working on something."

"Look, Sergeant, I'm only asking—"

"I told you, I'm *busy*." A half spin kept her from catching his eyes.

"I'm asking you for a few minutes, for heaven's sake, not a lifetime commitment."

"That's what you said last night. A few minutes."

"But this is life or death." She realized she sounded shrill and unprofessional, but Samuel Schulte wasn't just a runaway; he was a helpless human being, a target for every degenerate on the streets. Could any item on the police docket be more important?

"We'll have a meet later," he said. "Okay?" He sounded like a parent handling a persistent kid.

"For once in your life, listen!" she said. He stepped to the window. "*Sergeant*? I found his bike."

This bombshell produced a yawn and another glance down the corridor. Who was he expecting? "His bike, his *bike!*" she repeated. "It was downstairs in the bushes. In front of the building."

"Good. He has it back then, huh?"

Oh, Lord, he wasn't getting it. "So he didn't—run—away," she said, emphasizing each word. "Something—happened to him. He's *retarded,* and he left his bike *four blocks* from home and—"

"Left it where?" he asked without taking his eyes from the street.

"Behind the hedge, just to the right of the main doors. Where the winos sleep."

He nodded and said, "Where the winos sleep, huh?" Repeating back: another method of dealing with kids. When he turned from the window, his blond eyebrows came together in a glower, and his forehead furrowed as though his mind were in another country. Last night he'd seemed indifferent; now he seemed preoccupied. Whatever his problem, she had run out of patience.

"Sorry I bothered you," she said, heading toward the elevator. She would follow procedure: write a missing persons report and hope her sergeant kicked it up to the detective bureau to . . . Johnny Boon? Possibly. Or some other uninterested dick. Missing kids were their lowest priority; it took a good old-fashioned ax murder to capture their interest.

"Hey, *wait!*" he called out.

She answered over her shoulder without slowing down. "I really don't have time," she said. "I'm *working* on something."

He caught up at the elevators. "What's a troglodyte?" he asked.

"A . . . what?" she said, punching the button.

The doors slid open, and she stepped inside. "*You* know," he said, his eyes looking everywhere but at her. "A troglodyte?"

She waited till the doors had almost sealed. "Look in your mirror," she said.

Her report was half-finished when she thought of the dragon. She hadn't asked a favor of him in the five years since her father had retired, but he was the one who had fixed it up for her to do her research in uniform, and he still checked on her and insisted that she join the Mondragon clan for holiday meals and picnics.

But what about the manual?

The manual dictated that you typed your report and turned it over to your sergeant and went about your business. The police department couldn't have common ordinary patrolpersons skipping links in the chain of command, even if the common ordinary patrolperson was working on her Ph.D. That had been part of the original deal: she could do research on the job, but she had to be a cop in every way, including graduating from the academy and following all procedures to the letter. She had agreed, and now she was bound. . . .

She sighed and turned back to the typewriter. The manual made sense, in most ways. She remembered part of a letter her father had sent from his retreat a thousand miles away: "Well I got too much like the rest of them—thinking the rules are for other guys—going against my own advice. Every time you skip procedure and do it your own way, it gets easier the next time. Then somebody winds up in a wheelchair." The Andrew S. Wickham Doctrine of Gradualism. She believed it with every fiber, but she couldn't see how it would help solve the problem of Samuel Schulte.

A twinge of pain recalled her joust of the night before. What was that big guy so mad about? She'd overheard a little of his griping: his wife had run off with another man or stood him up or . . . some damned thing. Pierson must have written a report; she'd have to read it if she ever got caught up on the important stuff.

She typed a few more words, and the space bar jammed. An omen? She'd always been careful to stick to procedure, but what was bad procedure and what was good? Was it good procedure to let a twelve-year-old retarded kid careen about a dangerous city?

She aimed at the Q on the old typewriter and hit the A, tore the paper out of the machine, and opened her directory to "Mondragon, C. P., capt., dets." She dialed the number and cupped her hand around the phone so no one else in the office could hear.

"It's Tally," she said when his robust voice answered.

"Tally, sweetheart! Which bottom of a well you calling from?"

"Juvenile. Carl, can I, uh, see you a minute? Just us two?" Since infancy she'd never known him as anything but Carl.

"What do you have in mind, Tal? Dinner in a tatami room? A quick flight to Kauai? Hey, great with me! I don't know about Martha, though. You cleared this with your mom? Your boyfriend?"

"Carl, come *on!*" Sometimes his compulsive jocularity got in the way of real communication. Maybe that was the way he liked it. "I just want a few minutes."

"Something wrong?" His voice had turned solicitous.

"Can I see you?"

"Don't ask silly questions."

She had to walk through the detective bureau to get to

his office. An old plainclothesman with a purplish complexion and a cannon on his hip tried to impale her on the points of his cold eyes, but she was relieved to see that Boon wasn't in sight. She strode to the far corner, conscious that a few younger men had spun in their chairs to watch, and admitted herself to Mondragon's office without waiting for a clearance from his secretary. "It's *okay,* Amy," he was saying into the squawk box when she walked in. "She's family."

He was dressed in his usual three-piece blue suit, even though it was the middle of August and the building's central air conditioning had broken down and no one seemed interested in fixing it. "Tally! Come in, kiddo, come in! Hey, look at you! World's prettiest mule!" His Teddy Roosevelt grin and his flattery and his choice of words evoked someone else. Her father was built like a nightstick and the dragon ran to fat, but they both had gleaming halos of fine white hair and innocent watery eyes and long teeth that they displayed at the slightest provocation. And a quality of impishness she couldn't resist.

She kissed him on the cheek and backed away to stand stiffly in front of his desk, uncertain of the protocol. She'd been in uniform for eleven months, and this was her first visit. His walls were lined in cracked old leather, reminders of an era when police officials were considered important citizens, worthy of whatever decor they chose. The massive clump of mahogany that passed for a desk rested on lion's-claw feet, and a dusty sailfish in faded ultramarine surveyed the scene through a baleful eye.

"Take the load off your feet," he said, mopping a brow that was sprinkled with sweat. "You remind me of one of my lieutenants. Thinks he's still in the army. Comes in and says, 'Yes, sir,' 'No, sir,' or 'No excuse, sir.' I ask him, 'How's the wife?,' he says, 'No excuse, sir.'" The captain shook with laughter.

She told her story fast, eager to get in and out before

her conscience told her she was breaking the rules. She recited the facts of the Sammy Schulte case, carefully omitting Johnny Boon. She knew how the dragon would feel about using personal friendship to fink on a brother officer, and she felt the same. She watched closely as the old man's expression changed from polite interest to cool concern and back to polite interest.

"So whattaya got, Tal?" he said when she had finished. "You got a twelve-year-old retard that's been gone overnight, and you got his bike shows up on our front steps. And you got . . . a feeling."

"Carl, I—"

"Wait! I don't downrate that feeling, hon. It may be the most important thing we got here. Because to tell you the truth, the only difference between this case and a couple hundred other runaways in the files is . . . your feeling. Your dad was the same way, bless his heart." He turned sideways and adjusted the stained old venetian blinds to let in more light. "Intuition, you know? Something they can't teach at the academy. Or at Stanford either. It's an art, honey, not a science. Who knows . . . maybe he passed it along." He leaned forward, his belly pressing against the edge of the desk. "You hear about Mazanti?"

"No." She was ashamed to realize that she hadn't talked to Frank Mazanti in months. Somehow she found it harder and harder to keep up the visits to the young patrolman who'd once been her father's driver. She'd studied the old reports and come away in tears. Her father and Mazanti had picked up a harmless drunk for an on-view indecent exposure, and the captain had handcuffed him in front instead of in back. A few seconds later the harmless drunk had brought the steel loops down on the back of Mazanti's neck with enough force to split the nerves. Capt. Andrew S. Wickham had sentenced himself to early retirement.

". . . Frank and his wife, they're expecting," the dragon was saying. "And the doc says the way things're going he'll walk again. A little. I mean, he'll never win the police marathon, but he's already out of the wheelchair a few minutes a day."

The news touched her deeply. Why hadn't somebody told her before? "Oh, Carl, that's *so* nice," she said. "I'll call Frank. No, I'll go see them. Oh, I'll bet Dad was so *glad!*" The news made her want to laugh and cry and hug somebody.

"Your dad, he'd be in uniform today, honey," Mondragon said softly. "That's the sad part. He'd still be a cop. It tore him up that the boy was paralyzed. Anything less I think he coulda handled."

Tally looked away. Carl cleared his throat loudly, as though signaling that the subject was closed, and spoke in an official-sounding voice. "Okay now, so what do you want on this Schulte thing?"

"A detective," she said, aware that she was miles out of line. "Somebody with street sense and clout. I can be his . . . mule."

"Some mule." The captain shook his head. "I can't do it, sweetheart. We got unsolved murders, rapes. This is just a missing persons case. I'd never hear the end—"

"Carl, please. I'm going back to school in a month, and I don't even know what I've accomplished, rattling around from division to division. Let me have the feeling I did one tangible thing. *We can save this child!*"

He looked down for a few seconds. When he spoke, it was in a low voice. "We'll see. But don't count on anything." It was exactly what her father used to tell her. It usually meant yes.

"Thanks," she said.

He frowned and stood up. "You working plainclothes now?"

"It's my day off."

He walked slowly around the desk and took her hand with the delicacy of someone handling spun glass. "Tally, honey, do something for me, will ya?"

"Sure."

"Don't get in the habit of working on your days off," he said, walking with her toward the door. "That's a cop killer. I got a coupla dicks do it. Every time I see one of 'em, I say to myself, 'Carl, you oughta worn black today.' "

"I'll remember."

A half hour later she heard the news:

J. Boon was on the case.

17

"Do me a favor," Boon said, trying not to sound too harsh. "See, I been working alone two, three years now. So could you, uh, just sit there and not talk? If I wanna talk, I'll send you a signal, okay?"

Wickham didn't even nod. For a second he thought of explaining how he'd never been at home with words, never enjoyed gossip or small talk or big talk, either. No one had learned speech in the group homes; the preferred method of communication was more direct: a frown, a grin, a slap on the back or the face. With words, you got into double meanings, triple meanings, *hidden* meanings. He'd stick with his composers; look at all they could say without using a single goddamn word. The part of the Shostakovich Sixth where the long chord was repeated twelve or thirteen times always choked him up, and the screaming piccolo at the beginning of the next movement made him laugh. *That* was communication.

Besides, she pissed him off. A uniformed teenybopper with the street smarts of a cocker pup and a master's degree to confuse her even further. *Hey!*

A garbage truck swerved as Boon's Charger squirted

out of the police garage. He jerked the wheel and yelled, "Wake up, asshole!"

"How professional," his seatmate murmured.

"Oh," he said, chagrined. "I . . . forgot."

"Just be your own sweet natural self," she said. "Don't do anything special for me."

"Don't *talk,* okay? How many times . . . listen, this is work, is all, this isn't amateur night in the Turkish bath. I'm assigned to work one case with you, okay, that's fine, but that don't mean we gotta talk."

"I'm *terribly* sorry, Mr. Travolta, I didn't mean to offend. Could I just have an autograph? For my little niece?" Her face flashed splotches of pink, and a couple of twirls of light brown hair pulled loose from her temples and bounced around on her cheeks as she spoke. He gripped the wheel and thought of turning a couple of high-speed doughnuts so she could take another look at her lunch, but why lower himself?

"I didn't mean that," she mumbled after a few minutes of silence. "I'm just upset. I handled that boy before, and he's sweet, he's sad."

"You don't bother me," he said. "The only thing is, I'd rather drive and not talk, if it's all the same to you. I . . . got a lot on my mind." He'd be damned if he'd mention Annaliese.

"I understand," she said. He doubted it. "I *do,*" she repeated, as though she had read his mind. "Look, why can't we—did you ever hear of a *symbiotic* relationship?"

Shit oh dear, what next? "I'm married," he said. "Uh, separated."

She let loose a bored sigh, making his ulcers squeeze. This is exactly the kind of person the doc told me to avoid, he reminded himself. The kind that tries to make you feel dumb. She was a man, I'd erase that smirk fast.

He heard a silky rustling as she crossed one long leg over the other and shifted toward the window. He remembered what Foxy, the duty lieutenant, had said:

"Look, John, everybody on the force wants to ride with that cunning little stunt. Just blow a little smoke up her ass. It won't kill ya once." No, not if she went mute. Well, I'll go through the motions: interview the Schulte woman and her high yellow boyfriend for a while and then . . . back to my wandering snitch. That crazy Candy. How'd the sucker disappear between the lobby and the fourth floor?

He remembered Foxy's parting words: "And don't forget, John. This ginch is connected." That was the whole trouble with the PD; too many people were connected. A few hours ago he was closing in on a fool; now he was out looking for a *runaway*, for Chrisakes. A retard. Not that they weren't human beings, but how could you tell where a poor simple retard might wander? Where would you look for a lost cat . . .?

The Charger was hemmed in traffic by student drivers in Chevys and Medicare patients in Cadillac Sevilles. As they waited at a light, he flared up a Swisher Sweet and sneaked another peek; she was sitting erect and stiff as though she didn't belong. Well, she didn't. He hated to make people feel unwanted, but certain parties asked for it.

He turned off Fulton and eased past the Baltic Hotel, residence of Candy the vanishing snitch and a couple hundred other alkies and heads, none of them in sight. The sun came through the car windows like a heat lamp, and a warm breeze blew off the bay. He wondered where the hell Anna was on a knockout day like this. Maybe she took her flask to the park and sat under a tree the way she liked to do. He would check a few parks later. He thought how incomplete he'd been feeling in spite of the way they grated on each other when they were together. If he could only turn sideways and see her sitting there instead of Wickham. "How'd you swing this anyway?" he asked, overwhelmed by annoyed curiosity. "The dragon hasn't put a dick on a runaway since the sixties."

"Please," she said, waving the back of her hand at him, "I have a lot on my mind. If I want to talk, I'll send you a signal."

Boon sighed and turned away. A twenty-six-hour day stretched ahead.

18

Gamble stands on one foot and then the other as the red-faced police chief yells at him. ". . . You been butting in from the beginning. If you ever wanna see the subject alive, leave the police work to us. You're just making it hard for everybody."

"She's my wife."

"I don't care if she's your wife and your mommy and your whole goddamn family rolled into one tortilla!"

Gamble opened his eyes and saw his living-room ceiling. He started to turn over and realized that he had fallen asleep on the sofa, his legs dangling over the end. What time was it? Why was he asleep in the middle of the day?

His mouth tasted like rotting lemons. He closed his eyes till the nausea subsided. The sun was starting to fall toward the mountains, and the afternoon light was angling into the little house and overheating the air. He reached across the back of the sofa and lowered the matchstick bamboo curtain. He cocked his head as a fly buzzed and tapped and buzzed and tapped against the picture window.

How long had he slept? The mantelpiece clock said 4:07. He routed out his sore eyeballs with his knuckles and remembered coming home exhausted after distributing fistfuls of pictures of Margot to every precinct station in town. That had been a few minutes before four. He had started to listen to the five-minute hourly newscast for news of Margot. So he had slept . . . three or four minutes.

He stood up, wavered, and put out his hand for balance. His body felt as though the blood had run out through his toes. He recognized the symptoms of nervous exhaustion. The noon trip to the J-Building had been a total waste of energy, but he'd been drawn to the spot where she had disappeared. And learned nothing.

He wet his face and neck at the bathroom sink, carefully avoiding the ugly mauve bruise around his Adam's apple. He had to hurry; the stores would be closing.

He wondered if the managers would brush him off like the newspaperman. "Sure I'll listen," the editor had said in the anteroom at the *News*. "We're always looking for a Sunday feature."

"Not Sunday," Gamble had said. "That's four days off. I need you to run something *now*."

He had barely started to tell his story when the editor had coughed through the cigarette smoke and said, "Look Mr. Gamble, wives split, it's a fact of life. Ever hear of Joanna Roberts? Sunday school teacher, model wife, the whole *megillah*? Two years ago her kids come home from school, and she's gone. Coffee warm, house normal, no note, nothing missing. Husband says they never argued. Hey, *never!* A year later he sees her go down on a Great Dane in a pornie flick. He traces her to L.A., and her spade pimp beats him purple. I heard the story from a friend. The boss told me to shitcan it, we're a family newspaper."

"This is *different*," Gamble had pleaded.

"So was this."

He'd called radio and TV stations, but the reaction was the same old cynicism. A woman whose name he recognized from the "Nightly News" told him to "hang in there, she'll be back." A news editor said, "No, not today," as though dealing with a salesman. Three other stations told him to call when she'd been missing a week or two. All of them had treated him as if he were a little off. *Was he?*

Crazy or not, he had to distribute his sketch, tack it on walls and bulletin boards, tape it in store windows and around telephone poles. He couldn't rest. He had to make Margot the most familiar sight in town. *He sees her go down on a Great Dane.* But that had to be the act of a frustrated, angry, mistreated housewife. Margot was none of those; Margot had nothing to feel angry about. *Ciel?* But Margot didn't know about Ciel; Margot had no way of knowing. Unless Ciel herself . . .

No, no, that was impossible.

The Xerox copying bill had been forty-one dollars; the pictures of Margot filled the trunk of the little TR-3 parked out in front. He splashed more water on his face and sucked down an upper. Plenty left. He hoped he wouldn't need them.

19

By early afternoon the two silent companions in the unmarked black Charger had prowled parks and pool halls and malt shops and pinball arcades, looking for signs of Sammy Schulte, and all Tally Wickham had to show for it was a runny nose. She wondered what it would take to make Boon understand. She had wound her window down, reached back and opened the rear window, switched the air blower to Hi, and coughed and sneezed constantly, and still the idiot kept smoking those Chinese firecrackers. No wonder he always worked a one-man car.

He'd been his usual antisocial self all day. The visit to

the Schulte house had been wasted time: Betty had been dopey from too many sedatives, and Uncle George had been dopey from booze, and the great detective sergeant had been just plain dopey. He hadn't contributed a question, idea, or insight. And Sammy Schulte with his brown Keane eyes that filled so easily with tears was still out there. Wearing his horn-rimmed glasses and his white protective helmet . . .

She'd been surprised at how readily Boon had agreed to search the city's parks and loitering places with her. Maybe he had a vestige of professionalism left, enough to realize that a child's life was precious.

They spun around a corner in the Highland district, headed for the children's park with the blackberry bushes and the rabbits. His driving technique was making her seasick. He had two speeds: flat-out and full stop. He never eased into a turn or accelerated slowly or stopped gradually. Either his mind was elsewhere, or he was the world's worst driver. Or—he was trying to get even.

She heard the familiar sound of his fingernail igniting another kitchen match, and before she knew it, the words were pouring out: "If you're smoking those things to bug me, forget it." She set her jaw. "I'm . . . *not* . . . bugged!"

"Huh?" he asked, speeding through a red light. "You say something?"

"Forget it," she said.

A network of lines formed under the loose blond hairs that had drifted over his forehead. He lifted the newly lit cigar in the air and waved it in her direction. "You mean this?" He rubbed the ember out in the ashtray and peered at her through the smoke. "You shoulda spoke up," he said.

"I did everything but stand on my head."

"You did?" He sounded genuinely surprised. "What'd you do?"

"Oh, never mind." She was still trying to figure why

he'd put out the cigar. "Tell me something, do you actually *like* that taste in your mouth?"

"Swishers? Love 'em."

"Do you have any idea what you're doing to your insides?"

"Giving myself lung cancer and mouth cancer and the gout. So what? Nobody lives forever."

"Your mouth—it must taste *awful*. Can you imagine how a woman would feel, kissing—"

"I never give it much thought. My last partner was Ernie Belinsky. We hardly ever kissed."

"What about your wife?"

"Oh. Well, uh, I don't have one anymore."

"I can understand," she said, and was instantly sorry. He had *such* a knack for teeing her off. "Strike that," she said. "It must be the heat. I'm sure you have your . . . points."

"Oh, I do," he said coolly. "Like one is I mind my own business."

"I mind mine, too," she said, trying not to sound shrill, "till somebody tries to asphyxiate me."

"I got the answer to that," he said, reaching into the pocket of his shirt. "Here." He handed her a cigar.

She flung it out the window. "That's two bits you owe," he said.

"Bill me."

The small park was full of housewives rocking their babies, dogs chasing balls thrown by small children, and one old man in urine-stained pants sleeping noisily on a bench. She could see at a glance that Samuel Schulte was nowhere around, but Boon insisted on making the grand tour. His great disinterest in females didn't keep him from ogling every one in the park, even stopping to talk to a woman in halter and bra who looked like the last of the two-dollar hookers. She wondered how he spent his nights. Not hard to guess. Probably lining something up right now. Why should *he* be different from the other detectives? That's where their marriages went. Sacrificed to Bacchus for cheap thrills. Or was it Dionysus? She thought for a second. It was both.

Back in the car, he said, "That about does it, unless you wanna check Montego."

"Let's do it," she said. "I'd hate to think he's in the one place we didn't try." Montego Park was on the northern edge of town, a fifteen-minute drive. If Boon could stand it, she could.

They held their silence for a few minutes, passing out of the Highland neighborhood with its neat clapboard homes and its proud flower gardens and into a hollow where dingy frame houses clustered around a mill, a scene from a western Pennsylvania steel town. Whatever people wanted to say about this funky patchwork seaport, they could never say it was a bore.

Without thinking, she picked up a thick album that rested on the seat between them and leafed through the alphabetized mug shots. Under each picture was a short hand-printed résumé listing vital statistics, haunts, techniques, and known companions. "What's this?" she asked.

"Hmm?" He was off somewhere, thinking. She tapped the leatherette cover. "Oh," he said, "that's just . . . fools."

"You make this yourself?"

"Yeah." He didn't seem to want to discuss the matter. She took another look at the album. The printing was in the neat, primitive style associated with blackboards and small children: "MY NAME IS JOHNNY. I AM 6. MY TEACHER IS MISS . . ." The whole job must have taken him weeks. *Years*. Why so much involvement with— what did he call them? Fools? She glanced sideways. His brows were knit; he seemed to be wrestling with a private problem.

The car careened into Hyde Street, and the sun's rays bounced off his one-way glasses and made her blink. She held her hand up between them, but she'd forgotten that he never understood any message that wasn't communicated by tom-tom or sledge hammer. "Why do you wear those hokey glasses?" she blurted out.

He slid them up his tanned forehead without answer. In the bright light she noticed that his clear blue eyes were dark at the centers, as though a brown-eyed ancestor were fighting for recognition. He turned sharply into Market, and the glasses dropped over his eyes.

"Do you think those things make you look more like a cop?" she asked. She had an uncontrollable urge to keep pecking away.

"I don't worry about looking like a cop," he replied. "That's for you rooks." He hit the brakes to avoid rear-ending a taxi and said, "You got any more comments on my clothes? Let's get it out in the open. What about my Ike jacket and my lariat tie and my bolo clip? They meet with your approval? *Huh?*"

"The height of style in every bar in Reno."

"I'll run out and buy some designer jeans and sandals. And a nice purse."

"You do that."

He started to say something and subsided. They drove in silence for a few minutes, and she wondered if he was hurt or annoyed or just bored. She knew she'd gone too far, but everything about him infuriated her. Why?

On the freeway he surprised her by asking, "Uh, what kind of a name is Tally? Is that what they call, uh . . . black Irish?"

Oh, Lord, she hated pseudoscientific conversations about race and religion and national origin. On the other hand, she was getting tired of the tension; they would be together an hour or two more, and as long as he didn't smoke those noxious cigars and rail about spooks and broads and bleeding hearts the way most cops did, she'd make an attempt to treat him like a human being. Pro tem, anyway.

answered, trying not to sound embittered. "The personnel office keeps us kind of concealed. First I was in Traffic, and then I was down in the Ninth for a couple of months, third watch."

"Siberia."

"Colder," she said. "Lately I've been working Juvenile. That's how I met Sammy."

"Who's Sammy? Your boyfriend?"

She cringed. "Sammy is Sammy Schulte," she said sternly. "The boy we're supposed to be looking for. You forgot already?"

He fell silent. Had she hurt his feelings again? Thank the Lord they would be at Montego Park soon, and she wouldn't have to make any more conversation. "You never milked meters?" he asked after a while.

"They said I was overqualified."

"I didn't mean that in a bad way," he said, still sounding apologetic.

"I didn't take it in a bad way."

"I wasn't always a cop," he said.

"What's that have to do with anything?"

"You asked me awhile back if I always been a cop."

It was peculiar the way he shelved her questions till he felt like answering them. She wasn't sure if this proved he was methodical or just slow. "What were you before?" she asked, as though she gave a damn.

"Well, for a while I was a kid." He laughed. "Hey, just joking," he said. Maybe he was jollying her because he sensed her discomfort about her father. Something seemed to have changed since he'd learned who she was. Or maybe he was hitting on her. She'd ridden with too many cops whose whole discourse was a long stream of cracks and hints as subtle as a hand to the crotch.

She risked a peek. The sideways break in his nose was almost appealing in a street fighter sort of way, and the corners of his mouth were wrinkled in the faintest trace of a grin—whether antic or self-satisfied she couldn't be sure—but under his disorderly thatch of light hair she could see the worry lines deep in his forehead.

"I wasn't always a cop, no," he was saying, as though he still owed her an answer. That plodding mind again. "I was a roofer. Cedar shakes, mostly." He reached out and turned on the radio, as though further conversation might turn him to stone. She was surprised to hear classical flute fill the car.

"Rampal," she said without thinking.

He looked wide-eyed at her and said, "*You* know his stuff?" The question told her a lot about the company he kept. In her own circle of friends, nobody *didn't* know Jean-Pierre Rampal. "He's some piece of work, isn't he?" Boon went on, darting in and out of the busy lanes with one hand on the wheel. For the first time all day he seemed genuinely animated; she had to tighten her face to keep her surprise from showing.

They took the off-ramp at Colinwood Avenue, and she noticed that he had slowed to a respectable speed. Music hath charms . . . Well, Sergeant J. Boon, she said to herself, you may not be the troglodyte I thought. Not quite.

My partner the music lover.

Live and learn. . . .

20

As Gamble opened the front door of his house to walk to his car, he saw Ciel sitting in a splotchy blob of afternoon light on the bottom step, hands crossed in the lap of her thin sundress, small breasts visible from his angle almost to the nipples. Before he could duck back inside, she turned and smiled at him. *Ciel in the Sun:* one of her favorite poses.

"What're you doing here?" he asked.

"Waiting," she said, popping up effortlessly. "Oh, Severn, poor thing. Tell Ciel."

She took the stairs in her vigorous stride, short lemon-colored hair bouncing around her face, golden ear hoops catching the sun in glints and glitters. He was so confused that he retreated a step. Was this the onset of paranoia, shying away from a harmless woman, an old friend?

Meaningless bits of information about her flew through his brain, completely beyond his power to stop or alter: her name meant Sky; she was a potter; she jogged; she swam; she meditated; she was "into her body." And there was something else. . . .

. . . *Gamble and Ciel are sharing margaritas and sinsemilla in the hot tub. He hasn't smoked in months, but Ciel says it's exactly what he needs. Mood elevation; even doctors use it. Margot is at her mother's; Brooks has just gone on an emergency call. Gamble feels weightless, almost at peace for the first time since his show failed, but dimly aware of his nakedness, aware that being naked with Ciel alone is different from being naked with Ciel and Brooks. Now they are out of the tub, sitting on towels and bemoaning the life of the artist and drinking Sauza straight from the bottle and touching and giggling, and suddenly she is . . . His wife's best friend is . . . His best friend's wife is . . .*

"Severn," she was saying, "*Severn.* What *is* it? You're *white!*"

At her touch he retreated into the house. He had a feeling that Margot was watching from across the street, that Margot . . . knew.

"You're—you're pooped—you're out on your feet," she said in her jerky style, following him in. She made him take a cool drink of water and patted his forehead with a wet washcloth. "Lean back," she said, shoving him on the sofa.

He pulled the rag over his eyes and rubbed hard. He blinked and mumbled through the weave, "Gotta go put up her picture."

"Severn, my God, you, you can't *drive*," she said, the words pouring out. "You're *exhausted*—didn't you sleep? —that's why I waited outside. Brooks told me you—I had to—*you* had to sleep."

"I sleep, uh, slept."

"How much?" Her hand slipped under his neck, rubbed gently, and stopped. "My God, what's wrong with your throat?"

"Nothing." He had to get away.

"It's *not* nothing—it's—let me look. It's an ugly bruise! Severn, what—?"

"Gotta go now," he muttered, removing her hand.

"You can't help Margot by killing yourself."

"Please," he heard his voice say, "don't talk about Margot. Not . . . now."

"I'm just trying to help. You've *got* to get a little sleep —Brooks said—listen, put your head down. There. Close your eyes."

What kind of man would do what he did and then resent the woman for it? Had Ciel forced him to go through with it? To the end? Any schoolboy knew that was physically impossible. He'd been in control the whole time. Or else he'd have left when Brooks was called away. But hadn't Brooks insisted? *Stay in the tub, Sev! Relax, man, it's therapy.* Brooks trusted him—trusted them. It had always been unisex with the two couples: warmth, closeness, hugs and kisses, arms around the shoulders. Certain women turned him on, in a remote sort of way, but Ciel had never been one of them. She looked like a boy, with her chunky cheerleader frame and flat backside and small breasts. It would never have entered

Brooks's head or his own—or Margot's either, for that matter—that the two of them would come together like mongrels the second they got a chance. *Relax, man, it's therapy.* . . .

"Ciel," he said, sitting up, "did you say anything to Margot?"

"About what?" The small olive green eyes fluttered and gazed at the floor.

"C'mon, Ciel."

"Oh, Severn. How could you think—how could you imagine—oh, Severn, you *couldn't!*" As she looked at him, her eyes began to fill and glisten in the thin slits of aureolin sunlight filtering through the bamboo shade. "Do you think I would run to Margot and, *tell on you. On us?*"

She dropped to her knees and took his hand. "Sev, do you—for one minute—do you think—I could be that . . . *vicious?*" Her round face looked tragic, victimized, like early virgins painted by pious artists debasing their skills to please the priests. Was he being unfair? He couldn't tell; somehow in the long day he had lost the capacity to judge his own actions.

"I don't know what to think, Ciel. She had no reason to leave, unless—"

"I upset her?"

"Y-y-yes."

"Well, I didn't. The only thing was . . ." She stopped.

"What?"

"Nothing."

He sat up and grabbed her wrist. "Tell me!"

"That hurts!" She pulled away. "For God's sakes, get hold of yourself. I told you—it's nothing. You . . . talked in your sleep, is all."

"I what?"

"You said something in your sleep. About, uh, us."

"Margot told you?"

"Yesterday when we had coffee. She said, 'Ciel, what

have you and Sev been up to?' And I kind of laughed because I was, you know, shocked. And then she laughed, too—said you'd babbled something in your sleep—something silly."

"Oh, Jesus, what'd I say?"

"I didn't ask. We both acted like it was a joke. Margot thought it was—you know Margot—just, uh, funny. Oh, Sev, she'd never walk out on you— even if she knew. Don't you know she loves you? She'd never leave because of . . . the other woman."

The expression nauseated him. There was no "other woman." God, she made such sweeping assumptions. *What had he said in his sleep?*

As he walked toward the door, the floor moved under his feet like a ship's deck. His head spun with contradictions, probabilities, possibilities, but he had no time to sit and think; he had to take Xeroxes of Margot to the stores before they closed.

"Severn?"

"Good-bye, Ciel," he said. He hurried to his car as though he expected her to pursue, twisted the key, and breathed a sigh of relief when the warm engine jumped. Margot would never have deserted him over something he babbled in his sleep. Wouldn't she have confronted him if she had taken it seriously? Then why hadn't she? Her silence meant one of two things: that she was afraid to discuss his sleeptalk because she thought it was true, or that she thought the whole thing was just too trivial. But if it was trivial, *why had she brought it up to Ciel?*

As he steered the TR-3 down the street, cold anguish settled in his bones. The afternoon sun was bright, but his old neighborhood seemed dark, blurred, as though seen through a heavy screen. He was used to viewing all scenes as the raw material of his work, but he took no comfort from the familiar sights around him: the maple trees that arched and locked overhead; a boy dribbling a basketball down the cracked sidewalk; the old angled streets speckled with houses of frame and brick; the long hills sloping down to the gilded bay. In less than one full day his world had turned banal. Someone had pulled a plug; color and light had swirled away, and the smiles of strangers were curses flung in the face of his loss.

Did Margot know?

Ciel was right; he needed sleep. But he needed Margot more. He reached in his pocket and fumbled for the plastic container and swallowed two uppers with a gulp, making a face at the bitter flavor. He would sleep again: another time, another year. It didn't matter now.

21

Now that they had left the freeway, Tally had begun to notice signs saying *Farmacia* and *Bodega* and *Abarrotes*. The Precinct 17 beat men patrolled here in threes. "That's where I went to grammar school," he said as they drove past Saint Theresa's. "Me and my kid brother."

"You were . . . orphans?" The word almost stuck on her lips; it had a harsh Dickensian sound to it. She hadn't intended to sound patronizing, but she was afraid she had.

"Well, yeah, you could say that." His tone had changed. He'd picked up on her superior air. "I mean, we had a mother and a father like everybody else. We just didn't know who they were." Apparently it was a point of pride with him, as though she'd accused him of being manufactured.

"People always think of orphans as kids that don't have anybody," he went on. "Richie and me, we had each other, ya know what I mean, Tally?" She smiled and nodded; it was the first time he'd used her name. "I was his brother and his old man and everything. We laid in bed at night and made up a family, names and birthdays and all."

"I heard about your brother," she said gently. Every cop knew about the execution of Richard Boon; it was academy folklore.

"What'd you hear?"

"That he sent one of the Gratz brothers to prison and the other two Gratzes tied him to a fence and . . ."

"Rammed him with their pickup." He sounded defensive again, closed up.

"Is that what really happened?"

"Why don't you ask the Gratzes?"

"There's how many of them? Three?"

He nodded. "One was killed. One's . . . missing."

"Killed? How?"

"Me and my partner, we caught him dirty in a burglary," he said. "He, uh, rabbited."

She'd never heard that part of the story. "You *shot* him? For burglary?"

"He drew on me."

"Where are the other two brothers?"

"Willie went bye-bye. Louie's still inside."

She felt her eyelids go up. "Bye-bye?"

"Hasn't been seen in over a year. Maybe he moved." He sounded as proud as when he said he could spell *Natchitoches*.

The boastful voice chilled her blood. He was actually sitting there and bragging that he had executed two men. An eye for an eye might go over big in Saint Theresa's, but it was an appalling code for a law enforcement officer.

Maybe if she just didn't talk . . .

Montego Park was two blocks long and a block wide; they started at opposite ends and worked toward each other. When he was out of sight, she dictated a few words into her Minitex and slipped it back in her purse. By the time she realized that Samuel Schulte wasn't around she had almost reached the middle of the park and spotted Boon backed up to a handball wall by five or six excited Chicanos.

She grabbed at her belt. The police radio was still in its slot in his car. She rushed up in time to see him slapping the palms of a tall, swaying man with a red bandanna wrapped above a clay-colored forehead. "Hey, babe," the Chicano was saying as Boon started to leave, "we'll get the word out, dig?"

"*Mucha gracias,*" he called back.

"We'll, ya know, find 'er someplace," another one said in a slurred voice. "Don' worry 'bout it, Sarge."

Boon waved lazily and strolled her way. She was confused; had he told them Sammy Schulte was a "her"?

It was almost evening when they headed back down the freeway; the sun sent scarlet streamers across the sky. "The last Gratz brother," she said. "Louie? When will he be out of prison?"

"He got life."

'For killing your brother?"

"My brother and another guy and a fourteen-year-old girl they screwed to death with a bottle. Excuse my French."

"Life means what? Nine years?"

"His parole hearing comes up in '84."

"What'll you do if he makes it?"

His blue eyes darkened and narrowed. "He knows my plans."

"How's he know?"

"I told him and his brother. A long time ago." He ran a finger around the collar of his shirt. "I went to the prison on the first visitors' day after I got back from Nam."

They had reached the downtown exit; in a few minutes they would be inside the J-Building. "And?"

"Louie and Willie, I called on 'em, and we had a little . . . discussion."

"About what?"

"Life expectancy, actuary charts, things like that." He

paused. "I told 'em when they get out to look both ways before they cross the street, ya know what I mean?" He aimed his mirrored lenses straight at her. "I told 'em any second they might faw down and go boom." He spoke in a flat, emotionless voice. *Faw down and go boom*. One of those childish euphemisms that kept policemen from admitting out loud that they sometimes had to kill. But for Lord's sake, *not with malice aforethought*.

"So you've got four more—"

"Four more years to wait, right. Then I'll, uh, take care of the problem. Why? How would you handle it?"

"*I wouldn't!*" she said, hoping she didn't sound as horrified as she felt. "I mean . . . I'd leave it to the proper authorities."

He flashed his even white teeth. "That's me," he said.

"That's *not* you. Don't you believe in, in right and wrong?"

"My brother Rich used to talk like that. Look what it got him.'"

She couldn't believe her ears. "Don't you ever do something just because it's right?"

"Not if it don't work," he said, still smiling.

Her partner the killer . . .

She realized with a chill that she'd gone to Stanford to learn zero. She thought of junking her whole approach to the doctorate. Who gave a damn about quantifying public attitudes when there were wild animals running around with police badges? KILLER COPS: *The Rogue Complex*. Could she get it past the faculty committee? Shouldn't *somebody* blow the whistle?

The Charger shot up the ramp and stopped with a jolt an inch from the wall. Her fingers quivered as she signed their log. He was already halfway to the door.

A strange, confused, confusing man. Loved classical music and killed at the drop of a grudge. A faint buzz came from her pocket: the signal from her Minitex that it had run out. She realized with a twinge of guilt that she had accidentally left it on Record. Her partner's revelations were now on tape.

22

Just before midnight Johnny Boon walked down the dark halls and thanked God for arranging a calendar that included only one August 13 each year. The mystery was how it happened to fall on a Wednesday and not a Friday. He wasn't any more superstitious than the next cop, but there had to be a logical explanation for a day that included losing track of a prime snitch inside the J-Building and pissing away a whole afternoon on a grand tour of the city parks and not hearing one damn word from Annaliese.

Now where's the stupid elevator? he wondered. He checked his watch to time his wait. Everything went horseshit around here at night; he'd be glad when they moved to a building that worked, a nice clean rectangular structure without all the useless curlicues and cracked walls in this dilapidated carcass. It reminded him of an old movie set: all show, no substance.

As though in apology, the elevator doors opened in front of him, and he saw the maintenance man standing in the corner, his thin shoulder blades pressed against two walls. Boon nodded but didn't bother to say hello.

At the murky entrance hall he stepped out of the elevator and headed for his car. He often drove the police Charger home against regulations. Nobody complained.

He was headed for his apartment, but first he intended to swing by his wife's cubbyhole and see what the hell was going on. For the fourth straight night she hadn't called, and that was three nights more than usual. He was completely baffled. Did it mean she was finally learning how to function on her own, or did it mean she was trying to prove something? With Anna, you never knew.

The hyped-up car bucked and kicked till all six cylinders caught, then rumbled out the door of the garage like an Indy racer trying not to rear-end the pace car.

He wondered if things would look up in the morning. Not much chance, he realized; the overnight schedule showed him teamed again with Wickham's daughter. There had to be a way he could slide out of that. A word or two with Mondragon. The two of them went way back. . . .

But not as far back as the dragon and Andy Wickham, Boon realized. Those two had been best friends right up to the day Wickham left. Now he knew where Tally got some of her ways. If Captain Wickham knew he was right, he'd walk into a city council meeting and tell them all off. Once they said he had had a good shot at becoming chief, but Boon knew better; a cop who stood up to so many politicians and brass hats was lucky to end up a captain, let alone chief. A funny guy. All he ever wanted was perfection. Especially from himself . . .

He let the car idle in front of the Baltic Hotel while he ran in and knocked on Candy Diego's door and got no answer. The Charger's temperamental engine had died of boredom when he came back into the night air. Typical.

The streets were quiet, and a sweet coolness had rolled in from the bay. He liked to work on summer nights, when the stars and the fools came out. He swiveled his head as he studied the brightly lighted store windows and displays. One night about a year ago he had spotted a black dude doing a number on a furrier's window, outsprinted him for three blocks, and nailed him with a flying tackle out of a Ronald Reagan movie. Boon's last great play. The shape he was in now, he considered the hundred-yard dash a middle-distance race. He consoled himself with a Swisher Sweet, the next to last of his day. He would smoke one more after he turned out his bedside light, and then he would fall asleep. By dawn anyway.

Now that Annaliese was out of touch, something was happening to his head; he was starting to nag himself with the same questions she used to ask. It was as though a part of him required a steady diet of castigation and doubt. In the past Anna had been the one to question his choice of occupation; now he had begun to question it himself. For the first time he found himself entertaining the idea that he had sold his soul for the pure joy of chasing fools. He had a feeling that he was valued mostly because he took on the jobs that others wouldn't touch, like a high-iron worker or a swan geek. Maybe it was time to think about getting out of the fast lane and taking up . . . anything. Welding. Private security. Even roofing again. He would live longer. Make more money. Wouldn't smoke so much. His ulcers would heal, his nightmares fade. He'd be a better husband—assuming Anna ever came back. "And I'd be bored shitless!" he said out loud.

Wouldn't I?

He slowed as he passed the Arcade Motel, shack-up headquarters for the Western Hemisphere, closed-circuit movies available, dial *H* for your personal hooker. A woman with a slim, angular build like Anna's was weaving through the front door on the arm of a middle-aged man in a black rug. "Mr. and Mrs. John Smith, we just got into town." Sure, and the marriage would be annulled at dawn.

Could Anna be . . . with somebody? Stupid idea. She'd never been big on sex. He remembered how she used to ask him to take it slow and easy, told him that women enjoyed the build-up more than the act. He didn't want to chew over the whole four years of their marriage, but since she had quit calling, he found himself spending hours figuring out what he'd done wrong. Now he thought: if only I'd talked about something besides the job.

He knew he'd played it wrong from the beginning. He'd taken her to murder movies that made her sick, brought home paperbacks by Joseph Wambaugh and Dorothy Uhnak and Per and Maj What's-their-names and read passages aloud, hustled her off to watch parties and retirement parties and promotion parties. On the advice of a marriage counselor he'd taken her on a seven-day excursion to Hilo. He'd tried to walk on the beach with her, dance with her, swim, fish, eat pineapples with her, but his mind was an ocean away. On the third night he drove the rented Datsun to the Hilo police station, found a bunch of chubby cops sitting around in sweaty uniforms, and swapped war stories till the watch changed. On the fourth day he'd come up with a pretext and rushed her to the airport. In the back of the 747 over the Pacific, she'd turned to him with a wild look in her eyes and said, "John, even if you catch every criminal, don't you see— *Richie'll still be dead!*"

He braked the Charger for a red light and watched a young couple in a black Monte getting it on between signals. He remembered the silken rustle of Tally Wickham's long legs as she crossed one over the other in his car awhile ago. He wondered what it would be like with someone that smart. Probably stop you in mid-stroke and lecture you on technique. All he wanted was Anna. . . .

Driving slowly, alternating deep pulls on his Swisher Sweet with deep pulls of cool midnight air, he steered into the decaying West End and its termite-ridden old mansions and boardinghouses. Her efficiency apartment was the Walnut, formerly the Georgian Arms, formerly the residence of someone with very large bucks. He would climb the wide staircase quietly so as not to disturb the other roomers and slip inside to see what he could see. Four days were too goddamn many.

How had he let her get away? The booze, that was it. A few days after the miscarriage he'd noticed it on her breath, and soon he'd begun finding empties. He took the blame; he knew his obsessions had crushed her, made her feel unneeded. But he did have feelings for her, even though he couldn't talk about them. And now the feelings were coming on strong. He wished he understood, but he didn't. He only knew that nothing made him happy anymore.

Or was he just getting horny? No, that was an insult to both of them. He felt a different kind of stirring: an undercurrent, a feeling. For the first time Anna had gone days without calling; *she* had chosen to ignore *him*. He realized how much he missed her, how crucial the thread of communication had been to him as well as her.

Was that what they called love?

The sagging rooming house with its dormers and porches and gap-toothed slate roof was quiet as he approached in a burglar's walk. The heavy front door was unlocked, and the wide staircase was silent as he tiptoed to the second-floor landing behind the beam of his Kellite. He stopped outside 2F, tickled the wood with his fingernails, tapped lightly, and then knocked. He had expected no answer; his last act before shutting down the detective bureau had been to call her, letting the phone ring for a couple of minutes in case she was doing her Polish vodka number.

He pulled his Arco credit card from his wallet and slid it in to the crack. The old lock gave, and his breath caught as he stepped inside. What if there was a man? He touched the Chief's Special in his belt.

Her apartment was as neat as a downtown window display. No bottles were in sight; the dishes were stored in a breakfront; the white lacquered walls gleamed in the flashlight beam. He pulled the Murphy bed from the wall and saw that it was tightly made with Anna's old-fashioned hospital corners, something he thought she'd abandoned. He ran his fingers across a thick glass tabletop and came up with a light coat of dust that seemed inconsistent with the cleanliness of the apartment. Could the dust mean that she had cleaned up and left three or four days ago? The last time she'd called?

Feeling like a peeper, he opened a drop front desk that appeared to date from the building's better days. Fancy thin-line handwriting leaped up at him: "Dear Rose . . ."

He wondered if he should read the letter. God knew he wouldn't have waited a second if he'd been on a case. Rose was the younger sister in Baton Rouge, the one who taught. They were tight as twins. Maybe if he just read a little . . . He picked up the flimsy sheet of violet paper and noticed how the *I's* were dotted with circles and the underlines were made in long, gentle curves. Anna's hand, all right. He read:

> DEAR ROSE.
>
> Good news! Nothing to drink in a month and don't want to! The *longest* I've gone! I'm well and healthy and I think John and I can make it now. You know I've always loved him, Rosie—I just couldn't subject him to the way I was till I made sure I'd changed. And I *have!* I bought him a silly little gift (he gets so embarrassed about gifts) and I'm going to surprise him tonight and take it down to him (he's double-shifting, sound familiar?). After that—*back home*??? Excuse my gushiness, I'm so excited. Wish me . . .

The words stopped at the bottom of the page, and Boon couldn't find a second. Maybe she planned to finish it later. He looked for a date, but there was none.

He's double-shifting, sound familiar? He had double-shifted four nights ago, then again last night and tonight. The dust on the tabletop couldn't have accumulated in one day. She must have written the letter . . . four days ago. On August 9. Saturday. The last day he'd heard from her.

Where the Christ had she gone?

He picked up the paper again. "I'm going to surprise

him tonight and take it down to him. . . ."

He lowered himself on a scarred settee and tried to reconstruct her movements. She'd have planned her arrival at the J-Building for just before midnight, when he was due to go off; she didn't like to interrupt him during the watch, and she always avoided the other detectives. One night he had found her sipping from a flask in his car, another night standing behind a statue in the entrance hall. He tried to remember if he'd been in or out at midnight Saturday. For a long time he'd been typing up a report. Fordyce and Russ Smith had still been working when he'd checked out; he'd said his good-nights and gone home.

Why hadn't she met him as she'd planned? And why hadn't she phoned since?

He rummaged through the closet. Her coats and jackets seemed in place, all but the heavier ones that were still back at their apartment. Clothes were neatly stacked in drawers; her toothbrush and cosmetics were arranged in a row in the tiny bathroom, and her most valued possession, the full-carat opal engagement ring with the circle of garnets, was lying in cotton in a worn velveteen box in the top drawer of the desk; she had always said it was too precious to wear.

Had she gone to meet him and stopped at one of her bars to kill a few minutes? Took a quick drink . . . and couldn't stop?

Had some fool snatched her off the street? Boon decided to run a body search through the computer. City, county, state, maybe even adjoining states if she stayed missing much longer.

A puff of air moved across the warm room, as though someone had entered. He whirled. Was a window open? He checked; the place was sealed tight. *Anna, Anna, Annaliese, where did you go?* Fear crept into his stomach. It was a new sensation.

III *Thursday, August 14*

23

At dawn a fully dressed Severn Gamble lay in a nest of sweaty sheets, his mind seething. Running on Dexedrine, he had spent the night picking over the facts of his wife's disappearance; they had seemed like beach rocks, smooth and slippery and in all shapes and sizes. If only he had something tangible . . .

He raised the curtain and blinked into a gray soup; it looked as though a cumulus cloud had descended on his house. Rain slid off the broken downspout and hit the window in little clam spits. He padded into the kitchen in the same socks he had worn for their birthday date the night before last and swallowed two peach-colored tablets at a gulp. He dumped a tablespoon of instant Blue Mountain into a dirty mug and filled it with hot water from the tap. The thick mixture seared his mouth; it seemed logical that he should offer up the pain to Margot.

He slumped in the kitchen chair and squeezed his sore eyes tightly shut and pulled his hair back hard from his forehead with the knotted muscles of his hands. For a few seconds he lost track of time and place. Then he sat straight up, eyes opened wide, as another hypothesis crowded into his brain:

Maybe the cops had taken her.

It made no sense. But what did? He wondered why he hadn't considered the possibility before. Maybe because policemen were peace officers, defenders of the innocent, the city's "finest," all that crap. Maybe their image had lulled him to sleep.

But why would cops kidnap a respectable citizen? He had to admit there was no "why." He would get to motivation later. First he had to consider feasibility: *Could* the police have done it?

He built a scenario:

Margot walks in the rain toward the front door of the J-Building.

She passes the green and white police van parked in front.

A cop grabs her and pulls her inside.

A few minutes later Severn approaches the van, waving his arms. Afraid he has seen something, the cops speed away.

They take Margot . . . where?

It didn't add up. Too many holes. Too . . . crazy.

But a guilty face *had* stared out the window of the van as he ran up to ask for help. Had that meant something? What about their seeming unconcern about Margot? They had practically laughed at him when he'd called at the end of the required twenty-four hours and asked to speak to the detective assigned to the case. The deskman had made it only too clear: no detective had been assigned. Or ever would be.

Was that significant?

If cops had been involved, how many? One or two? A conspiratorial clique? *All of them?* He fantasized a bulletin:

ALL PRECINCTS BEWARE OF SEVERN T. GAMBLE. SIX
FIVE, 250 POUNDS, BROWN EYES, DARK HAIR, REDDISH
BROWN BEARD. MAY TRY TO RESCUE WIFE

Ridiculous, yes, but no more than Margot's disappearance. What was he to believe? That she had evaporated? Fled to Mataiea like Gauguin? No, someone had taken her, and it could have been cops. He wasn't in a position to discard any theory, no matter how far-fetched.

He paced the bungalow, trying to decide what to do about his newest brainstorm. Call up the police commissioner? The mayor? Go to the papers, the TV stations? "Those bastards, they already laughed at me!" he said aloud. Ask Brooks to help? Yes, but only as a last resort. Brooks was married to Ciel, and Ciel was . . . another problem.

He stirred up the dregs in his cup and sloshed them down. He would have to reconnoiter the scene of the crime, and if anybody wanted to know what he was doing, he would play his role: the blundering husband whose wife had run off. He thought of the patrolman asking him if he had checked the bars. Supercilious son of a bitch. Well, he had one big advantage over the cops: they didn't know that he suspected them.

His hands shook as he stalked from room to room. He had an idea, a place to start. It wasn't much, but it was better than sitting around feeling sorry for himself.

He poured one more cup of coffee and began to lay his plans.

24

Boon opened his eyes to slits: 5:25 A.M. For three hours he had thought about Annaliese. The alarm would go off at 7:00, and he'd probably be in a dead coma by then and sleep another five or ten minutes, and then it would be the same old story: another day, another $79.80.

He pulled the pillow over his head and tried one of his favorite sleep-inducing techniques, "counting wouldas":

1. What woulda happened if I hadn't missed that trick

question about the *Miranda* on the test for lieutenant? Nothing. The department hasn't made a lieutenant in three years. The way the budget is, I'll be a sergeant till I put in my papers.

2. What woulda happened if I'd told the dispatcher I couldn't leave the tearoom snuff for a juvenile runaway? I wouldn't be riding with a female partner, that's the main thing woulda happened.

3. What woulda happened if I hadn't been in Nam when they mashed him on that fence?

He pushed the pillow off his head and twisted his lean body till his ligaments gave off a cracking sound. His "wouldas" always seemed to circle back to Richie's execution.

Goddamn, he needed more sleep. A guy had to be rested to handle that Wickham broad. Master's degree, big vocabulary; probably read the *Reader's Digest* every week. He hoped she'd just stay quiet. Maybe if he asked her politely? No, he'd tried that the day before, and they both wound up talking their heads off. Why hadn't he been able to talk to Anna like that?

Oh, Christ . . . *Anna.*

He sat up. He was glad nobody could read his thoughts: mushy stuff, unmanly. He felt ashamed. He had never been close to another human being except Richie, and look what happened. And now he was alone again.

He told himself that he shouldn't have gone straight from her apartment to the Czech joint where she hung out. Shoulda kept myself ignorant a few days longer. That bartender was a nice kid. Mark? Marcus? *Marko.* "Anna Boon?" he'd said, wiping circles on the resin-topped bar. "Sure I know her. Nice lady. Why?"

"I'm her husband," Boon had said, clocking the room. A big relief map marked "PRAHA" had hung behind the bar under a polished brass lamp. The only other light had come from candle butts flickering in pimpled blue glass jars.

"You're Sergeant Boon?" The kid had stretched a damp hand. "How's she doing? I thought the two of you run off someplace by now."

"Whattaya mean?"

"Anna told me about you getting together again. You know how she is: if she's your friend, she don't hold nothin' back."

Sitting at the half-moon bar, he'd felt guilty. If Anna had gone public with their problems, whose fault was it? Human beings had to talk to somebody, didn't they? But a bar? His own goddamn fault. He had driven her from the house with his unconcern.

"What's wrong?" the kid asked, voice all tense and compressed. He was maybe twenty-five, and Boon had trouble relating to bartenders who were younger than he was. They were supposed to be mellow old dudes, not boys working on their first mustache.

"Uh, she been in lately?" he asked just above a whisper.

"The last time was, let's see . . . Saturday night. She was all excited, on her way to the J-Building to see you. I figured you two were in Baja or somethin' by now."

"She never showed."

The kid took a step backward. "You're jivin' me."

Boon shook his head.

"You didn't get the thermos?"

"Thermos?"

"She bought you one of those new stainless steel jobs, said you were always losing her glass jars."

Oh, Christ, that was something else he'd never explained to her. She packed applesauce and potato salad and sauerkraut in jars in his lunch, but sometimes he had to use the empties as urinals in his car. A good detective would piss his pants before he'd leave a stakeout. Some of the men rinsed their jars and took them home. Boon couldn't. Silly. And sillier yet that he hadn't come right out and told her.

Marko refused a Swisher Sweet, but Boon lit one himself and spoke through a tinge of blue. "I'm worried about her. She called me every day." He tried to imagine her sitting in this dark neighborhood bar, getting juiced with friends he'd never met. Men, maybe. Separated or not, she was still his wife. "Did she ever say anything, uh, personal?" he asked.

"Well, we, we . . . *knew*, if that's what you mean."

"Knew what?"

"The, uh, temporary separation. She always emphasized *temporary*. She was really hipped on you, man. Used to be a couple of guys would try to hit on her, but they quit trying 'cause all she wanted to talk about was Johnny Boon, Johnny Boon. It got, you know, boring. Nothing personal." He smiled, and a glint of light caught and held in his teeth.

"Eh, Marko." Boon leaned forward. "When she was in here Saturday night, did she, uh, take a drink?" He felt like a cheap divorce investigator, looking up crotches for a living.

The kid didn't seem offended. "Yeah. The usual: mineral water. Most of the time I just charged her for one drink and then kept refilling her glass the rest of the night. I mean, you don't have to worry: she didn't leave no tab or nothin'."

Lying in his bed, remembering at dawn, Boon felt unaccountably saddened by the bartender's words. It was as though the two of them, Boon and Marko, were standing over her grave, paying tribute. *Good old Anna, she didn't leave no tab. . . .*

His watch showed ten after six. Might as well go in and knock off some paper work. He sat up on the side of the bed, lit a cigar, and sent a smoke ring pulsing across the room.

He flicked on the classical station while he dressed. *Lieutenant Kije.* The offstage trumpet was announcing the birth of the fake officer. He wondered why life couldn't be that simple. If you needed a hero to impress the czar, you just invented one. If it was all that simple, he could bring Annaliese back, make her up, breathe his own life into her. . . .

The trumpet sounded again, faintly. He wished he could take it as a sign that somewhere she was well and happy, offstage. But he'd never believed in crystal balls or horoscopes or omens; Kije wasn't alive and never had been, and maybe Anna wasn't alive either. Reality. That's where he lived, not in the imagination of some dead Russian.

He needed a shave. He hadn't felt so down since the night ten years before, when an orderly had come into the rec hall in Cao Xiem and interrupted a run of eleven balls with a telegram that Richie Boon was dead, and all his buddies had clustered around and said it didn't make sense for a soldier in Nam to get a telegram like this from the States.

But what did?

Chasing fools till your ulcers bled?

Made as much sense as anything else . . .

The phone rang over the whir of his antique Remington shaver. Who the hell could be calling at this hour?

"Johnny?"

"Yeah."

"Gorman, dispatch office." Robbie Gorman: an old bike cop with a steel femur and a glass eye and lucky to be able to hold down a dispatcher's job after being sandwiched between a wall and a truck. "The garbage collectors just found a DB."

"Garbage collectors?"

"The body was in a Dumpster back of the building."

"Back of *what* building?"

"*Our* building. The J-Building."

Boon said, "Male?" and caught his breath. To himself he kept repeating, *Say, yes, say yes, say yes. God damn you, Robbie, SAY YES!*

"Female. Garbagemen almost put her through their

grinder, but one of 'em spotted a hand."

Anna? Jesus, who else? He had waited too long to look for her. How many times had he told her to stay off the city streets at night? Bringing him a new thermos. Rotten, scummy neighborhood. Midnight Saturday, when all the fools were loose. Why were they just finding her body today?

"I'll, I'll be down to help, Rob. Gimme . . . a few minutes."

Down to help. How? By standing around blubbering? Every cop's nightmare was to work a case involving his family. He grabbed the clothes he had thrown over the chair and began pulling them on.

The two of them stood side by side in his mind, Richie smiling and beckoning to him, Anna holding out a shiny new thermos. He had loved them both. He could say it now.

25

Tally Wickham had spent the night with Johnny Boon and a Greek chorus of retarded boys with soft brown eyes. She remembered waking up and looking at her digital clock just about every hour, but the bad dreams had always swept her back into plots and plights that made her tremble with anxiety.

She knew from her psychology courses that sleepers composed their own dreams. Why was she wasting perfectly good dreaming time on a killer like Boon? To come to grips, she decided. To decide what to do about that tape. She had already violated her oath of office by keeping it overnight. Shouldn't she go right down to Internal Affairs and turn it in?

She took a few deep breaths to clear her head so the dream wouldn't resume; she was getting enough of J. Boon by day without taking him into her bed—metaphorically speaking, of course. Literally speaking, she'd just as soon go to bed with a great white shark. At least it wouldn't be smoking cigars.

Naked on her futon, lips slightly parted, she had started to doze off again when the timer turned on her police scanner and she heard, "Robert Six, you pick up the ME yet?"

"At the door. Where'm I taking Doc this morning?"

"Police garage. Code Two. The DB's in a Dumpster by the back wall."

She reached across and turned up the volume. "Received," the car acknowledged.

The DB's in a Dumpster by the back wall. That was where the J-Building's trash was stacked. The trashmen collected just after dawn. This morning they'd found . . . *a dead body?*

She rolled on her stomach and pounded the thin bedding with her small fists and said, "No. No!" Her FTO's warning came back: *Don't get personally involved. You're not a social worker out there; you're a cop. . . .*

She remembered the green and gold bike concealed in the shrubbery by the front door of the building. And how he'd smiled at her through his horn-rims and held her hand like a baby. And Betty Schulte's faltering voice: *He missed work today. He never misses work.* And Johnny Boon: *You start falling to pieces every time a kid runs away, you're gonna be spread so thin you'll be invisible.*

She'd been right from the beginning. She patted her eyes with the end of the sheet. Lordie Lord, how she wished she'd been wrong.

26

Boon forced another look at the lump in the Dumpster. His first reaction had been a gasp of relief that it wasn't Anna. But now he felt only rage. God damn it, he thought. "God *damn* it!" he said. He ground his fist into his palm and turned away so the uniformed cops couldn't see his face. Now his only lead to the tearoom killing was dead.

Look at the poor bastard, he mumbled to himself. Laid out on a couple tons of trash in a parking garage, and three harness bulls drinking coffee out of plastic cups for a wake. You deserved better, Candy. You were kinky and quirky, but as a snitch you gave good weight.

"Somebody said you could identify him," a young officer said, sidling over.

Boon nodded once. "Street name's Candy Diego. Ralph, I think."

The cop paused as though reluctant to pry, then said, "Jeez, that's a beautiful black dress, huh? She musta went for a bundle on that little number. Him, I mean."

Boon nodded.

"Uh, you're gay, too, huh?" the cop asked out of the side of his mouth.

"Hmmm?" Boon said, still deep in his thoughts.

"I, uh, just wondered. I mean you identifying the body and all."

"Just wondered what?"

"I mean, I thought you and him being friends and all, that you, I mean, you might be, uh, you know . . ." He held up one hand and shook the fingers loosely.

Boon clucked in annoyance. The academy must be recruiting at the Montessori School. Do I look fruit? With

a nose broken about fifteen degrees and a face nicked
with scars and a .38 jutting under my jacket like a
hard-on, for Chrisakes? *Do I look fruit?* "I'm with Homicide," he said, flashing the tip of his tin. "Who the hell
are you? The Vice?"

"Oh, gee, I'm sorry, I—"

"Don't be sorry, kid. Not for me *or* him. You bust as
many fools as that DB there, you'll be famous."

"I was just—"

"You were just flapping your mouth." He looked around
at the growing knot of cops. "Did any you guys think to
call the ME?"

"District car's picking him up," a young cop said.

"Tell 'im call me when he gets in. I'll be upstairs." He
started to walk away, then turned back for one more look.
The body appeared unblemished under its shroud of used
Kleenex and milk cartons and butts and paper; not a
drop of blood or a bruise visible. The lips were faintly
glossed in pink; the eyes were smeared with mascara as
though he'd rubbed them before he died. That was the
last way he'd have wanted to go, Boon thought sadly.
With his make-up smudged.

But it was the mouth that made his ulcer twinge and
pinch. It was stretched wide open. The neck cords were
distended like night crawlers.

The fool who'd killed him had tortured him first.

27

Something was happening inside the police garage as
Gamble drove by in the mist—cops were milling about,
and roof lights from police cars were throwing elliptical

red and blue smears against the whitewashed walls—but
he didn't stop to gawk. His business was upstairs. He
needed information, and his only chance was to act before the big shots came to work and threw up more
obstacles.

His head spun with questions as he parked the little
Triumph almost exactly where he'd parked it on her birthday night. Was there any conceivable reason why cops
would kidnap his wife? Did it have something to do with
her work? The lawyers she dealt with? Some of them had
offices upstairs, and some of them had connections with
the cops, with organized crime, with all kinds of ques-
tionable people.

He wished he'd paid more attention to her recent jobs.
Maybe she'd been typing something hot: a police brutality
case, systematized graft, a scandalous miscarriage of justice that could topple the city administration.

Would that justify kidnapping an innocent woman? A
bystander? Cops and politicians played a power game,
and the rules were changing fast. Look at the rest of the
world: women, children, even babies were kidnapped,
held hostage, murdered, over . . . what? Politics. Religion. Was this country so different?

But wouldn't she have mentioned it if she'd been working on something explosive? No, she wouldn't. She'd have
sheltered him from the news. Ever since his one-man
show she'd been treating him like an invalid.

He pounded down the pavement toward the front entrance. The chill of the short summer night still hung in
the air; the overcast would hold down the August temperature. It would be a cool, enjoyable day, for men whose
wives weren't missing. He tried to remember what life
had been like before. Another hoary cliché, all the more
true for its hoariness: We never know what we have till
it's gone. . . .

He stopped outside the big brass doors and leaned
against the marble facing. He had to collect his thoughts

before he went into the entrance hall with its awful decor and its awful memories. He couldn't afford a single mistake.

He dug at his eyes with his big knuckles and tried to straighten out the kinks in his theory. If Margot had been typing something volatile, wouldn't she have left copies somewhere? He tried to remember the names of her lawyers: Rosalie Richards, Ron Perle, Gabe Granger, Kerry Buckhorn, Peter—Pedro?—Garibay, Somebody Barnes . . . the list was endless. It would take a week to question them all. And how could he be sure they would tell the truth? He didn't trust lawyers any more than he trusted cops. They were part of the same machine.

He wondered if Margot had left a note somewhere, a memo to herself that could provide a clue. He doubted if she would have taken the time. Lately she'd been overworking even by her own tough standards. They needed every penny while he built up a portfolio of paintings for a new show. She would sit at the Selectric for hours without even getting up to stretch, and he realized that if she'd been working on something hot, her main interest would have been to finish it and collect the money, not waste time writing memos or sharing her fears with a husband who was already deeply troubled.

He leaned against a tall column next to the doors and closed his eyes. For a few seconds all of his ideas seemed absurd.

The gray morning turned darker, then black. *Margot steps out of the Triumph and starts to walk away from him. "See ya 'round," she says, and disappears.*

"Margot!" he cries out, then louder: "MARGOT!"

"Sir. Sir?"

He opened his eyes and saw a woman standing next to him, forehead squeezed into fine lines under a straw summer hat. "Are you all right?" she asked, taking a step backward as he stared down at her.

"Huh?" he blurted out, "Oh, yeah. Okay. Fine, thanks."

The woman tilted her head like a sparrow, then hurried past him into the building. He was upset at himself for falling asleep on his feet; the woman might have been a cop, like the one who choked him the other night. He'd have to keep a better grip on himself. He lurched through the doors and walked down the hall and joined several nodding heads in the coffee shop.

Through its grimy faceplate the clock above the griddle showed 7:15. He ordered coffee to wake himself up and a large Coke to soothe his parched mouth. He popped a couple of pills with the icy drink and accepted a refill of the coffee. His heart pumping behind his eyelids, he headed for the patrol office.

Another new deskman was on duty, and Gamble asked to see the officer in charge.

"Pertaining to what, sir?" the deskman asked.

"My wife. Margot Gamble. She's a missing person."

"Missing person, huh?"

Was that another goddamn smirk? He bit his lip as the deskman studied a clipboard. "Uh, listen," Gamble said, aware that he must look like a street bum with his red-rimmed eyes and straggly beard. "I just wanted to discuss the case with, uh, the officer in charge."

"The watch commander's down in the garage."

The run-around again. He wasn't surprised. He arranged his face into a smile and said, "I'll wait."

The deskman motioned toward the wooden bench.

After a few minutes a tall cop with a long face and a mop of black, curly hair sauntered in. The deskman motioned toward Gamble. The tall cop turned and said, "You're waiting for me?"

Gamble noted the silver bars on the collar. "You're the, uh, watch commander?" he asked.

"Jack Estes," the cop said, beckoning toward a door behind the counter. "You're—"

"My name's Gamble," he said, following the man's tired

shuffle through the door. "My wife is . . . Margot Gamble?"

"Do I know her?" They were in a small office with the barest essentials of plastic furniture and three tall green lockers with slits like gills.

"She's been missing since two nights ago," Gamble said. The watch commander showed his interest with a huge yawn that revealed gold crowns in the back of his mouth. "Uh, listen, Commander—"

"Commander's my job, not my rank," the tall man said, motioning his guest to a wooden chair. "Just call me Lieutenant."

Typical cop, Gamble thought. Wasting time on his title, as if it mattered. Well, I'll get right to the point. "When my wife disappeared, there was a police van parked in front of the building."

"What building?"

"This building."

"She disappeared from *here*?"

Gamble blinked back his annoyance. They knew damned well she disappeared from here. "Yes," he said evenly. "She came inside to pick something up, and that's the last she's been seen. But there was a police van. No windows, a pair of rear doors—"

"One William Victor. Our evidence wagon."

"It was parked out front when I went looking for her. It, uh, pulled away." He had to be very careful. He was looking for information, not a showdown. "I was just wondering . . ."

The watch commander's faded brown eyes fixed him like darts. "What's our evidence wagon got to do with anything?"

"I don't know," he said, trying to maintain a look of puzzled innocence. "I just thought the men inside might've seen something."

"Like what?"

"I dunno. They were there the whole time. One of your

officers was closing the back doors of the van when I first walked by, and then, when I came out of the building looking for Margot—uh, my wife—they were just driving away. I hollered, but they . . . they didn't hear me." He wanted to grab this skinny straw boss by the collar and yell that those cops had acted pretty damned suspiciously and what in the goddamn hell was going on, but he couldn't jeopardize Margot's life.

"What time was this?"

"Just after seven. Tuesday night."

"You sure of the time?"

"Positive."

The lieutenant walked to a wall where eight or ten files dangled from ringholders, each thick with papers. "Tuesday night," he mumbled. "August twelve. Let's see here. Yeah. One William Victor. Checked into the shop eighteen hundred hours for a new radio, on the street after that. First run of the night, let's see . . . eighteen forty, that's twenty to seven. So it couldn't been here when you thought."

"What kind of run? Does it show there?"

"Homicide. At the beach. Their job is, they go out and dust for prints, preserve evidence, help out the detectives."

"Does it show what time the van got back here?"

"Sure. Twenty-one hundred. Nine o'clock. Some of these evidence men, they'll take an hour to dust a shot glass. I say, put 'em back on beats, but then my opinions don't count for much, or I wouldn't be working stiffs in Dumpsters, know what I mean?"

Gamble realized he was getting exactly what he'd expected: double-talk. "Thanks, Commander," he said, backing toward the door.

"Sure," the tall man said, smiling again. "And good luck with the missus." He winked and added, "These things usually work out." The party line. Gamble glanced over his shoulder as he left. Jack Estes had already picked up the phone.

The cop at the counter gave him a searching look. "Say, where's the city jail these days?" Gamble asked.

"The jail?" the cop asked. "Or the holding cells?"

"What's the difference?"

"Holding cells is where we keep prisoners till they go to court. Jail's where they serve time. Both units been moved to the new building. Sixth and High." The cop turned away.

"Thanks." Gamble started off, then spun on an afterthought. "Didn't the jail used to be here? In this building?"

"The holding cells. In the basement."

The hairs stiffened on the slope of his neck. Basements made him think of rats and roaches, sticky spider webs, cold drips of water, and, worst of all, the feeling of being closed in, helpless, isolated. Could Margot be there?

He hurried into an open elevator and pressed the lowest button on the panel: "B." When the doors opened again, he saw that he had arrived at the first-floor lobby. He jabbed at the button, but the ancient mechanism refused to take him any lower. After a few minutes a middle-aged woman entered with a dripping umbrella, and he stepped past her into the entrance hall.

As he surveyed the dim corridors, several men in suits walked past, looking like a delegation of judges. His watch said 8:10. Before long the place would be swarming. He hurried along the corridor toward Fording Street and passed a door that led to a down staircase. It was boarded.

Was the basement sealed off from the rest of the building? Why? Maybe every office down there had already been moved to the cereal box. That would explain why the elevator wouldn't go below the main floor no matter what button he pushed. Or maybe there was another reason. Margot was being held somewhere; what better place than an abandoned basement?

A few feet closer to the elevators he found a door bearing the word *Maintenance*. It was locked. As he turned away, he heard a creak. He whirled and saw that the door was opening.

"Excuse me," he said, "but I'm looking—"

The door started to shut.

He grabbed the knob and yanked. A small man fell back into the shadows, his body turned sideways as though he expected to be attacked. "Excuse me," Gamble repeated, slightly unnerved by his own violence. "How do you get to the basement?"

The man faded from sight without answering, and Gamble caught a smell like Clorox. An unfrosted bulb dangled from its own wire just inside the door and bathed the contents of the room in flat light. He could make out tangled skeins of tubing and pipes, a row of fuse boxes, a control panel with assorted buttons and switches, a jumble of machinery and brooms and cleaning equipment. "The basement," he repeated, stepping inside. "Where's the door to the basement?"

"Izza closed," a familiar voice replied.

He stepped inside and saw the night janitor in the shadows. What was he doing here so early in the morning? Maybe he loved his work so much he slept in the room. Right now he was cowering in the corner under a bulbous duct swathed in leaky insulation.

"Please," Gamble said, "there must be a way down. You got a key?"

The little man held up his hands as though warding off evil spirits, and for an instant Gamble felt ashamed of himself. Why bully the guy? He was obviously a defective, more to be pitied. But why was it so hard to get downstairs? He could almost hear Margot calling. ESP, maybe. Or hallucination? How could you tell them apart? He'd read of couples who could communicate through walls. He had never believed it before, but now he wasn't so sure. There were . . . vibrations. Inexplicable. *Margot was near.*

He took another step forward. The man ducked behind a box covered in sheet metal. "Hey," Gamble called, "I'm not gonna hurt—"

The bulb flickered and died. Something brushed past. The door opened wide, and the light from the lobby splashed inside. The little man was gone.

Gamble tried to find him, but there was a choice of three corridors, and by the time he decided which one to take the halls were empty in all directions. He walked fifty or sixty feet, rattling doorknobs, and when he gave up and returned to the elevator banks, the janitor was standing in the wake of a silver-haired man in a police uniform. "What're you looking for, sir?" the cop asked in a voice that surprised Gamble by its calmness.

"Uh, nothing," he answered. "The men's room."

"Ugo here said something about the . . . basement?" The old cop flashed telltale rows of pearly teeth, as even and straight as new tile, but his hand rested lightly on his club.

"I thought the men's room was in the basement, Officer. Didn't it, uh, used to be?"

"Everythin' used to be," the cop said, taking his hand off his belt. "Basement's shut off now. Elevator don't go there; stairways and doors are all boarded up. See, they're gonna start demolition in a month or so."

"But the men's—"

"Right over there," the guard said, pointing. "You got business in the building?"

"An appointment."

"Who with?"

"Estes. Commander Estes."

"Lieutenant Estes? Fourth floor. Patrol office." He pointed to the elevator.

"Thanks," Gamble said.

The cop sauntered off, and the man called Ugo retreated behind his door. Gamble heard the lock click as he walked toward the exit, but he didn't turn back; he couldn't help Margot by antagonizing the building's personnel. A new guard would come on in a few hours. Time enough . . .

He aimed the TR-3 toward the waterfront, headed for coffee and a snack, if he could get it down. Illuminated by the sun, thin sheets of fog hung like silver dust, glary and harsh. A block down the hill on Fulton, he squinted at a familiar sign:

CITY BELOW THE CITY
Underground Tour Starts Here

An idea was forming in his mind. It was no more reasonable or logical than the other strategies that had obsessed him through the night. But it was a plan.

Underground Tour Starts Here. So would his search for Margot.

28

Ugo stood behind the maintenance room door, his ear pressed against the crack. His lips barely moved as he reverted to the soft accents of his native Bolognese dialect. "For a favor, Blessed Virgin, make the *gigant'* to stay away."

He closed his eyes, but the image remained. The bearded giant in the paint-spattered shoes was evil of eye; men of the *malocchio* were of Satan. The clown shoes fooled no one. A long time ago a group of German soldiers commanded by a *malocchio* like this one had lined up the Ruggiero family of Monte Sole for a family photograph, and when the dark hood had been whipped off the tripod, it hadn't been a camera at all. . . .

Ugo squeezed his eyes shut and turned his pinched face

to the wall, cringing at the memory of the machine-gun bursts. They'd come so fast: *Brppp. Brppp. Brppp. Brpppppppppppp* . . . Like someone tearing along a dotted line, stopping and ripping, stopping and ripping. Then a few extra bursts: *Brppp brppp brppp* . . .

Mamma . . .

Babbo . . .

He sees the members of his family twitch as the slugs from the machine pistols pierce their flesh. A bullet stings his arm and spins him to the ground, and his mother sinks slowly on top of him, still smiling for the photographer. Pink tears seep from her blank eyes. Her teeth are edged in red. . . .

More bodies crisscross atop his small frame. He hears the muffled shouts of the Germans: *"Tutti partigiani! Tutti kaput!"* But the boy knows no partisans. The only fighting man in the family is his cousin Oreste, stationed in Bosco Marengo with the bersaglieri. Why are they saying we are all partisans? Why did they promise to take our picture and then turn the guns on us?

He opened his eyes in the little maintenance room, but the scenes continued on the wall. He covered his face with his arm as the soldiers with the lightning on their collars began kicking the bodies and firing into the heads of those that moved.

Will they see me?

Will they shoot into my head, my face, my eyes?

Ugo Ruggiero, twelve years old, tries to slow his pounding heart while his blood runs down his mother's arm and across her face and joins the watery pink flow trickling along the curb. . . .

The janitor opened his eyes again and saw that he was in his room. *Safe!* Safe for a while, till the wreckers came and took away his last hiding place.

Unless . . . unless . . . hadn't the Blessed Virgin promised him something? Promised *what?* He closed his eyes and tried to remember.

Pictures of his family passed before him in delicate cameo frames with intricate edgings of gold filigree: *Mamma, Babbo, Nonna.* Angels on earth. His little brother Maximiliano, "Maxmcin" in the mountain dialect, wearing the tin helmet of the Sons of the Badilla . . .

He saw his brother staring blindly from his soft brown eyes. "Do not die, Maxmein," he whispered. "Stay with Ugo. . . . No, Babbo! No, Nonna! I beg you. Do not leave me! Mamma, raise your head. Raise it! DO NOT DIE. . . . !"

He muffled his voice in the little room, but he couldn't hold back the sobs. He cried because no one had said good-bye, and he cried because he had waited till dark, trembling under his dead, and then abandoned his dead out of fear that the Germans would come back. And he cried because when he went home after the *liberazione,* the whole mountainside lay silent and unrecognizable except for a few wells and the remains of a wall. No birds sang; rats darted among old bones in the desecrated *zimiteri* where the tombstones and statues dated to the Etruscans.

He opened his wet eyes and saw that he was safe in the room next to the elevator shaft. Safe, yes, but . . . for how long? Machines were coming to destroy the place he kept spotless with his bare hands. His marble, his granite, his statues, his *eleganza* murals, his vaulted ceiling that touched the sky . . . The *assassini* would come with the steel cable and the murderous swinging ball, and then— what would be left for Ugo?

The city had offered him another job, but this time he would not run away. His smile returned. He had felt so desolated when they told him. His life destroyed again! For hours at a time he had hidden in his hiding place, crying, imploring, until he felt his head would burst. Then suddenly there was an answer. It was as if a bright shaft of sunlight had illuminated his little room. *She* had come. Let the wreckers wreck; life held something better for him. The Virgin had promised . . .

He would be reunited with his family on the day of *ferragosto,* the Feast of the Assumption. Tomorrow! The dead would rise. *Un miracuel!* Already most of them were here. Their hearts, red and strong, would ascend together. He clasped his hands together and did a mountain dance step around his workbench.

But wait, he had a responsibility. He must warn the Virgin tonight.

He must tell her about the giant with the clown shoes and the *malocchio.*

One more day.

Nothing must interfere.

29

"Okay, Doc, what killed my snitch?"

"Sergeant," the medical examiner answered in a voice made even more nasal by a scratchy telephone connection, "you are just having to be patience for a while." Boon knew he meant "patient"; the ME was a refugee from Latvia, and English was his third or fourth language. "It doesn't help, you ringing up every ten minutes. Already we're doing the best we can."

"Doc, you had his body two hours. You must know something. Gimme a hint. What's the diagnosis? A shiv? A slug? The heartbreak of psoriasis?"

"I am prevented to tell you what happened. Do you understand my meaning? Can say only he suffer severe attack of death. *Very* severe."

"Death, huh." Dr. Yevgeny Madona's favorite source of humor. The Latvian Peter Lorre loved to leer out over the top of his bloodstained apron and tell visitors to the morgue, "See you later." *Not me, you won't,* Boon always said to himself, as though warding off demons. He'd known Madona since the days when medical examiners were coroners.

"Terminal case of death, yes," the doctor repeated through his nostrils. "We're seeing very many of that this summer."

"Doc, can't you gimme some kinda hint? I mean, Christ, it's my case."

"No. Already I told you: *orders!*" He sounded exasperated, jolted out of his usual good nature. "I tell you this much, John. Preliminary tests are negative. But I can say, my friend Boon, your world-class informer inhaled much amounts of cocaine in his life."

"I coulda told you—"

"*But*—cocaine did not kill this specimen. Pathologically he is healthy: one hundred sixty-one centimeters tall, sixty-eight point five kilograms—"

"Pathologically how come he's dead?"

"It upsets my tripes, John. Nobody should be dead like this. Now give me some break, huh? I'm as mystical by this as you are."

Listen, Doc, Boon felt like saying, *nobody's* as mystical as I am. The whole goddamn world's falling around my ears. "Doc," he insisted, "the guy's dead, so there's gotta be a cause, right? I mean, *he did die,* didn't he? He's not laying on that slab helping you sort his guts, is he?"

"You're having fun of me."

"I'm just trying to get a simple answer to a simple question. When did he die?"

"Sometime yesterday afternoon. I am authorized to say you that."

What the hell was going on? Why was Madona holding back? He was usually a nonstop talker, full of technical crap about angle of entrance and weight of gall bladder in grams and state of the victim's gonads. Who was shutting him down? It had to be high up; nobody had any real authority over the medical examiner except the voters.

Boon had a silly idea. "Is there such a thing as being scared to death?"

"Ah *hah!* You saw mouth? The look? Fright cannot kill, no, but it can . . . contributing. Very bad scare can make the initiation of a heart attack. Anoxia, yes, that can open wide the mouth, but anoxia by itself doesn't mean many."

"Anoxia?"

"Lack of oxygen. You get when climb mountains. Also sometimes when die."

"Could that be the cause of death?"

"More tests, more tests. Liver's at the university now; lungs going next." Boon had a mental picture of Candy Diego's organs commuting to college, lungs now, heart later, the brain on the 5:15 express, fumbling for exact change.

"What about the heart?" he asked.

There was a silence. "The heart, Doc, what about the heart," Boon repeated.

"I told you I am under orders. Please, Sergeant, off my back!"

"I'm under orders to break this case!" Boon exclaimed. "How the Christ am I supposed to start with the ME holding out me?"

"You're sure you're the assigned officer?"

"Come on, Doc! Would I lie to ya?"

"I am getting you back."

Five minutes later Boon's phone rang again, and Madona's voice whispered, "First, you are sworn secret. Understand? Not to tell other detectives, not to tell wife, not to tell girl friend. Okay, you inquire of heart. I didn't telling you for one reason. Heart cavity empty. Heart . . . missing—"

"You mean one of your men—?"

"No! *Not* one of my men. Before we find body, somebody remove cadaver's clothes, make incision below sternum, excise heart, wash body so is not one drop blood, dress body again, and place on Dumpster where is found this morning."

Boon thought they must have a bad connection. "Say again, Doc?"

"Already say!" Madona answered, louder now. "Somebody steal heart after body moribund."

"Moribund?"

"Dead. Defunct."

"*Somebody stole Candy's heart?*"

"Correct. And remember, is hundred percent confidential. Highest authority. If newspapers find out, I go back Latvia. And I take you with."

"But how was he killed, Doc? You must have some idea."

"*No* idea. Still checking. Is uneasy without heart."

"You got his clothes?"

"Yes. Bra, thirty-two B cup. Black lace drawers. Long black dress, very simple. Peasant clothes. Plain black shoes, low heels. And rosary with a gold cross."

"Well, at least he was dressed normal."

"Normal?"

"For him."

The ME said he had to go. Before he could say, "See you later," Boon slammed down the phone. Then he picked it up and called Anna's building. No, the quavery old voice said, he hadn't seen Mrs. Boon since before the weekend. No, she didn't leave any word. Yes, he would see what the other tenants knew.

Boon thought how little he'd given her. She'd come to the J-Building Saturday night to tell him she was off the juice, that she understood the way he had to work, that she . . . loved him. And he'd never had a chance to thank her for the thermos and put his arms around her and explain that he loved her, too, but the words were always hard to say, they just didn't come readily, they didn't feel right, but he'd work on saying, "I love you," and on being a good husband and . . . Oh, Christ, she was gone.

And some fool was cutting out hearts.

30

Tally Wickham sat idly in front of the cool green cumputer keyboard the way a child plays with a familiar toy, expecting neither surprise nor reward. Available at her fingertips were millions of bytes of information from city, state, and federal data banks, but what good were millions of facts if you didn't know what you were looking for? She remembered the cardinal rule of computer programming from one of her courses at Stanford: Garbage in, garbage out. What could she put in that wasn't garbage?

When she'd arrived at work this wet Thursday morning and learned that the body in the Dumpster wasn't Sammy Schulte, she'd had a stirring of insight, and now she entertained the hope that somehow, if only she knew the key, the computer would validate her feminine intuition. She could imagine the gales of laughter if she ever mentioned those words aloud. But there *was* such a thing as feminine intuition, and hers was telling her loud and clear: Samuel Schulte and the dead body are connected.

Incoming patrolmen straggled by, talking and giggling and ragging each other—"jacking around," they called it —but she ignored them. Nobody on the PD seemed to realize that it took concentration to wring secrets out of a computer; the terminal should have been set off in an alcove of its own instead of square in the middle of the patrol office.

She tried to remember her single computer course. *First, state the problem.*

Is there a connection between a twelve-year-old boy's disappearance and the death of a gay informer?

The only apparent common denominator was the J-Building; Sammy's bike wound up in the bushes out front, and Boon's snitch wound up in the garage. Not much, but still . . .

Translate the problem into the language of the computer.

She punched "289," the code number that tapped into the city's data banks, typed the locator number and the legal address of the Justice Building, "600 Fording," added "MP" for "Missing Persons" and "?" for "query." If anybody was missing from the area of the J-Building, let the computer now provide the names or forever hold its peace. The computer held its peace. Then she realized she had forgotten to tell the dumb machine to "execute." She punched "Exec" and was greeted by more silence.

She wondered why the stupid thing didn't at least spew out the data on Sammy Schulte, but then she realized that the boy would have been entered into the computer memory as having disappeared from his home, four blocks away. Evidently the Crime Data Section had failed to feed in the fact that the bicycle had been found in the bushes in front. A plain case of "garbage in, garbage out." There *was* a J-Building connection, but the computer hadn't been informed. Which made the computer worth zilch. She pushed her chair back and reached for the Off switch just as the printer begin to clack. At 540 words per minute, it snapped out: "MISSING 8-12-80 MARGOT WILLIS GAMBLE (SF)."

She shielded her eyes with her hand so she could concentrate on the surprise information. She felt like someone who hit the dollar jackpot while walking away. Did this silly computer realize what it had just said? It had told her that another human being had disappeared from the J-Building in the last three days.

What in the name of God was going on?

"SF" meant "see files." She switched the machine off and looked at the clock. She still had twenty-five minutes before she had to report to her partner the killer.

The file on Margot Willis Gamble was pitifully thin, typical of files on missing mates. A report signed by Ptn. Billy Pierson said tersely, "Subject reported missing by husband, Severn. Last seen vic. Justice Building 1900 hrs., Aug. 12."

She couldn't believe her good luck. *Last seen vicinity Justice Building . . .*

Exactly like Sammy Schulte and Boon's informer.

She grabbed the roster and found Pierson's home number. The second watch deskman answered sleepily, "Pierson."

"Bill? Tally Wickham. Listen, I'm sorry to bother you so early—"

"Oh, hi, Tal—"

"—but what do you remember about Margot Willis Gamble? Missing since, uh, Tuesday night? Husband, Severn, made the complaint?"

"What do *I* remember?" Pierson said, laughing over the phone. "You don't remember?"

"Remember what?"

"The guy you assaulted Tuesday night?"

"With the beard? He's—?"

"The husband, right. Severen Gamble. An artist, I think."

Tally was confused. How come she hadn't been told about this Gamble and his missing wife already? Then she remembered: she'd rushed out of the J-Building the night before last to check on Sammy Schulte, and that had been the end of her contact with Mr. S. Gamble, nine feet tall. He'd been manhandling a brother officer, and she'd subdued him: a routine night's work, except that it had scared her half to death.

"What's the status?" she asked.

"The wife? She's still running, far's I know. I put out a bulletin. Didn't you see it?"

Tally hated to admit that she hadn't. Every officer on every watch was supposed to read and assimilate all bulletins, arrest reports, and FIRS, field interview reports. There were cops who never read anything but the sports pages and *Guns & Ammo,* but she wasn't one of them.

Well, she'd been busy on other things. She asked herself if that was a legitimate excuse. *Negative.* For Sammy Schulte's sake, she should have come in and gone over the whole missing persons file and *every* bulletin and *every* arrest report and *every* FIR for at least the last week. Her father would have. Johnny Boon would have. She remembered his meticulously kept album of "fools." That was how the best cops worked. Mules . . . When would she learn? There weren't any secrets or tricks.

She thanked Pierson and dashed for the bulletin clipboard. There it was, eleven sheets down, initialed by three different watch commanders: "MARGOT WILLIS GAMBLE 8743 STINSON AV. N.E. 446-9210." She dialed and gave her name and number to the recording machine that answered. She looked again at the bulletin: ". . . MISSING FROM FORDING & FULTON SINCE 1900 HRS DATE. . . . UNK REASON FOR LEAVING."

Unknown reason for leaving. Just like Sammy Schulte. The woman disappears around the J-Building, and the child disappears from his nearby home, but his new bike turns up here. And this morning a dead man is found in the garage. That's three J-Building connections in three days. Two could be a long shot coincidence, but . . . three?

She picked up the phone and dialed Mondragon.

31

"John," Mondragon said from behind his desk, "I'm depending on you and Tally here." No wonder he's wearing that friendly grin, Boon said to himself. He needs all the help he can get.

"We'll assume these cases are connected," the old man went on, looking at the policewoman. "I still doubt it, but we'll handle 'em like they are. Tally, you're the expert on the Schulte case, and John, Diego was your contact, so the two of you combine those two cases with the Gamble case and take it from there."

"Oh, Lord," Wickham put in, "not Gamble again. I almost lost an arm."

"I heard about that," Mondragon said.

"About what?" Boon asked. It would be nice if they let him in on their secrets.

"Your partner here." Boon wished the old man would stop using that word. He didn't consider her his partner and never would. She was a passenger in his car, period. "She decked this Gamble the other night. When he came in to file the missing persons report on his wife, he got physical."

"*You knocked him out?*" Boon asked.

"I just helped subdue him," she said, turning a little pink around her prominent cheekbones.

"With a chokehold," Mondragon put in. "Shut him right down. He's six-five. About two-eighty. Pierson said she rode him like a jockey."

Boon stared through his own smoke. He'd have to hear it from Billy Pierson before he believed it.

"Both of you pay attention," the dragon said, leaning

forward in his swivel chair. "Give these cases the full treatment, but keep in mind this could all be a big fat coincidence. The kid could've wandered off, hopped a bus, a ferry, hitched a ride. He'll turn up in a campground playing Huckleberry Finn with some thirty-year-old pervert, you mark my words. And this Gamble—he's a painter, a sculptor, one of those hippie types. Beard and all. I wouldn't be surprised he's got his wife up in his attic. In a box. If she's missing at all . . ."

Boon looked over at Tally. Her face was a total blank. That was the best way to listen to Mondragon. He was probably right, though. The idea of a snatcher roaming the J-Building was pretty far out when you thought about it. "You can't put too much faith in a story told by a hysteric," the old man went on. "Back when we took missing persons seriously, we'd spend three weeks looking for a guy's wife, and then we'd find out they had a big fight and he practically threw her out, only he didn't bother to mention it. Am I right, son?"

"Don't ask me, Cap," he said. "I don't go back that far." He wondered if he should jump in and mention Anna; her disappearance was uncomfortably like the other ones.

No, he shouldn't. An hour ago the old man had sounded bored with the subject. "Again?" he'd commented when Boon had mentioned that she was missing. Forget it, Cap, he said to himself, I'll find her single-o. If she's alive to find.

After they left the dragon's office, Wickham said, "Where do we start?"

He turned up his palms. "Who knows? This is nuts, lumping these cases. I wonder where he got an idea like that."

"From me," she said.

On the way to Gamble's address in the Charger, she tried to explain her reasoning, starting with something about the computer, but he barely listened. Young cops were always ready to talk your ear off about their achievements. She was eager, he had to admit that. Overeager. And now he was stuck with her for Christ knew how long. "There's something sick behind this," she was saying. "Some twisted kind of mind. Or some . . . force."

A force, huh? *Whoo-ee!*

"I keep thinking about Sammy," she went on, more to herself than to him. "Anybody who would hurt that child would have to be sick."

"You got yourself convinced some poor sick fool snatched the kid, don'tcha?" he said to shut her up. "Listen, get one thing straight: cops don't like that word *sick*. It's always being jammed down our throat: 'That poor man, he sliced up a mother and four kids with his machete, but he couldn't help himself, he's sick.' Well, lemme tell ya; not all fools are sick. Some fools are just plain bad." He waited for her to argue, but she rolled her eyes and turned away. "I hate the sons of bitches," he said.

A light rain had started again. He didn't want to hear a load of sanctimonious bullshit about turning the other cheek and loving the downtrodden. There was a clique of born-again cops who talked like that, and every one of them had to ride alone. Nobody wanted to hear that crap night after night, least of all law officers. He'd been force-fed the New Testament in Saint Theresa's: faith, hope, and charity, and not a word about what to do when a guy kicks you in the nuts. "For God so loved the world, that he gave his only begotten Son. . . ." Yeah, and I gave my brother and two marriages, he said to himself. Win some, lose some. . . .

"Hate's a sickness," she said. He knew the silence had been too good to last. He glanced sideways; her eyes were wide and full of light. "It destroys people. You're halfway there, Sergeant." She paused and said, "The funny thing is I think you're mostly a fake."

"What's that suppose to mean?"

"I think you work at your hate," she said, the words coming faster. "The way some people work at their looks.

Or their marriages." He wished he had a marriage to work at. "You cops that run on hate," she said, her voice softening a little, "you're mostly method actors. Trouble is, you start believing your own act. Pretty soon you hate yourselves. And that's the end for a policeman."

"They teach you that in college?"

"They didn't have to. I grew up around cops. To me, *you're* the rookie."

He wanted to laugh at her superior attitude, but a fiddler crab was chewing too hard on his ulcer. He never expected to hear a female cop talk to him like this. Method actor, for Chrisakes . . .

"Think about it," she said.

All that came to his mouth was a sarcastic "thanks, Reverend." He wished he knew more about talking to women.

She made a little aggravated moan and turned half away, as though she found the campus scenery more interesting than talking to an idiot. Well, maybe it was. These goddamn college women; it was like trying to communicate with somebody from another planet. They didn't even use the same language.

But he couldn't let a green rook shut him down, so a few blocks before they reached the Gamble address, he downshifted behind an unmuffled white Trans-Am and called out, "You keep on treating fools like sick people, and I'll keep on treating 'em like fools! We'll see who comes out in one piece!"

The Pontiac dropped into second and almost popped its heads. "YOU'RE ASSUMING YOU'RE IN ONE PIECE NOW?" she shouted back.

"YEAH!" he said. "TWO LEGS, TWO ARMS, ONE HEAD . . . EVERYTHING RIGHT WHERE IT BELONGS!" He lifted his hands from the wheel and spread them wide: a method actor taking a bow. "LOOK AT ME!"

"I'M TRYING TO!"

*   *   *

A tall bearded man with startled eyes and flecks of dried spit at the corners of his mouth answered the door at the Gamble address. Boon showed his ID and brushed past him into the living room of a damp bungalow littered with empty cups and paper. He didn't want a long hassle about warrants or credentials with a coked-up hippie who liked to jump cops.

Nobody was invited to sit. Boon glanced at the pictures that covered almost every inch of the walls. There were a few good paintings of the harbor, but most of the stuff was just plain silly: lines and circles and streaks and sloshes of paint like the ones the kids used to make in kindergarten. They called it fingerpainting then; now it passed for art. He wasn't surprised. Punk rock passed for music, too.

The man admitted that he was Severn Gamble and after a brief hesitation began pacing the bare wooden living-room floor as he told a jumbled story at a jitterbug pace: how he'd let "Margot" out of the car at the J-Building and he'd been waiting two days for her to come back and he'd begged the police department to work on the case and *nobody* would *listen*. When the guy was finished, Boon realized with relief that they could scratch one mysterious disappearance; this dude *was* a goddamn hysteric, just as Mondragon had said, and doped to the eyeballs to boot. His wife had gotten fed up and split, and if she hadn't, she should have.

"The first thing you gotta do, Mr. Gamble," Boon said when the tirade was over, "is you gotta cool it a little, quit blaming everybody else. That only makes things harder."

"Ah, God," the big man said, cupping his face in hands the size of hockey gloves, "you think I'm paranoid."

"No, I don't," Boon said. "But you could fool some

people." He glanced at Wickham; she looked concerned, but at least she was keeping her mouth shut. If the Margot Gamble disappearance turned out to be a false alarm, what happened to the great J-Building mystery they were supposed to clear up together? It went up in smoke, that's what happened.

The young bartender's story came back to him: Anna had been on her way to the building. Sure, but that gave her forty blocks to travel on a Saturday night. She'd fallen off the wagon before. There were a hell of a lot of bars and motels to pass in those forty blocks. Besides, she still had a few more days to go to break her record for longest disappearing act.

The same kind of reasoning applied to the retard: his bike had been found in the front shrubbery, but lots of kids misplaced their wheels, and lots of kids took off. He could be anywhere. Candy, though—that was a puzzle. The missing heart; no way that made any sense . . .

"You'd act paranoid, too," the bearded man was mumbling through his fingers. He lifted his heavy-lidded eyes; there was a Jesus look about him, an air of martyrdom. For the first time Boon felt sorry for the guy. Freak or not, he was suffering; it was painful to watch the shifting planes and angles on his face, like looking at exposed nerves.

"Wives leave," Boon said gently, realizing what an expert he was on the subject.

"My wife didn't."

The room grew quiet except for the rattle of rain from a leaky downspout. Boon pulled up a velvet-covered chair and said in the mildest voice he could manage, "I know how you feel, man. You're positive your wife would never leave you. But you *never* know. I was just as positive about my own wives. *Twice.* And now I'm living alone. Get my drift? Don't make me spell it out. No husband ever knows their own wife. They only think they do."

Boon looked at Wickham; she had a funny look on her

face, as though he'd said too much. Well, this big guy needed some honest advice. He'd been dumped, no doubt about that, and he wouldn't start to get over it till he faced it square. "Wives, husbands," Boon went on, "they take it into their heads to go, and . . . they go! Understand what I'm saying?"

Gamble looked up, then lowered his head again. It was hard to tell if he even heard the words.

"I seen this movie," Boon said, moving closer. "Some old man's trying to tell a kid why people commit suicide. He says, 'You get yourself a little spot on your hat, and . . . that's an earthquake.' That's all it takes sometimes; a spot on a hat, and a man jumps off a bridge, a boy runs away, a wife takes off. It's not the big things, Mr. Gamble. People can handle the big things."

The artist looked up again. He seemed calm enough, but his dark eyes kept blinking. He started talking in just as soft a voice as Boon's, but in a tone that suggested he'd given up all hope of convincing them or anyone else. "There was nothing like that. There was no . . . spot on her hat. My wife and I, we were tight. If she was getting ready to take off, I'd've known."

"Uh-huh," Boon said, giving up but trying not to show it. What the guy should do is find a counselor, check out his church, the community relations program, anything but the PD. "Look, you oughta be sleeping. You been getting any rest?"

"I've been busy."

"Rest awhile. You hear anything, give us a call." He fished out one of his cards and handed it over. "Me and the lady here, we'll do what we can."

"You won't go out and look for her," the artist said. "Nobody will. That leaves me." He sounded as if he'd had a lot of time to think things over. Well, he was right; no cop in his right mind was going to waste time on a missing wife. Where would you start?

Boon stepped to the window. Through sheets of rain,

the visibility reached eight or nine blocks down the slope: hundreds of houses and apartment buildings, thousands of hiding places. He swept his hand toward the bay. "Tell me where to look," he said, "and I'll—we'll look. But where? You want us to check the parks? Tree by tree? The public toilets? We did that yesterday, looking for a missing kid. It's a pure waste of time, Mr. Gamble. Your wife could be anywhere in this city—or any other city."

"She's . . . somewhere," the artist said. The furtive look behind his beard gave an indication that he knew more than he was telling. A sudden thought struck Boon: *How much more?* Worth thinking about. He realized that Gamble had been giving him a lot of those looks during the interview, as if silently gauging his reaction.

It wouldn't be the first time that a wife killer had laid a false trail by pushing the cops to find his wife.

He caught Wickham's eye and jerked his head a few degrees toward the door: the senior partner's prerogative.

Maybe they should keep an eye on Severn Gamble.

32

As Gamble pulled away, freshly fortified with coffee, he noticed a green and white patrol car a half block down the street. He gunned the TR-3 around the corner, doubled back through the alley behind the bungalow, and sped off, untrailed.

He had to get to City Hall before the place emptied for lunch. As he drove through the wet streets, he thought about the blond-haired detective with his little cigar and his garbled quote from *Death of a Salesman*. He wondered if Margot would have considered Ciel a spot on her hat. . . .

The bell in the tower was tolling noon when he entered City Hall and studied the black index board in the front lobby for the city surveyor's room number. Off to one side he saw a guard approaching and broke for the stairs at a fast walk. At the top of the landing he sneaked a look over the spiral-twist iron rail. The guard was standing by the main entrance, looking out.

Gamble squeezed through the shutting doors of a crowded up elevator. He rode a few floors and stepped off. A thickset cop with an oyster gray complexion and eyebrows like caterpillars sat square in front of him at a desk. The city crawled with uniforms.

He strolled past with his face averted. The cop appeared to be hunched over some papers. As Gamble stretched out his stride down the silent hall, he could feel the eyes boring into his back from beneath those bushy eyebrows.

He turned at the first hallway, ducked into a door marked "Exit," and dropped down a flight of concrete stairs to the next floor. He shoved the door open and almost knocked down a woman with rhinestone-studded glasses and a single hibiscus that looked planted in her head. "Uh, excuse me," he said. "Where's the surveyor's office?"

"Ninth floor in the annex," the woman said, staring up at him.

He didn't return to the staircase till she disappeared into an office. He was puffing when he stepped out on the ninth floor, but for once no cops were in sight.

Before he was allowed to look at documents, Gamble was asked to sign a paper by a man who looked like Uriah Heep atop his three-legged stool. Gamble hesitated and scribbled "Willem de Kooning." The clerk held the scrawl in the light and nodded slowly as though to confirm its authenticity. Then he disappeared for a few minutes and returned with a wary look on his face. "What was it you wanted?" he asked, avoiding eye contact.

Gamble needed to find out exactly where the old streets had run before the lower town had been lifted by caissons and fill. He knew that the job had been completed by 1890, so he asked for charts from the years before. The clerk led him to long, thin drawers where the yellowing maps were preserved in clear plastic.

At first the documents seemed to swim before his stare —his eyes weren't focusing properly, and he saw blurs and glitches that he knew couldn't be there—and when he was finally able to focus, he was confronted with strange street names, tidal flats and creeks and drainage basins that meandered across the middle of downtown, and elevation markings for hills that hadn't existed for ninety years. But a trestled Fulton Street was there, and it gave him a locus for the rest. In 1880 a wharf had stood where the J-Building was now, probably for provisioning ships. And Exposition, the street that ran along the back of the J-Building, had been called Canal, although no trace of a canal showed on the map. It must have been drained. But had it been filled? And if it had, were there gaps that a man his size could get through?

He returned the maps and took the elevator to the first floor. He walked briskly into the moist noon air, looking for cops and feeling stupid for thinking that they might have taken Margot. One part of his mind knew well that he was only keeping himself busy. He cursed under his breath when he reached the Triumph. A thin envelope was tucked under his windshield wiper. "Overparking, $5." He'd forgotten the meter. Meters were of no importance now.

He drove to the Old Town office of Underground Tours, Inc. A sign on the door said that the tour left at 10:00 A.M., 2:00 and 4:00 P.M., two dollars each, children under five free. "Uh, you have any literature?" Gamble asked an auburn-haired woman at the ticket desk.

She put down a magazine, handed him a white and blue pamphlet, and collected fifty cents. He walked back to the sidewalk and flipped the pages impatiently till he came to a hand-drawn map of the route. A dotted line showed that the tour started on Fulton at the bottom of the steep staircase he had inspected the first night, meandered to Pine, went two blocks south under Wells, a block west under Sumner, and then zigzagged back to the starting point.

He visualized the 1880 surveyor's map and mentally superimposed it over this one, making allowances for the different scales. As near as he could figure, the underground tour came within a few feet of the J-Building's sealed-off basement. As he had hoped . . .

The auburn-haired woman was half-concealed behind teetering stacks of coins. "Tell me something," he said, trying hard to conceal his intensity. "Are there any underground streets or alleys that the tour misses?"

"What do you mean?" She had a squeaky chorus-girl voice that didn't go with her aging face.

"I mean, could a person, uh, get lost?"

The woman looked insulted. "Not if you follow the guide," she said. "We're electrified the whole way. You'd have to be trying."

"The lights stay on all the time?"

The woman sighed and looked up again. "Only during the tours. Obviously. Did you want a ticket?"

"Please," he said, digging in his pocket.

She handed him a long blue strip bearing a line drawing of a bearded gold miner and told him to return promptly at two. "And don't worry," she called in her canary voice as he walked through the door. "We keep good track of our people."

I hope not, he said to himself.

"How'd *you* get in?" he asked Ciel. She was dusting feverishly, her backside waggling in vermilion jeans that looked painted on.

"Your key was where it always is," she said as she rubbed the feet of a walnut armoire that had belonged to his aunt. She looked up and blinked her olive eyes. "Am I —are you saying—Ciel's an intruder all of a sudden?"

It grated on his ears whenever she referred to herself in the third person. Next she'd be using the royal *we*. Well, he had forty-five minutes to check his phone calls, grab some equipment, and be back for the start of the underground tour; he had no time for chatter.

"Ciel," he said, "thanks anyway, but—go home. Please?"

"I—"

"I need to be by myself for a while. Okay?" As he spoke, his vision blurred again. He stepped toward her, but she slipped away and turned into a pair of Ciels, both of them holding a dust rag like a shield. He stopped just short of the wall.

"Severn, listen to me!" she said. "You're not yourself. Please, Sev, *listen!*"

"No time." He realized that he was wired: high on uppers, low on protein, and something less than rational. A couple of cheeseburgers and a quart of milk and a few hours of sleep would change all that. But first . . .

He strode to his studio with Ciel in his wake and pulled his Wilderness Experience climbing pack from the closet. Into the flat bag he stuffed a point chisel, a claw chisel, a compass, and a small flashlight. He took his long-sleeved bush jacket off a hanger; he would need it against the subterranean damp. Luckily it was a cool day for August; the jacket wouldn't look too conspicuous on the street.

"Severn? You're not listening!"

"Huh?" He rummaged through his closet, looking for an old lead-cored chipping mallet.

"Can I explain something?" she said. "Sev, look, you're having a guilt reaction. It's not just Margot. Do you hear what I'm saying?"

He didn't answer. The damned mallet used to be in this corner in a box. Now where the hell—?

"Severn, the other night—it wasn't your fault. It was *me*, not you. Oh, God, won't you *listen*?"

He found the box, but it was empty. He couldn't chisel through obstructions without a hammer. Well, he'd just have to buy a new one. Extra flashlight batteries, too. There was a hardware store around the corner.

As an afterthought he threw in his Swiss army knife: twenty-three blades, including a screwdriver, scissors, and a hacksaw. When he returned to the bedroom from his studio, Ciel followed and dropped into Margot's dressing chair.

"Sev," she pleaded, "I—"

"I gotta get going," he said.

"Where? What're those chisels for?"

"Find Margot."

"Where's Margot?" she asked nonchalantly.

"Never mind."

He felt her hand on his arm. "Severn," she said, "don't do this to yourself. It's not your fault. You didn't do anything wrong."

He looked at his watch: 1:05. He had to make a detour to the hardware store. That would take five or ten minutes. He felt dizzy again. Maybe . . . if he just . . . sat. . . .

He slumped backward on the bed, his backpack clinking. He shut his eyes to steady himself and far in the distance heard Ciel's muffled voice babbling that Brooks had fallen in love and this morning they had agreed to separate; she'd suspected for weeks; she'd known that all those nighttime emergency calls couldn't be legitimate; she'd found out for sure the night of the hot tub, and . . . she'd taken revenge. She hadn't meant to involve Severn; it could have been anyone. A neighbor. The plumber. She'd been out of her mind with jealousy and pain. Surely he understood . . .?

He opened his eyes. "I *used* you, Severn, can't you see that? Oh, God, I'm *so* sorry. And now you—you've got everything mixed up in your mind—Margot and, and—

what happened with us. But there's no connection, Severn
—*no connection!*"

He lifted his long legs off the bed and saw her standing
in the hallway behind the shell curtain, clawed fingers
touching the sides of her head as though auditioning for
a tragic role. "I know what I did," he said. "I'm not looking
for a cop-out."

"It's *not* a cop-out, Severn," she said, running in and
grabbing his hand. "It's the truth. You're dear to me, but
not . . . that way. You understand?"

Why did she always seem to be playing a role? *Ciel
enters stage left, takes Severn's hand.* He felt wobbly.
"On the sink in the bathroom," he said. "Some . . .
pills. Get me a couple, will ya?"

She came back with his entire Dexedrine supply
clutched in her hand. "Severn, you'll *kill* yourself," she
said.

He reached out, but she jerked the peach-colored pills
away like a frivolous child. He lunged and knocked them
loose. He groped on the floor and shoved a couple into
his mouth. The phone rang, and he heard Ciel's hushed
voice: "Oh, yes. . . . *Worse.* . . ."

She dragged the phone on its long extension and held
it against his ear. He smelled her light lime scent and
heard a distant male voice. "Sev. *Severn!* You there, man?"

"Here," he said, holding the phone by the mouthpiece.

"It's *me.* Hey, pal, what's happening?" Brooks's thera-
peutic voice. "What're you up to?"

He jerked his head hard. "What?" he asked.

"This is Brooks, Sev. *Brooks!* How you feeling, pal?"

"Gotta go now, Brooks," he said, frowning at the phone.
"Go where?"

"The underground tour. Margot." His head was clear-
ing. Good old Brooks. It helped to talk to him.

"You think Margot's . . . underground? Why don't
you call the cops?"

"They're no help. See ya, Brooks. Don't tell anybody.

I'll find her." His strength was coming back.

"How're you gonna find her by yourself?"

"People'll help. You'll help, won't you, Brooks?"

"Wait! I'll be there in a few—"

"I'll be gone."

33

Ugo smiled down at his grandmother, resting peacefully in the tiny room he had chosen for her. Nonna looked as young as she had in 1944. He stroked the long black peasant dress, lifted a swatch of the coarse material, and pressed it to his cheek. Tears wet his face. He fell to his knees and prayed his thanks to the Virgin.

He still trembled with fear that something would go wrong. The sacred date, August 15, *ferragosto*, was just a day away. But where was his father? All the others were here now, even Uncle Duilio. . . .

He hadn't known what to think when he first saw what the Virgin had sent. A man made up as a woman, mouth open as though screaming! For a while he had been fooled. Sacred name of Christ, what a blasphemy!

But then he had recognized the body of his uncle. The one who made the family laugh. Wasn't it just like him to arrive dressed in women's clothes and painted face? Always the buffoon . . .

But . . . still no Babbo. The head of the family! Babbo, you must come. . . .

Now that his loved ones were almost assembled, he wanted nothing more than to sit quietly in their company, but he had to perform his maintenance duties for appearances' sake. In the *Stati Uniti*, Pentecost Eve and

Pentecost Day were ordinary workdays, and there was no feast of the Immaculate Conception. He shuddered at the prospect of going upstairs and bumping into the *gigant'* again. *Where was he now? Did he still walk the halls?*

The tall *malocchio* had stormed into the maintenance room and screamed words Ugo couldn't understand. For once he was sorry that he had refused to study English. It would enable him to deal better with menaces like the *gigant'*, turn them away with a soft word or an explanation. One night ten or twenty years ago he had recited all the English words he knew, expressions like "Thank you," "That's okay," "Hello," "See you later." Maybe he had a thousand words of *inglese* now, all of them squirreled away for the rare occasions when he had to deal with the public, and even then he always tried to appear stupid because if he revealed too much, someone might discover that he had fled his GI foster father's strap thirty years ago.

Soon the nightmare would be over. The Virgin had told him that high in the heavens the mountain home of his childhood was still intact, as untouched and unspoiled as when he had crawled from his cold bed every morning to milk the goat. She had come to him in the night and explained that they would all go home together: Babbo, Mamma, his brother, Maxmein, his Aunt Livia, his Uncle Duilio, his angel Nonna.

Transported: that was the word she had used. To a fertile *podere* on a mountainside. To the pungent white truffles that grew on the roots of the chestnut trees. To the glint of morning sun that warmed their terra cotta roof. To the wind that blew down from Trieste and heaped the snow into caves and crevasses where children hid and played.

To Monte Sole.

He took his whetstone from its cloth pouch, reached inside his belt, and carefully slid out the J. Marttiini filleting knife that gleamed like quicksilver. As he stroked it gently back and forth, he had a vision of the moon gleaming down on the *casa colonica* where the Ruggiero family had lived with the rest of the Marchese Triolo's tenant farmers. Touching the sharp blade with his thumb, he thought he caught the faint scent of smoke from the old church of Casaglia, the one the *Nazi-Fascisti* murderers had burned down while the congregation was trapped inside. He pictured the blue flames devouring his favorite painting on the wall of the church: the dripping heart framed in black over its own eternal candle. His knife rubbed against the sharpening stone—*ssst ssst ssst*—as he thought of the engorged carmine heart, veins and ducts as real as in life, paired angel wings sprouting from the sides, a few drops of scarlet blood in trail, soaring toward the celestial light at the top of the painting. The Sacred Heart of Jesus, bound for heaven . . .

He thought of the years of silence, beginning with the first days in America with his *benefattore*, when he had suppressed all but the vaguest memories of his mountain. Then bit by bit, relaxing in the familiar confines of his building, he had blocked in the cracks of his memory like a mason working with tile, reconstructed almost every minute of his twelve years on Monte Sole. But not the massacre.

And now he remembered everything, but it no longer brought him pain. The Virgin was returning his dead, the loved ones who had been dumped into a hole in the mountaintop cemetery overrun with tangled weeds and wild marauding cats. . . .

He put down the razor-edged knife and touched his Nonna's cool hand as he recalled the unmarked wooden cross he had found atop the common grave when he had first come out of hiding, the shell-shocked priest with the smashed face and black stumps of teeth pulling him away from the depression in the earth again and again: "No, my son, you must not try to dig them up. They are dust. No, *no*, Ugo! It is a mortal sin."

"But my Mamma, my—"

"It is not just your family, my son," the *reverendo* had told him. "It is all the families of the mountain. The *Nazi-Fascisti* spared no one. At least allow them the peace of the grave."

"How many, how many—?" he could not bring himself to say the word.

"*Tutti.* They are buried everywhere."

"*How many, Father?*"

"Some say eighteen hundred, some two thousand. Nobody knows. The mountain died. You are the only survivor. *Solo tu* . . ."

He thought about the money he had sent back from America to care for the graves, more money than he had kept for himself, so that his family could rest in copper-lined boxes with fresh flowers purchased every day in Bologna, arrays of candles in red cut-glass containers set in front of each crypt in the shape of a cross, the *mausoleo* walls in fine Carrara marble of a rosy hue, polished to a gloss and surmounted by a jade statue of Saint Anthony in his robes, one hand upraised toward heaven, and just inside the thick brass-barred doors a deliberately broken column to symbolize the incomplete life of a child, his brother Maximiliano, and the family name RUGGIERO carved across the front above the quote from Alighieri: "And thence we came forth, to see again the stars."

Through the Virgin's intervention, those heavy brass doors had opened in the night, and the Ruggieros were here now, together, all but his Babbo. It was only fitting; his father was always the last to come in from the fields, hands scarred and gnarled from the work. The one they depended on . . . He would arrive any minute.

Ugo reached down and brushed the backs of his fingers across the kind old face of his grandmother and thought his heart would burst. The generator sent an odor of ozone through the maintenance room, but he was already smelling the *ferragosto* feast. He sat on the edge of his sagging cot, closed his eyes and saw fresh-cooked salami and polenta and envelopes of tortellini stuffed with sausage and fried pork bits and the flaky *crescentina* baked of pastry and ham between hot bricks. He saw wooden bowls heaped with soft red pimientos, truffle-stuffed eggs, beefy mushrooms, blanched cauliflower that snapped to the tooth, platters of tender lamb and pork served with his mother's *salsa piccante,* fresh-killed chicken and rabbit cooked hunter style in a pungent tomato-pepper sauce, and side dishes of turkey and guinea fowl sliced thick for the heavy eaters like his Babbo and his Uncle Duilio and the *prete.* And of course, four different kinds of pasta and a half dozen cheeses.

Nobody went to bed hungry. Ugo smiled in his little room. *On* ferragosto *night, nobody went to bed at all!*

He turned his face toward the door that led to the hall of the Justice Building, and as he did, he saw his father delicately pat his buttered mustache with a single sheet of the newspaper *Il Resto di Carlino* and clap his hands for dessert, and the women of the family appeared in stately procession. First his dear graying Nonna as the oldest, then his saintly mother, Felice, with hair as black as Negretto wine tumbling to her waist, and last his beautiful Aunt Livia, her skin the color of the first cream, and each holding aloft her own *specialità:* berry tarts, the sweet chestnut pastry *mistocce,* Spanish spice cakes, the big soft jelly rolls *ciambelle* and *crostate,* warm sweet loaves beaded with honey and marmalade . . .

Smiling and nodding in the maintenance room, oblivious to the sounds around him, Ugo tried to remember all the preparations he still had to make. Was today August 13? No, *no,* he must get it straight. There was no more time for his typical forgetfulness. *He must remember!* Today was Thursday, August 14, and tomorrow was . . .

Ferragosto!

He glanced at the plastic Christ on the cross that hung from the wall, crossed himself and kissed his thumbnail, and renewed his thanks to the Virgin. He was prepared for her visit, his soul cleansed, his confession taken the evening before by the mission priest around the corner. He could never thank the *Madonna* enough, could never repay the miracle that she was bringing to pass even if he devoted a thousand years.

The Holy Mother had shown him that death was only a human concept. Back on Monte Sole, the family Ruggiero was listed under a black cross in the municipal records, but that was the work of *ignurant* clerks who did not understand that the holy immortal soul resides in the human heart, and the soul does not die!

"A thousand thanks, blessed mother of Christ," Ugo said passionately in the darkened room. *"Grazie mell, Madonna. Grazie grazie grazie . . ."*

He heard a sound.

Hush!

Someone was in his room.

He fell to his knees on the concrete floor and shut his eyes and lowered his head as the presence revealed itself with a noise like the far-off gathering of wind. He heard the peal of bells, closer and closer, and the powerful chords of a great organ. "My son," the voice said, and he opened his eyes.

She floated in space between the air duct and the vent, shimmering in cold fire, a twinkling ring of light above her head. The Virgin had returned.

34

Gamble walked beside the tour guide as the group followed an overhead wire strung with lights. He had taken another upper just before the descent; his head was light, and he could feel his heartbeat. But he was *doing* something. The solution to his problem seemed simple: if he kept trying different approaches, one approach would lead him to Margot. It made perfect sense.

So far the guide's monologue had been heavy on whimsy and light on facts. He needed to know exactly where they were, so that he could slip away from the group near the underpinnings of the J-Building and take off on an inspection tour of his own. If he had it figured right, that would be in ten or fifteen minutes.

The group entered a low-ceilinged chamber held up by the thickest beams he had ever seen—they could have been squared-off cedar trunks—and the tour guide pointed out a wooden sign with indecipherable printing. "This was a store," he said into a bullhorn. "Your helpful hardware man, 1880." The twenty or twenty-five tourists shivered in the unaccustomed chill. Gamble saw a splintered cask, broken wooden dowels, a flattened high-top work shoe, a wooden counter that had been crushed by fill.

From a niche in the brick wall, the guide produced a yellowing book of payroll records for men named Alonzo, Rudolph, Josephus, Homer. "Good old American names," the college-age guide intoned as though he were reading from a script. "The names that made our country great. You remember President Alonzo Lincoln? And the father of our country, Josephus Washington? They all worked here. For a buck fifty a day. No wonder they went into politics." Gamble faked a smile. He didn't want to look conspicuous.

The party shuffled out of the room and down a narrow passageway past dangling iron pipes, ruined storefronts, rotting boardwalks, brick arches over musty waterways that the guide explained had been sewers, sagging walls of buried buildings, and the charred remains of warehouses and docks from the fire of '86. Shapes wet and dark, rodentiform, scurried past their feet, peered at them with hungry yellow eyes from slits in the walls.

"Creepy, huh?"

He turned to see a padded man in a business suit picking his way along. "Uh, yeah," he answered.

He needed to check his compass; he thought they were still headed east under Fulton, but they had been in and out of several rooms and down a few curving pasageways, and his sense of direction had never been a precision instrument.

"Big fella like you, you gotta duck a lot, I imagine?"

He turned again. It was the same man, closer now, evidently craving companionship against his fears. A claustrophobe, maybe. Gamble had suffered an attack of claustrophobia the first time he'd made this tour, but this time he felt light-headed and energized and . . . fearless.

"Yeah," he said, slipping the compass out of his bush jacket pocket and cupping it in his hand.

"Where ya from?"

Just what I need, Gamble said to himself. A self-appointed tour companion. "Uh, here," he said.

"No *kidding*?" the man said, as though the news were exciting. "I'm from Dubuque, Iowa."

Get lost, Gamble thought. *Get lost!*

"What bidness you in?" his new friend asked.

"Huh?" The compass showed they were headed a few points north of due east, almost exactly the way Fulton had pointed on the old maps. They should cross the old canal under Exposition Street in a few minutes. Time to slip away.

"I'm in snap fasteners, me," the man persisted.

Gamble stopped and looked at the wall. The mortar had receded in places, and a few bricks had fallen out, giving it the look of an old man's mouth. As he leaned forward for a closer study, the tour group flowed past till he was the last in line. Now all he had to do was clomp along behind till he came to a convenient opening and . . . disappear.

"Keep up, friend!" Gamble heard the familiarly irritating voice. "Don't get lost in the shuffle."

The tour poured into a room dominated by a mired old donkey engine lying on its side. A rusty piston had pulled loose from a cylinder and fallen on the floor. On a broken water tank girdled by rusted bands someone had written, "Perelli sucks," and underneath was scrawled, "Whoever wrote this better watch their ass."

A gathering of wildlife squeaked from a split in the side of the tank. "Don't let them get away!" the guide bellowed through the bullhorn. "They didn't pay!" He dropped a few scraps of bread into the tank, and the rodent family quieted. Gamble wondered if there were any other tame rats down here and if they'd been carefully conditioned to put on their show. When the group spilled out of the room, he found himself up front again, alongside the guide.

So was the man from Dubuque. "Sumpin', huh?" the man said.

Gamble nodded and looked for an escape route. Maybe he was overreacting, but his companion was coming on too strong to be real. Any normal person would have noticed Gamble's coldness a long time ago and looked for other companionship. The man was sticking with him for a purpose. Why?

Was he a cop?

If he was, he wasn't a very bright one.

Huddled in the clear white light of a lantern held by the guide, the group made a short side trip into a cavern where water dropped from small stalactites. The guide pointed to a slanting wall of rock slabs and boulders and said, "That's ballast. Came here in ships, and the city used it for fill." He rapped a piece loose with a small steel hammer. "This might be from some exotic place: Genoa, Lisbon, Baltimore." He pretended to toss the fragment to a woman, who giggled as though it were alive. "Take it home!" he said. "No extra charge. Free real estate."

They squirmed out of the cavern through a jagged hole in the crumbling wall wide enough for one at a time. The guide led the way, followed by Gamble and the man from Iowa. Over their heads, traffic rumbled and whirred. The place seemed like a city under lava: an American Pompeii, but where were the smashed amphorae? The shattered statuary? Here the *objets d'art* were broken toilet bowls, rusty machinery, old boots. He wondered if Pompeii was so musty, so . . . banal. If there was an esthetic ordering of ruins, this one must rank near the bottom.

Plodding behind the guide, he followed down a long, straight stretch of tunnel. At first the paving consisted of loosely set cobblestones, but after a few minutes the flooring turned into thick logs, the interstices filled with what looked like plaster or mortar.

The canal!

If he was right, they were directly below the corner of Fulton and Exposition, give or take a few feet. Margot had disappeared somewhere above.

Time to bug out.

But the damned busybody dogged his steps, still acting like a gawking tourist but never straying more than a few feet away.

Just beyond the filled canal they came to an intersection of tunnels. Unlighted voids reached left and right.

The guide explained that a narrow-gauge railroad had crossed here at grade level and that the pufferbelly train had kept bringing in rock till "it filled up its own right of way and couldn't get out. They called it the little engine that couldn't."

"*Severn!*"

He turned at the sound of his name. At first he thought he was hearing things, but then the voice came louder, echoing and reechoing in the passage. "Severn! SEVER-R-R-R-R-nnnnnn! Wait up. WAIT!"

He knew that voice. Oh, God, he whispered under his breath, deliver me from my friends. Just when I felt like I was accomplishing something . . .

He squinted down the long corridor. A hundred feet away Brooks and two uniformed policemen approached under the overhanging bulbs.

Everyone had turned to look. Gamble edged sideways into the railroad tunnel. "Hey!" he heard a voice. "*You!* Where—?"

He spread his hands to guide himself between the unseen walls and moved along in a sped-up Groucho shuffle, head lowered to keep from scraping it on the ceiling.

He had no idea how long the tunnel extended. Any second he might slam headlong into a dead end or a mound of fill, but he didn't dare slow down. His fingers touched algae that grew along the walls, and once he slid on something squishy and almost fell.

He looked back and saw that the light in the main corridor behind him had turned into an indistinct cadmium yellow. He was fifty feet down the right of way by now, and there was no pursuit.

Then he saw indistinct forms entering the tunnel mouth.

"*Severn!*" Brooks's voice rolled down the corridor and bounced back at him from dead ahead. *A wall!* He was almost to the end.

He reached ahead into emptiness. He took a step and

felt the flooring change from smooth to rough. In two more steps he was halfway up a steep gravel slope that reached to the ceiling. There must have been a cave-in. End of the line.

He backtracked to the tunnel floor and groped on both walls. There was an opening on his right.

Was it another corridor? A vault? A room? Was it one of the vertical bores that fell to tidewater?

He inched into the opening, sliding his feet before him like a beginning ice skater. He had barely started when one of his Saucony running shoes hit something solid. Behind him a strange voice called, "We're not gonna hurt you. *Nobody's gonna hurt you!*"

He fumbled inside his pack for the small flashlight with its two C batteries.

"He can't get far," one of the voices said, much closer now.

He played the light against the break in the wall. A brick arch sheltered an opening. He knelt down and saw that it was the entrance to an old square sewer; the guide had pointed out several along the way. A thin stream of water topped by a dirty froth of bubbles fell a few inches in a miniature waterfall and disappeared under a ledge.

He poked the beam of light up the opening. A pair of reddish yellow eyes died like drowned sparks. Slime the color of garden slugs grew on the brickwork. The air was fetid.

"Severn!" The familiar voice was near.

He raked broken bricks and stones from the entrance to the culvert and forced his body inside. He wriggled upstream on elbows and knees, the flashlight clutched in his right hand. He was totally unafraid; he felt that there was nothing in the world that he wouldn't do. Or couldn't do. For her . . .

He crawled till he was out of breath and then stopped; he didn't want his hoarse gasps to carry down the line and give him away. He wondered what would happen if there were a cloudburst and the pipe filled. He would be swept from the culvert like a mouse from a fire hose. What a ride!

"Come on, man, give it up!" a new voice said. It seemed to come from ahead and behind at the same time. The whole underground was a resonating chamber; it sounded as if his pursuers were talking into his ear.

"Don't panic him," he heard Brooks say. "Let me handle it. He's in a state."

He turned off the flashlight so that the others wouldn't spot the glow and inched forward again. His big body scraped against all four sides and over pebbles and pieces of broken brick. He wondered if he were slowly wedging himself into a trap; it was barely possible to move forward, and it would be harder to get out. Were they gaining on him? He stopped to listen. All he could hear was his own breathing.

Something wet and sharp ran across his hand and jumped to his head and made its escape down his back and legs. A rat, or . . . he couldn't imagine what else lived down here. He remembered a childhood story about baby alligators that thrived in city sewer systems, but surely that was only a story?

Okay, go ahead and be rats! Just don't be alligators!

He was tiring. He wished he could reach the uppers in his pack, but there wasn't enough room to twist his arm around.

He stopped, completely out of breath. The air tasted like mildew; he decided it must be like this inside a tomb. He opened his mouth wide to clear his air passages. When he had drunk in his fill, he held his breath to hear.

Mixed noises came from behind. He reached forward to pull himself along and touched something slick and cold. *An eel!* His flashlight turned the eel into a short length of rotting canvas hose, swaying sinuously in the trickle.

He raised his head and pushed on, no longer bothering

to be quiet. His breathing sounded like a bellows in the confined area. He banged his sides and his head on the ragged brick and took a noseful of cold water.

His shoulder slammed against the side of the culvert, and he realized that he had come to a sharp turn. He slithered around the bend and found an opening above his head. He flicked on the flashlight and saw that an avalanche of ballast had holed the roof of his pipe.

He pulled himself through the fractured edges and clambered across the rock face. Ten or twelve feet up, beneath a solid ceiling that rumbled with heavy traffic, he came to a ledge. He pulled himself over the lip and stretched out. He couldn't be seen from above or below; if he kept quiet, he could wait them out.

35

"Have a seat, Officer," Carl Mondragon told her in his official voice. His round face bore a fat man's haggard look, jowls curved down like a bassett hound's. Tally wondered what was troubling him. He looked at Boon, seated to one side in a smog bank of smoke, and said, "We've got to talk. I been getting heat on these disappearances. What've you got I can show 'em? I mean—"

Three sharp tones cut him off. He held up his pudgy hand and punched a button on his desk. She watched him lean forward and say, "Go."

"The pigeon flew, Cap," a male voice crackled from the speaker. "On the underground tour."

"What the hell was he doing down there?" Mondragon asked.

"Dunno. He just went in with the regular crowd and ran up a tunnel. He can't get far."

Boon called out, "I'll be there in a minute."

"He'll be right there!" Carl barked into the squawk box as though the imminent arrival of Johnny Boon would solve all problems.

"Received."

"I told you there was something kinky about that guy," Boon said as he went out the door.

Tally ran to catch up. "Where're *you* going?" the old man asked.

"With my partner," she explained. The dragon started to say something, but she didn't wait to hear what it was.

36

As Boon jogged along the underground corridor in the wake of a tall cop in uniform, he thought how much his job depended on instinct. I took one look at that Gamble freak, he said to himself, and I knew there was something going on. Maybe not Murder One, but something. *How did I know?* How would I explain it to a class at the academy or to a judge? What did I have to go on? Just a look in his eye. A couple of hesitations when he talked. That's what experience does for you. You get so you can tell a fool a mile away.

He'd never been in the underground before. "You got a flashlight?" he asked.

"Yeah," the cop answered, slapping his baton ring. A long black anodized tube hung down. It looked less intimidating than the old-fashioned baton, but a six-cell Kellite could drop a horse.

"Can't we go faster?" a female voice called out. Wickham had tagged along. Little Miss Superglue.

"Can't go any faster'n the guy in front," Boon huffed.

"Ought to quit all that smoking," she said.

"Send me a letter." One thing about Wickham, she was generous. He could write a whole new manual with the suggestions she'd offered him in just two days.

After a few minutes they stopped at a side tunnel, and he reached in his dampened shirt pocket for a Swisher. "Uh, no smoking," said a kid in a gray probationary police uniform, standing in the mouth of the tunnel. "Throws off the dog."

Boon touched the cigar to the flame and made a round yellow fireball that lit up the walls. "No crap?" he said, flipping the match away.

Beams of light bobbed in the distance; they put him in mind of an old prison escape movie. "Who's that?" Boon asked.

"Search party," the skinny young cop answered. "That's where the guy disappeared." A dog yipped and howled as if there were an underground moon to bay.

Their escort unsheathed his Kellite and poked its quavery cone into the tunnel. Boon wished he'd worn a hat. He didn't want a flight of bats to swoop down and tangle his hair. Or a rat up his pant leg. He wondered about his partner. Didn't women scream and jump on tables when they saw rats and mice? He turned. She was following closely, looking calm. Probably didn't realize what they were up against.

Halfway down the unlighted tunnel they were stopped by another uniformed cop, twirling his night stick. Boon recognized an old friend who was finishing out his years walking Fulton. "Hey, Eddie, what's happening?" he asked.

"Our dog's got him cornered, John," the cop said, wiping his forehead. "At the next mine shaft. Better take a canary for safety."

"I'm with one," Boon said, flicking his thumb over his shoulder.

"I'm safe, too," Wickham piped up. "I'm with a turkey."

About thirty feet farther a man in coveralls and police cap was wolfing at a German shepherd: "Go, Schatzi! *Get in there!*"

Boon said, "Whatcha got, Angelo?" The dog circumnavigated the group, sniffing, then licked Wickham's outstretched palm.

"Schatzi!" the handler shouted. "Hit the hole! Get in there!" The dog looked ferocious enough to tackle a bear, but she cowered behind the newcomers.

Boon knelt and saw the problem. An arch of brick covered an old culvert about three feet in diameter, leading . . . where? The dog had sense.

"He went up that pipe?" Wickham asked.

"Must've," the handler said. "She tracked him here on the dead run."

"Shoulda brought a carp," Boon said. "What's up there? Where's it lead?"

"No place. Dead end."

"Sure?"

"Tour guide says there's nothing in any direction but landfill. So our rabbit, he's gotta—"

"Come out sooner or later," Boon finished. The dog handler nodded, and Boon turned to the uniformed cop who'd led them in. "Where's your sergeant?"

"He couldn't stay. He had an appointment." Boon understood. For the first time in his life he felt uneasy about a chase. But fools had to be caught, no matter where they were hiding.

"Did anybody order him out?" he asked.

"Eight or ten times," a cop answered. "No answer."

"Maybe he's dead," Wickham put in. "Suffocated or drowned or something."

"Not likely," the dog handler put in. "There's plenty of air and hardly any water. Probably he's waiting for us to leave. Course, he could be stuck."

Boon lowered himself in a reverse push-up over the mouth of the drain, his face a few inches above the brownish scum. The place smelled like every summer swamp he'd explored as a child. "YOU IN THERE?" he shouted. His words died away without echo.

"Angelo, whatta you got in a smaller size dog?" he asked, standing up. The beam from a flashlight froze on a small bat hanging from the ceiling.

"Nothin'," the handler replied. Boon felt something brush against his coatless back. He realized it was Wickham's nipples. His balls raised in his jocky shorts; he hoped it was from fear.

"All's I got is shepherds," Angelo was saying. "They always done the job before. Schatzi here, she has sixteen citations." He sounded betrayed by the four-legged creatures that defined his worth.

Boon brushed brick dust off his acrylic slacks as the dog nuzzled his ankle. "Bug off!" he said, shaking the back of his hand at her. A bad cop was a bad cop. The mutt went over and sat by her master's boots.

Angelo cupped her muzzle and said, "Put her on a scent aboveground, she'll—"

"She's not aboveground," Boon said. "Take her outa here."

"You don't hafta talk like that in front of the dog."

"That might be a killer up that pipe," Boon said.

"People think 'cause they're dogs, they're suppose to be perfect. You perfect?"

"No," Wickham said, sliding between the two men.

As the handler led the dog away, the woman asked, "What makes you think he could be a killer?"

He was tired of explaining himself. "Why'd he rabbit? That seem normal to you?"

"Maybe something scared him, and he, he just panicked. You saw how edgy he was when we talked to him this morning. Look, his wife walked right out of his life. Some men can't handle things like that."

More professional advice. Another couple days with her, he'd have a philosopher's degree of his own. Of course, she had things back asswards as usual. Annaliese'd walked right out of *his* life, hadn't she? Had he had a nervous breakdown about it? But then he'd had practice.

They made the short hike back to the lighted tunnel, where an excited young man in an Underground Tours T-shirt told them how Gamble had fled at the sound of a friend's voice.

"Where's the friend now?"

"In our office."

Boon turned to the cop who had escorted them in. "I want an officer posted where these two tunnels meet and another up at the door to the street. If he backs out of that culvert, he's gotta pass one or the other."

The kid looked worried. "What's this guy, uh, wanted for, Sarge?" he asked. "I mean, what's the shooting policy here?"

"The shooting policy?" Boon hadn't considered the possibility.

Before he could answer, Wickham jumped in. "The shooting policy is . . . *don't*," she said.

The young cop looked relieved. Boon said, "Tell your sector sergeant not to change these orders without checking with me." He nodded reluctantly toward the woman. "Or, uh, with Officer Wickham here." Like it or not, the case was hers, too.

They followed the guide through the main tunnel and up the stairs and blinked in the gray, misty daylight as he led them around the corner to a storefront marked "Underground Tours Inc." Inside, a medium-sized man with half a head of hair introduced himself as Dr. Brooks Asbury, a psychiatric resident at Bales Memorial. He begged Boon and Wickham, "Please, whatever you do, don't hurt him."

"Nobody's gonna hurt him," Boon said. "He your patient?"

"My friend," Asbury said.

"What's the problem?"

"His wife disappeared a couple of nights ago," the shrink said, running his hand across his damp pate.

"We know," Wickham said. "We FIR'd him this morning."

"You . . . what?"

"She means we did a field interview report on him," Boon said. Rookies loved to talk in jargon; it made them feel like veterans and puzzled hell out of civilians.

"He seemed distraught," Wickham went on.

"He *is* distraught," the head shrinker said. "Couple weeks ago he had a one-man show. His best stuff. About six people showed up, and he hasn't been the same since."

Wickham nodded. "The artist in the provinces," she said, whatever that meant.

"Then he takes his wife to the movies for her birthday and she—"

"We know the story," Boon said. "How'd they get along?"

"Get along?" The doctor frowned.

"Fight? Argue? Threaten each other?"

"Never. They're close. That's why Sev flipped out like this. He can't imagine where she went; he can't imagine living the rest of his life without her; he can't imagine why the whole damned city isn't out looking for her. Especially the police department."

"We got a few other things to do."

"Try telling *him* that. He's lost his perspective. Soon as he told me where he was headed, I grabbed the first two cops I found and tried to stop him before he did something dangerous. When he saw us, he panicked. He's in a crisis: up one minute, down the next. If I were you, I'd approach him gently. He's big and strong, and he's out of touch. Keep that in mind."

Boon didn't know how to respond to the diagnosis. Maybe it was accurate, and maybe it was bullshit. He'd never heard of a deserted husband running from cops. The opposite. They ran *to* cops and stayed *with* cops till they found the wife or the body. Maybe this shrink was involved in the scam, whatever it was.

"Can we reach you when we get him?" Wickham was asking.

Asbury scribbled some numbers on the back of a card and handed it over. A cop burst in the door and said, "Sarge? Cap'n Mondragon wants you right away."

"I'm sure," Boon said.

A squad car rushed them two blocks to the J-Building. Boon was surprised to see uniformed cops roaming the halls, looking as though they were all on Search and Destroy. Could that big stoop artist have crawled out of the underground and got loose up here? The place was never this full of uniforms except when the watch changed, and the next shift wasn't due till eight o'clock tonight.

He grabbed an old beat cop. "What's up, Willis? Chief drop his contact lens?"

The cop turned away from a broom closet he'd just flung open. "Roll up your sleeves, and help us look, John," he said, breaking into a snaggle-toothed grin. "Somebody mislaid a judge."

37

Gamble heard the barks and whimpers coming from the other end of the brick sewer and tried to imagine what he would do if a salivating Doberman bounded up the pile of stones and aimed its canines at his throat. He got out his Swiss army knife and pried open the long blade. It was dull and splotched with color. In the life he had chosen, knife blades were for stirring paint. He realized how poorly cast he was for violence.

Not that it mattered. He could spend the whole night steeling himself for the act, but he could never hurt a dog. The idea almost nauseated him. The best he could do would be to raise his hands and try to grip the animal under the front legs and throw it back with his long arms. And if the dog got him by the throat . . . ? *Could he kill then?* He didn't know. He hadn't been thinking too straight lately.

The dog stopped barking. Was it approaching? He peeked over the small parapet where he hid and shone his small flashlight down the rocky slope.

An object too small to be a police dog pulled its pointy noise back into a crack. Were there muskrats down there? He decided it must have been a large rat. He had no qualms about killing rats, but with what?

They would have to coexist. He had heard them on the cobblestones below, chirring back and forth like raccoons, as though laying plans. They were probably scared of him. But not so scared that they didn't appear in his light every time he checked.

He waited till 4:00 P.M. before creeping down to the broken culvert. He poked his head into the opening and heard the drone of male voices. They were talking low, and their words weren't carrying.

He thought about wriggling back out, but he was still suspicious of anyone in uniform. His only hope was to outwait them. The dog had already gone or shut up—he didn't know why—and the men would have to leave sooner or later. He clambered back up the rocks and arranged himself in a painful U on his stone bed.

After a while he closed his eyes. There was nothing to see, and they felt as hot and dry as coals. Two hands at a time, he tapped his fingers on the rock. He was bone-tired. He might as well sleep; there was nothing to do but wait, and a short rest might clear his mind. Maybe he could produce a brilliant plan for evading the cops. His mind kept returning to Margot: where she was, whether she was suffering, whether she was . . . dead.

He thought about others who had disappeared without explanation or return. Kidnap, amnesia, runaway, unrevealed murder, suicide . . . What pain, he thought. What terrible inhuman pain. Death was a thousand times easier to take. Death was sharp; death was final; death ended when it ended. Two years ago the cops had searched for a thirteen-year-old honor student who hadn't come back from Sunday school, and Gamble had felt then how much easier it would have been on the parents if the child had died in their arms. She was still gone; every morning the mother and father woke up to the same loss. Faded old posters hung from telephone poles in the neighborhood: WE LOVE HER. PLEASE HELP US. Down at the bottom was the most pathetic word of all: REWARD. As though it took cold cash to excite interest in a missing child.

Would Margot still be gone a year from now? Two years from now? How the hell would he survive an ordeal like that? He'd go crazy first. He'd *try* to go crazy first. . . .

A few feet above his face, traffic thumped and bumped. He wondered how thick the paving was. Caissons and fill and crossbeams supported it, but there were plenty of settling air spaces like the one that sheltered him. Every few years one of the streets opened up, and a truck or a bus fell through. He had a momentary vision of his head poking up through the cab of a Peterbilt truck, the driver pointing angrily at his sign: NO RIDERS.

After a while his thoughts began to fade, and he slipped into a sequence of dreams, one following the other like movie shorts. He woke with a start when a siren went off overhead. His mouth felt stuffed with steel wool. He tried to revive the interrupted dream: He had been transplanted intact to the star Sygnax, and since Sygnax was forty light-years away, the events of the last three days were unknown there. It would be forty more years before Margot would disappear, and by then he would be beyond grief, in his grave. It seemed logical till the noise woke him, but he couldn't recover the thread.

He turned on his flashlight to look at his watch: 4:58. He had been holed up for nearly an hour. The light from the flash was yellowing. *Christ!* He had forgotten to pick up extra batteries. And a chipping hammer. He snapped the light off and sank back into blackness: literal blackness, the total absence of light, no reflection, no diffusion, no edges or spots or shadows—the black of the womb or the tomb, the black of death, a black few humans ever saw or imagined.

His head felt blown up like a balloon, and his body ached where he had cut and bruised himself crawling through the culvert, but most of the pain of his loss had localized itself in his throat, as though objecting to his refusal to cry. It was the stuck ice cube again, and he tried to sob to relieve it, but the pain was too intense.

If I knew Margot was dead, would the pain go away and a different one take its place? Where is she today? What is she doing?

> *She is dead; And all which die*
> *To their first elements resolve. . . .*

He wondered if John Donne felt cursed or consoled by his love poems. He must have felt consoled; he wrote so many of them.

> *Oh do not die, for I shall hate*
> *All women so, when thou art gone.*

. . . When thou art gone . . . When thou art gone. When thou . . .

Oh, Jesus, he said to himself as he shone the flashlight on his watch, I've slept four hours. I don't have that much time! It may be too late already.

He sat up and bumped his head lightly, rubbed it hard,

and realized that he had a violent headache. It was as though an ax blade quivered in his skull. He thrust his head between his legs and snorted the damp air, but the pain didn't let up. He fumbled in his pack for the Dexedrines, the only medication he had, and forced two down his parched throat.

After a while his brain began to function, starting slowly and then seething and racing the way it had before. His first realization was that the cops might have given up on him, assumed he had found another exit and slipped up through a manhole or a sewer opening.

Or were they waiting at the end of the tunnel with more men, more dogs, ready to grab him when he emerged?

He had a disturbing insight that he was not capable of orderly thought, that he had slid over the edge into hallucinatory behavior. Somehow he had to recover his reasoning powers. But how? By swallowing more uppers?

No—by finding Margot. That was the only way.

He sat up and thought: My God, what am I *doing* down here? Does it make any sense to try to get into the basement of the J-Building? *Why?* Because a few locked doors set off my paranoia? But they *should* have been locked! The basement's empty; everything's been transferred to the new building.

Was he psychotic then?

How could he tell?

The hell with give-up thinking. He would carry out his plan. No one was looking for Margot, and the basement was a good place for him to start. The cops, at least a few of them, had acted suspiciously from the beginning; they could hide a prisoner down there for months, until the wreckers came and the victim was buried under thousands of tons of rubble. Hadn't a police van been out in front the night she left? And hadn't a watch commander looked him straight in the eye and lied that the van hadn't been there at all? *Why the lie?*

Four hours of doubled-up sleep had left him stiff and

cramped. Or *had he slept . . . sixteen hours?* His watch said eight o'clock, but that might mean eight in the morning. Could anyone sleep that long without waking up? Bent in half on a slab of rock? He listened for the sounds of traffic and caught only fragments of wheel noise. It was eight at night. Morning traffic would be much heavier. A punch line flashed across his mind: "I might be crazy, but I'm not stupid."

He cocked his head. Another sound came to his ears, not so much a hum as . . . hundreds of small boys drumming lightly, approaching slowly in lock step.

Rain.

He wondered why he hadn't noticed the downpour before.

He tried to imagine what effect a storm would have. Would it cause a flash flood that would rise under him till he was flattened against the roof, sucking air like a beached fish?

No. The underground would drain. He remembered the tour he had taken with Margot and her parents. It had been raining hard that day, but the corridors had been dry.

He grabbed his pack, held it in front of him, and slithered down. He took his flashlight out of his breast pocket and dropped it into the deepest part of the pack, where it would stay dry. He wouldn't need light on the short crawl back through the brick sewer.

He reached the base of the ballast slope and heard a sound like white water running over rocks.

He moved forward on his hands and knees and lowered his hand toward the hole in the culvert. Cold water slapped his hand backward at the wrist and wet his arm to the elbow.

He played his flashlight across the opening where he had climbed out hours ago. His escape route ran full. He was entombed.

38

Tally tried to keep her face composed while Carl Mondragon spoke in a voice like steam from a pressure cooker. "You two," he said, "you better damn well find Judge Holder. You had the inside track. Now"—he grabbed the short overhang of hair on the back of his round head and gave it a pull—"now everybody's on *my* case. 'How can all those people disappear under your nose?' Crap like that. The chief, the mayor, the council, the other judges —my damn phone won't quit. And all because—"

She squirmed on his old sofa as the phone rang.

"Mondragon!" he growled, then said gently, "No, nothing. . . . Maybe a little later. . . . Yeah, Holder. H-O-L-D-E-R. Betty Jane. Criminal Court. . . . I dunno, about fifty, fifty-five. . . . Okay, Blair. . . . No, not right now, Blair. . . . I told ya, we'll find her. . . . She's gotta be someplace. . . . Right. . . . Right. . . . *Right*. . . . Anytime. . . ."

Tally blinked hard as Carl slammed the phone down and rearranged his features into a glower. "That was Seabury. The *Post*. TV's been calling, too. Everybody but the WCTU. What can I tell 'em? Three or four people disappeared from our own building and we didn't do a goddamn thing about it? Didn't even realize it was happening? *Can I admit we been that dumb?*"

"You joined those cases and put us on 'em yesterday, Cap," Boon put in. Tally had to admire his boldness; most cops would have sat silently under the barrage and griped later to somebody else. "What more—?"

"I joined them and gave them to *you*," Carl said, ham-

mering the air in front of his face like a Latin dictator.
"And what'd you do? You let one of the main witnesses
disappear underground like a goddamn mole, and your
own snitch walks in the front door and turns up dead in
a Dumpster, and now a judge leaves her court for a ten-
minute recess and goes up in smoke like some cheap
magic trick. Jesus Christ, Boon, we look like, like . . .
amateurs!"

"I did all that?" Boon said. She wished he would shut
up. The old man was just blowing off steam. A desk cop
needed an occasional catharsis; Boon could act out his
frustrations in the street.

She looked over at her temporary partner. He was
studying the floor and rubbing his nose between his
thumb and index finger. In the back of her mind she
realized that sooner or later she had to inform on him for
executing the Gratzes. No PD had room for a killer cop.
But first . . . there were missing persons to find.

"Captain," she said, still trying to glean some hard
news, "can you run the new thing by us? The judge?"

"She called a recess," he said, leaning back in his
leather chair as though the incompetence of others had
sapped his strength. "She likes to run downstairs and
have a drink every afternoon. Coke syrup, lemon ice
cream and fizz water, if you can believe it. Won't send
her clerk for it 'cause she says it goes flat."

"Did she ever reach the coffee shop?" Tally asked,
jotting notes in a spiral pad.

"She finished her drink, paid at the door, and walked
out. Then—what's the word? She dematerialized. That
was an hour ago. Her clerk put in the alarm, figured the
old lady'd had a heart attack or something. We checked
her car, all the other cars in the garage. Checked the
ladies' rooms. Now we're checking every broom closet
from the roof down. And door to door in the neighborhood . . ."

Boon muttered, "It's just like—"

"All the others," Tally said. "Who saw her last?"

"The cashier."

"Nobody noticed her in the lobby?"

"Well, it's obvious somebody must've," Mondragon said as though it were a stupid question. "But we can't find 'em. We weren't shooting movies in the lobby, ya know. Tell you the truth, we weren't even expecting her to disappear. Know what I mean? Kinda caught us by surprise."

Tally withdrew under the sarcasm.

"Who's on it?" Boon asked in a low voice.

"Who's on it?" The contorted features showed what Carl thought of the question. "The whole department's on it. This is a *judge,* man! I got troops coming in off traffic control; I got bikemen changing into street clothes. Jesus Christ, son, this is serious!"

Tally thought about Sammy Schulte. Where was the whole police department two nights ago? Where was the detective bureau when she was begging for help, when she was telling anyone who would listen, "We have to find this child. This child is not a runaway." She remembered Boon's smirk as he said, "You got a feeling, huh? . . . Gimme a call they find the body." But a judge—that was different. Judges were *important.*

As she watched, Boon lifted his gaze from the carpet. His eyes were red; his face was pale. Had something finally pierced that thick hide?

". . . Get moving now," the captain was saying, shooing them away with the backs of his thick hands. "Start at the beginning. Don't flub it this time. Lean on your snitches. Turn something, even if it's nothing."

In the hallway she heard Boon muttering to himself, "Dead. They're all dead."

She grabbed his arm and said, "How can you say a thing like that?"

"Huh?" he asked, turning sharply. "A thing like what?"

" 'They're dead.' "

"You heard wrong. They're missing, is all. They're

missing!" He sounded almost strident.

"What now?" she asked.

"Things to, uh, do," he said.

"Well, let's do them!" Against her better instincts she was beginning to think of them as a working partnership. At least for the moment.

"I mean by myself," Boon said. "You heard the captain. We gotta double-check everything. You work on the Schulte kid and Margaret Gamble—"

"Margot."

"And I'll take the snitch, the judge, and . . ." His words trailed off as he started toward his desk. He turned after a few steps and said, "If you turn anything, set up a meet through the duty lieutenant. Don't put a word on the air."

She shivered at the implication. "You think we might be looking for a police officer?"

"We can't rule anybody out," he said. "People are missing; people are dead. Somebody's capering. Vampires, maybe."

A lieutenant in uniform came by at a trot, headed toward Mondragon's office. "Henny?" Boon called out. "You finished the sweep?" The lieutenant nodded. "What'd you find?"

"Four cannabis plants, a cigar box full of numbers slips, a dime bag of heroin, a case—"

Boon held up his hand. "No judge?" he asked.

"No judge."

"No trace?"

"No trace."

Tally felt cold.

39

In all the hours he had spent in the underground, Gamble had barely thought about his claustrophobia. The symptoms came only when he felt trapped, when he found himself in a situation over which he had absolutely no control—in a stuck elevator, in a plane—and so far there had always been a way out, even if it meant giving himself up to the police. But now his only exit route swirled with cocoa-colored water; he was sealed off from the rest of the world, and the familiar chills began to come over him.

He scrambled up the slope of the ballast rocks to the ledge that had sheltered him for nearly five hours. The steady thrum of the rain filled his ears, louder than before. These summer storms blew in from the coast and went on and on. Maybe he could outwait a short sprinkle, but he'd never make it through hours and days.

He squirmed on the edge of the flat rock and tried to fight off his welling panic. Brooks had mentioned a technique. "Concentrate on externals," Brooks had said. "Make lists. Sort things. Count your heartbeat, your breathing, anything you can count, and then start over again."

He grabbed his pack. Inside were two chisels, a weak flashlight, a Swiss army knife with dull blades, some Dexies, and a couple of pieces of fruit that he had grabbed from the refrigerator and hadn't the slightest urge to eat.

He sorted them by feel, trying to force his mind to focus on the simple operation. He lined them up, mentally assigned each a number, rearranged them in reverse, then started over. He fought against switching on the light; the batteries were almost gone, and he had no extras. Still working by feel, he opened each of the knife's blades, identified each by touch and assigned it a name, sheathed and resheathed the ivory toothpick, did the same with the tweezers, then closed the blades and started again.

The rattling of the rain grew louder. He made a mental list of what it was doing: washing specks of salmon and crab off the decks of the fishing fleet; laying the dust on the old logging roads that spiraled into the mountains; dappling the flowers in Margot's little garden; granting free car washes; refilling reservoirs; raining out children's games; swirling and whirling through the gorges where the steelhead and the cutthroat lived.

And through the drainpipe below.

The only escape route.

His heart beat erratically, the first sign that he was losing control, and he began to feel the light-headedness, the hollowness in the stomach, the clutching of an invisible hand around his throat.

There had to be a way out!

He groped above his head, scraping his fingertips along the underside of the street. It was rough and pitted with stones.

His ledge was cool, but the sweat dripped down his body. His windpipe seemed to constrict, as though preparing to seal itself. He thought he might pass out again and hoped to God he would.

But oblivion didn't come, and a pressure built in his head. Just when he feared he would lose control, he thought of Margot.

She was lost, kidnapped, maybe hurt, maybe dead, and what was he doing? Nursing imaginary fears, indulging himself in infantile feelings.

He clenched his right hand and slammed it into his left. He raised his head and called into the blackness, "I'll be *goddamned* if I'm gonna let myself be trapped down here when Margot needs me. I'll be *goddamned* if I'm gonna let those cops keep me cornered. I'll be *goddamned* if I'll let my wife suffer another minute."

The claustrophobia began to yield. The fear of fear dissolved into pure rage. Do it now! he ordered himself. NOW! There's a way out of this place, and I'm gonna find it. Maybe . . . maybe if the water's running strong enough, I can shoot the pipe. If I don't make it—well, I tried. I didn't give in to phantom fears.

He gathered the knife and the other contents of his pack, sealed the top with clumsy fingers, bumped to the bottom of the ballast rock, and crawled toward the culvert on hands and knees.

It still ran full. Water was backed up behind the entrance, swirling around, waiting its turn. He tried to remember how far it was to the other end. Maybe thirty feet, maybe fifty. It didn't matter if it was fifty miles; *it was the way out!*

He wondered if his long body would stick in the tube. He remembered an elbow turn near this end, rubble and rock and protruding bricks. He already hurt from cuts and bruises. Would he snag on rocks and drown?

Possibly.

But if there were the thinnest air space above the flume of water . . .

And if he could float on his back and keep his head up . . .

And if the thrust didn't spin him out of control before he even got started . . .

He could make it.

He started to lower his body into the opening.

He looked back toward the slope, imagined giving up and secreting himself on the same black shelf, imagined the long hours waiting for the rain to stop while Margot was somewhere suffering.

The water sucked and tore at him as he gave his body to it inch by inch. *Control!* He had to maintain control!

He held the top edge of the drainpipe with his hands, like a man chinning himself horizontally, and allowed his legs to be swept into the hole.

The pressure tore at his big feet; it felt as though one of his shoes were already gone. Now only his head and arms were out, and his hands were beginning to slip. He inhaled deeply, huge sucking gasps, then inhaled again, ramming the oxygen into his lungs. . . .

And let go.

In seconds his feet hit the elbow turn. He twisted his body into a sidestroke position and maneuvered around the bend. If he could only hold his ears against the roar . . .

He inhaled a mouthful of water and forced it out. His cheeks bulged, and his head banged something hard, and red tracers flew across his brain.

He had to find air; he couldn't make the whole distance underwater.

He twisted till he thought he was floating on his back and pushed his head upward. Water covered his face. He blew his burning lungs clear with his last reserves of air and spread his feet to brake his speed.

Still moving too fast, he felt an outcropping and held on. He lifted his face toward the surface of the water and found—

Air!

His ears rose above the water momentarily and were battered with noise; he had the feeling of being trapped inside a jet engine. But there was an inch or two of free space. . . .

He swallowed a mouthful of froth and blew it out and told himself to stay cool. *Stay cool, and you've got a chance!*

He knew he couldn't maintain his position: floating on his back, feet and hands spread wide, head rammed upward. The water splashed across his tilted face. He tightened his grip on the sides of the pipe and tried to keep his face level with the surface. If he yielded to the reflex of raising his head to clear his lungs, his scalp would bump the roof and his nose would go under again.

He was getting ready to loosen his grip and release his body when a fresh bore of water slammed through the pipe and filled his nostrils and his mouth, catching him at the end of an exhalation.

He pushed hard against the sides of the culvert and raised his face till his nose touched the top again. He tried inhaling, but the air space was even narrower than before. He took a few snorts and let go.

His body shot ahead feet first. When he felt himself running out of air, he braked to another stop.

This time he found a sliver of clearance between the surface of the water and the roof. He poked his nose up and took in more air till his lungs felt full.

Not much farther now, he reassured himself. *Hang in!* It can't be more than fifteen or twenty feet. You—are— *making it!*

He let himself go with the current, gaining confidence, lifting his body by his fingertips in buoyant little shoves to keep from scraping the rubble below. But the next time he raised his head, there was no air.

His heart thumped. Where was the top of the culvert? In the black water he couldn't tell up from down. He reached out with a hand and felt his body start to rotate. *Where's the air?*

He batted at the water like a drowning cat and bashed his forehead against an airless tube, solid with water from bottom to top.

His lungs were empty. He was on the verge of having to inhale with all his strength—water or air, it didn't matter. The colors in his mind faded to gray and then black. He was no longer able to struggle or plan. His universe had become this whirling bore of roiled dirty water that would drown him and carry his body out into the bay, where it would be found by someone who would never know how he had died.

Margot!

The memory of his wife returned and settled into the repetition of her name: Margot Margot Margot *Margot Margot . . .*

He opened his mouth in surrender and listened until the voice came from too far off to hear. Then he thought: This is your birth. When you come out, you'll be born again. *Margot, honey, look! I'm born again.*

The words *Hello Mr. Death* passed through his mind, and he wondered why he kept remembering Donne, or was it somebody else—Stafford? Cummings? Annie Dillard? He felt a hard final thump of his head and realized that he was cured of his claustrophobia relieved of all his ailments his pains his guilts his hurts his losses cured for now and forever. . . .

40

Anna's gone for good. . . . The words played in Boon's mind as he brooded at his desk under the calendar from Lou's Tire Hospital, satisfaction guaranteed. *She's gone God damn it she's gone for good.* Now I know why she hasn't been seen, hasn't come around, hasn't called. Some fool is whacking people out in the J-Building. Or grabbing them here and killing them someplace else. Wickham was right, making that stink about the retard. Most likely it's a cop. Some poor bastard that got passed over again. Or his third wife left him. They flip all the time. If the public only knew . . .

He sifted the contents of his in box and grabbed a yellow slip that said, "Call ME."

A female voice told him that Dr. Madona was out.

"What'd he want me for?"

"I haven't the foggiest—"

"Then check his desk!"

After a few minutes the woman said, "This might be something. It says, 'Notes on Harrier protocol.' Says, 'Call Boon.'"

"Read it, will ya?"

"His handwriting's *so* bad. It says, uh . . . I better spell it." He grabbed a stubby pencil. " 'P-E-T-E-C-H-I-A-E. On mucosal and serosal surfs—'"

" 'Surfs'?"

"I guess that means 'surfaces.'"

Boon threw the pencil halfway across the bull pen. "For Chrisakes—"

"Sergeant, if you'd *just*—I'll let you talk to Clancy. Maybe he can interpret."

Boon had played poker with Clancy Carroll, a chain-smoking coroner's assistant who was one of the few around the ME's office who didn't refer to shit as "fecal matter." Not exactly the man you'd bring in to operate on your kid, but plenty bright for his job, which mostly consisted of prepping DBs for autopsies. He liked to brag that he'd never lost a patient.

"John?" the wheezy voice came on. "What's happening? You found Judge Holder?"

"No. Listen, Clance, take a look at Madona's scribbling and read it to me in English, will ya?"

Carroll read: " 'Petechiae on mucosal and serosal surfaces and conjunctival membranes of eyes.' Say, is this that dead snitch of yours? The one in the dress and the bonnet?"

"Yeah," Boon said impatiently.

"Heartless bitch."

"Clance, I don't have time, okay? Is there anything on Madona's note that says what killed him?"

"Petechiae, they're pinhead-size red dots," the diener mused. "Hemorrhages from tiny ruptured blood vessels."

"*Meaning what,* for Chrisakes?"

"Hey, John, cool it, will ya? I'm just reading what he scribbled here. A coupla lines is all. Lessee . . . Nope, no conclusion. These are just notes."

"What causes peteek—peteekki—"

"Petechiae? A lot of things. We see 'em in, uh, suffocation—"

"Suffocation? You mean, like . . . *strangling?*"

"I don't think it was that violent, John. I opened the body for Doc. The only mark was a six-inch incision below the rib cage. If he was suffocated, it had to be with a pillow, a plastic bag, something like that. Something that wouldn't make a dent."

"Thanks," Boon said. "Call me you get anything definite."

He hung up and looked around the empty bull pen. Every duty man must be out looking for the judge. He knew what they'd turn: a handful of air. Four missing persons, and not a clue. Nobody could hide that many live humans for long. Anna Anna Anna . . . Why'd you ever leave? We could of worked it out, babes. . . .

His words sounded fake. What kind of asshole would ignore his wife for four years and then go into mourning?

But how were they killed? *Something that wouldn't make a dent* . . . It didn't add up. A kid like the retard, he might sit still while some fool arranged a plastic bag or a pillow over his face, but an adult would scream and punch and claw and raise the dead. Candy Diego would kick the crap out of anybody came at him with a pillow. Even Anna—frail, tired Anna—would put up a fight. But—how could something that violent happen in the J-Building? People were crammed in like anchovies, and yet no one had heard a sound. Did the victims walk into the building and die noiselessly, like squashed ants?

He took the elevator down to the main floor and walked to his Charger. He still couldn't bring himself to report Anna missing, but that didn't mean he wouldn't work on the case. Working on one of the disappearances was the same as working on all; he only wished he'd realized that sooner. Well, that was one of his problems: he never took time to think. He was so anxious to bust fools he just waded in with his machete.

He was getting too old to be acting so dumb.

41

Gamble dreamed that a hot, bitter fluid kept squirting up from his insides. Long after the last spurt his esophagus squeezed, and his mouth opened and shut in spasms.

At last the vomiting stopped, and he heard the sound of gently flowing water. He touched his forehead and felt something warm and sticky. He held his hand in front of his face and opened his eyes to darkness. Then he realized that he wasn't dreaming.

Did death hurt this much?

That wouldn't be fair.

Was he still atop his slab?

No. He remembered leaving the hiding place to hunt for Margot.

Then this must be his tomb.

At the thought of being buried alive, his heart beat faster, and he moved his legs in a running motion. He stopped when he realized he wasn't moving. His feet were cold; he bent his toes and twisted his feet and felt a light pressure against his legs.

Running water.

He pulled his knees up to his chest, but he could still feel the flow against his legs.

The culvert! He was still in the culvert!

He opened his eyes again and tried to wrench himself

upright, but it was too much of a task. "God, God, *please,*
God," he said, "let me go."

He knew he had to get out of the drainpipe before the
next torrent came down. He didn't want to go under again.
If only he could see . . .

He remembered his tools. He stretched his cramped
right arm and felt behind him for the pack. One of the
straps had torn loose, and the flat plastic bag was twisted
around on his side. He found the opening by touch and
groped inside and pulled the flashlight from the soggy
insides.

He slid the metal switch.

A clear white beam illuminated a ceiling of porous
rock. He aimed the light down his body and saw that he
was lying across the mouth of the opening where the
sewer line met the old railroad right of way. His head was
butted up against a broken brick, and the rest of his frame
lay like a broken doll in the main watercourse.

But now it was a trickle.

The storm was over.

He *had* been born again. Blown through the pipe and
out the opening where he had first entered . . . how
long ago?

His watch said 9:15. The information was useless.
Was it even running? He held it to his ear. Old faithful.
Like the flashlight. But it could be 9:15 in the afternoon
or 9:15 in the morning, and it could still be Thursday or
Friday or a week from Friday for all he could tell. And
this time no overhead traffic gave him a clue.

He noticed a flicker and then a change in the texture
of his light, from clear white to the beginnings of a soft
aurora yellow. So the resurrection of the flashlight had
been strictly temporary. He stuffed it back in the pack.
It clanked against the other tools, and he knew it would
be next to useless from now on.

One by one he checked out his limbs: all joints flexed;
all bones were intact. The arm had been torn from one

sleeve of his bush jacket, and his pants had been ripped. He couldn't tell if his body had been scraped and bruised; his skin was too cold to feel such subtle injuries. He tried to remember what time he had made his decision to shoot the rapids. Late in the afternoon. Had that been Thursday? Yes, Thursday. Two days after . . . Margot. He had been unconscious in this culvert at least four hours, maybe longer.

Well, he'd needed rest.

A throbbing began in his head. The warm fluid dripping across his right eye had to be blood. He must have cut his scalp. Painful, but not disabling. God, how he wished he could sleep in a soft bed. The amphetamines must have burned out his system. Now he felt weak and lethargic.

He thought of Margot again and stirred.

But how could he help her now? He barely had enough strength to help himself.

He remembered that he had taken no nourishment in two or three days. He still felt queasy, but he groped into the backpack and pulled out a gooey mix of apple and banana in a flattened plastic bag. He stuffed the mush into his mouth and swallowed it like medicine.

He narrowed his eyes and saw a glow. A light had been turned on . . . somewhere. He craned his neck. The main tunnel! All he had to do now was walk out.

The cops! Wouldn't he stumble right into them? Or one of their dogs? It was a trap. Why else light up the place? They must have heard him splashing around, and now they were waiting. The searchers. The ones who might have taken Margot.

But how could he help her lying in this ditch?

He had to take the chance.

He tried to pull himself into a standing position and flopped back hard. After a few minutes he tried again. This time he made it.

No matter what happens, he thought as he staggered

along like a newborn stork, I won't die. I've done that number already. I'm playing on house money. . . .

He was barely making headway as he neared the junction with the main tunnel. He heard a clanking sound, stopped and listened and heard nothing, resumed and heard the clanking again.

Someone was following.

He turned and realized that he had been listening to the tools in his pack. He slid out of the straps and rolled the bag into a curl and held it in a tight grip. If cops were stationed in the main tunnel, they'd find him soon enough without advance notice.

At the intersection he dropped to his hands and knees, laid the pack aside, and listened.

Silence.

Was a guard sitting out there? Reading a magazine? Dozing?

He eased his head into the tunnel and looked both ways.

Empty!

Where were the cops?

Maybe he *had* been lying in the sewer for days. Maybe so much time had gone by that they'd given up on him. But why was the tunnel lighted?

Another tour group must be on its way.

He had to take the chance of being seen. This time there would be no escape. He could barely walk; the circulation was slowly returning to his legs, but with it stabbings of pain. His right shoe was missing, and the sock was gone.

He retrieved his pack and slumped against the side of the tunnel for a few minutes of rest. Somehow he would have to find the filled-in canal and follow its course toward the basement of the Justice Building. That had been his original plan anyway. He could no longer judge whether it made sense. What had made him think Margot was in the basement? He wished he could remember.

He had just started down the main tunnel when he heard soft whistling.

About 150 feet away a figure appeared, walking toward him.

He edged back along the wall toward the entrance to the railroad tunnel. His foot hit against a mound of rocks, and he almost fell.

The whistling continued.

He stepped around the fill and dropped to his knees. The intruder was apparently unaware that he wasn't alone. Or he could be faking, trying to get within close range before making his move. Gamble recognized the song he was whistling: "She's Leaving Home." Must have been a teen-ager when it came out ten or fifteen years ago. That would put him in the prime of life now: twenty-five, thirty. He'll run me down like a cheetah. . . .

He stretched out on his belly and looked through a space in the coarse rocks.

It was a cop. He was swinging his club as though walking a beat. He flung it out to the end of its thong and made it tumble through the air like a matchstick. Gamble couldn't help notice the resemblance to a baton twirler. He must practice in front of his mirror.

Whistling and twirling, the cop came on.

When he was about forty feet away, Gamble stopped breathing, afraid that the strange acoustics of the underground would amplify the sound.

Could he jump another cop?

Not this time. He was so weak he'd barely be able to throw his arms around the man and try to weigh him down like a dancing bear. The fight wouldn't last a minute.

But anything was better than giving up.

Closer now. Yards away. He tensed. Not even this preoccupied club swinger could fail to see six feet five inches of fellow human hiding behind three feet of fill.

The heavy footfalls crunched on the floor. The stick

made a slapping noise as it hit the cop's palm. *She's leaving home, bye-bye.* . . .

For an instant he wondered if he should stand up and surrender to keep from being shot. But then who would search for Margot?

The footfalls had stopped.

He looked through his crack. The cop stood motionless, then sniffed the air, flipped the polished wooden club toward the rock pile, drew it back to himself Yo-Yo style, and executed an about-face, whistling faster. His figure became smaller and smaller and finally disappeared out the other end of the tunnel like a Charlie Chaplin fade-out.

Gamble held himself rigid for several minutes. He still suspected a trick. It wasn't impossible that the cop had seen him—a protruding tip of his one remaining Saucony shoe, a bit of matted hair sticking up over the rocks. In a few minutes he could be back with reinforcements.

It was probably close to midnight. That would explain why only one man was on duty. When daytime came, the place would be swarming again. More cops, more dogs. Exhausted or not, he had to move out.

It took ten minutes to reach the filled-in canal and turn into the unlighted tunnel that followed the waterway under Exposition Street. If his original computations were right, the northeast corner of the Justice Building was about twenty yards away. *If* the tunnel didn't run out. *If* he didn't run into a wall. *If* a rockslide didn't block the way . . .

The light at his back faded slowly as he dragged his feet along the pebbled floor.

Hadn't he walked twenty yards by now? He looked at the wall and found nothing but hard clay and embedded rock.

He struggled through the passageway and came to more loose rock angling to the tunnel floor. A slide. He clawed at it with fingernails already cracked and ripped.

Under the rock slope he found more rock slope and then a vertical face that broke off in his nails like chalk.

He pulled out his flashlight and found a gray white concrete surface under a scabrous layer of a yellowish substance like saltpeter.

The foundation!

He snapped off his dying light and pushed slowly ahead in nearly total darkness. In a few minutes he came up against another wall. He ran his hands across the face; it was smooth, cool.

He wondered if he should risk the light again; it couldn't have more than a few minutes of life left. What would he do later when the batteries were dead beyond recall and he was inside the dark basement looking for Margot? He ran the flat of his hands up and down the wall like a blind man.

It was solid concrete, probably a corner pier of the old building. Impenetrable. Well, what did you expect? he asked himself, and answered angrily: *a break*. One lucky break. The last goddamned thing I need now is a dead end.

He walked to the other side of the face, sliding his hands against the smooth hardness, and found . . . an opening.

A new tunnel?

He had to risk the flashlight.

The hole trailed off into darkness around the back of the concrete pier. He stumbled behind the dying light and saw a shattered metal staircase with missing steps and risers and holes the size of his feet.

Teetering like a tightrope walker, he climbed the stairs to a rotting wooden door that looked as though it had been carved from a heavy slab. He grabbed the porcelain knob, and it came off in his hand.

He checked the other edge of the door. The hinges were long and thin and eaten by rust. He took out his point chisel and pried them off in seconds. Then he slid the blade into the crack at the top of the door and twisted.

The door gave at the top but held at the bottom. He turned the chisel again and heard a crack. The wood was yielding. He rested on the top step to catch his breath and felt a little stronger. He put his shoulder into the door, and the top half broke with a snap.

He stepped into a large room. Two grimy windows, recessed below sidewalk level, emitted thin slits of streetlight.

He turned and looked at the door. The broken top bore the words AIR AID SH LT R.

As his eyes grew accustomed to the faint light, he saw that the room was stacked with desks, three and four high: typical institutional green models, most of metal, a few of wood, none relieved by the slightest attempt at ornamentation or style.

He picked his way through the stacks to a door on the far side and pushed through.

A dim reddish light sent irregular shadows against the walls of a large room. He walked toward the faint light and banged into a dense shape that didn't yield. Two or three more of the shapes appeared in a row, like barges in a fog. He thought they might be packing crates, but when he touched one, he felt a tilelike surface with gutters down both sides. Another gutter ran down the middle to a depression the size of a soup bowl at the end.

He slid his hand along the slab till he touched something stiff, like dried-out hide—a dead rat, an old glove. As he jerked away, his hip caught the edge of a small table and sent something clattering to the cement floor. He leaned over and saw a pair of empty cans. Afraid the noise had been heard, he backed away.

He stopped at a wall covered with hexagonal white tiles. Wires dangled like snakes from the ceiling. Large drains ran along the floor and the walls, connecting with the smaller drains that he had felt on the three stone tables.

He walked along the wall till he came to a metal

handle, one of many that jutted from drawers aligned atop each other like ice trays in a refrigerator. Just as he reached out to give the handle a pull, a scene from one of his favorite movies flashed across his mind—Brakhage's *The Act of Seeing with One's Own Eye.*

Now he knew where he was.

The scene had been filmed in a morgue.

He sniffed and stepped away. How many drawers were there? At least six. Maybe as many as eight or nine.

He had to open every one.

42

Ugo was combing his little brother's hair when he heard the sound from down the hall. Instantly he knew it was the cans he had stacked on the table; his other tin-can alarms were on the floor and wouldn't have made that much noise.

"Wait, Maxmein!" he said in *dialetto Bolognese,* patting the boy's still head. "And do not fear the dark."

He slipped off his heavy work shoes and tiptoed toward the abandoned morgue, inching along dark corridors that he knew as well as a blind man knows his home.

He peered through the cracked door and heard the sound of metal scraping metal. Inside, a flashlight blinked and captured a face.

The *gigant'!*

He was trying to open the drawers!

Ugo was stunned. Hadn't the Virgin promised to protect him from the *malocchio* in the clown feet and the beard? What was he doing down here?

Ferragosto was threatened again. Holy Mother of Christ, where is my Babbo? Send my papa, Madonna, I beg you! He will know what to do.

He slid the fileting knife from its scabbard inside his overalls and waited.

43

The first three drawers Gamble had tried to open were either locked or jammed. Then one slid out smoothly, as though recently oiled; in the poor light he could only tell it was as wide as the average human body and about seven feet long. He knew what it was designed to hold.

He turned on his flashlight; its filament glowed dimly, barely illuminating itself. Useless.

He felt dizzy as he reached into the drawer and groped around to feel its contents.

It was empty.

He shut his eyes and breathed a silent thanks.

The next drawer was jammed. He wrenched, but it held. He broke off his point chisel in the crack. Whatever was holding these drawers shut was stronger than his tools. He wondered what was inside. Hadn't the basement been closed off? Who would go to the trouble of locking empty drawers?

He stood back, more puzzled than ever.

Were the drawers refrigerated? No. There didn't seem to be any electrical power; the fixtures had been ripped out, and the sliding drawers were at room temperature, slightly cool.

Mummified bodies?

Severn, Severn, he thought, get it together! They may have imprisoned Margot down here; they may even have killed her. But why would anyone have mummified her? It was an idea left over from childhood movies. He had to think straighter than that. There would be thousands of feet of dark basement to check out room by room. Jumping from one hysteria to another wouldn't get the job done.

He tried to remember how long it had been since his last meal. Days, really, except for a few mouthfuls of mashed fruit and gallons of black coffee. *Coffee!* He thought of his stash of uppers, reached in his pack, and found the little plastic bottle. He opened it and shook out his last two pills. They tasted like unripe persimmons, bitter and dry. He swallowed hard and wondered if there were a water fountain around. He'd never find it.

He pulled the handle on another drawer and felt it give. He paused to control his hands. Amphetamines worked fast on a hollow stomach, almost like an injection. He felt confused; for the first time in his life he would be opening a drawer hoping *not* to find something.

It slid easily on silent rollers, moving him backward. The contents were in full shadow.

His fingers touched something hard and round. He squinted and reached for his flashlight again. He had to see whatever was lying in that rack.

He felt stupid for not stopping to buy extra batteries. How had he made a crucial mistake like that? He knew the answer. By not sleeping or eating, by mistreating himself till his thought processes were blurred. Cheap atonement. And typically self-indulgent. Now he was in a position where light had become a precious commodity, more valued than gold, something to be doled out in tiny portions.

The flashlight was dead. He would have to inspect the drawer by feel.

His fingers danced against a round surface. Cool, metallic. *A casket?*

Too narrow. Wincing, he encircled the object with both hands. As a casket it would hold only a pet or a baby.

Then he realized it was a metal tank. Too big for scuba

diving, too small for welding. An old, empty tank . . .
He started breathing again and slid the drawer shut.

He had to find a way to open the others. He reached
into his pack for his claw chisel, but after slipping it into
the crack between the drawer and the opening, he realized
it would only break like the other.

Somewhere there must be a stronger tool.

He backed away from the drawers, trying not to bump
into the dissecting tables again. He didn't want to touch
a slab where hundreds, maybe thousands of human
bodies had been stretched out to be bled and cut and
peeled.

He walked toward the soft glow in the far corner. He
found a counter and a small thick candle in a red glass
illuminating a tray bearing the words COKE REFRESHES
YOU BEST. Centered on the tray was a wide-mouthed jar
with a white crepe ribbon tied about its middle.

He leaned closer. Wilted flowers helped mask a pungent
smell that seemed to reach his nostrils all at once, as
though it had lain in wait. He pulled back, then found
his eyes drawn again to the tray and the bottle.

He changed position for a better angle and saw something darkly bulbous inside the jar. He bent and read
"Hellman's" on the lid. Through the glass he could make
out a purplish maroon lump that looked like meat. Or
liver.

He moved closer till his eyes were inches from the jar.
The smell again. Alcohol.

He recognized the unbalanced shape of a heart.

Animal? *Human?*

Left over from an autopsy?

But why the candle and the white ribbon and the
flowers, as though someone were preparing services?

Maybe winos had found a way in. Or psychos. Or a
splinter group of religious maniacs . . .

His head turned slowly toward the dark mass in the jar.
Hers?

He backed away from the improvised altar and discovered that he had lost his night vision while staring
into the flame. Instead of waiting for his eyes to readjust, he felt along the wall till he came to a half-opened
door. He stepped through into more blackness.

Which way to turn? He had a primitive need to put
distance between himself and that heart, no matter whose
it was. How he hated the dark! His slight fear of it was
turning to rage. He remembered Claudius's command:
"GIVE ME SOME LIGHT!"

But who would come if he called out?

He was alone, wasn't he?

He needed a heavy piece of steel, an ax, a sledge, something with enough weight to slam through the front panels
of those drawers. Margot could be lying in one. Or what
was left of her . . .

As he stood outside the morgue, he became aware of a
break in the darkness, like the first thinning of clouds
after a storm. At first he thought it was his imagination
again, but then he realized that there was light in the
distance, and he was in a hall.

He struck out unthinkingly, bumping into walls, kicking over more empty cans, unconcerned about the noise.
GIVE ME SOME LIGHT! He came to a room that seemed
to glow softly from an indistinguishable source.

He made out a row of doors about six feet apart. He
tiptoed up and touched one: solid wood, thick and heavy.
Just below his eye level there was a small depression, a
few inches square. He ran his fingertips over it and found
it was made of wired glass.

Cells! He'd been thrown off at first by the absence of
bars.

One door was open. He stepped inside. Half-seeing,
half-feeling, he found loose chains and eyebolts that once
had supported a pallet. In the back he saw a toilet bowl,
unadorned by a seat. Just above the cracked porcelain
bowl a pipe had pulled loose from the wall, leaving a

small hole, and from the hole a pale Naples yellow shone through. The air held a trace of a volatile scent. Some kind of petroleum product? Oil? Gasoline?

He slid to his knees and peeked through the hole, like a child looking into a candy egg. A small kerosene lamp guttered on a wooden table a few feet away. A slab of bed hung from the far wall on tight chains; it seemed to be covered with drab old clothes.

Then he realized the clothes contained a human form, stretched out on the slab, immobile. Everything was covered except the head and a pair of slender bare feet, toes pointed upward.

He heard a noise and turned slowly. He couldn't see anything behind him.

A rat, maybe. The constant companions of his search. But the sound had had a human quality. A suppressed sigh, a brief exhalation. There'd been something piteous about it. Did rodents sigh?

He listened in the near darkness, muscles tight, heart pounding. He knew his imagination was out of control; he knew that stimulants distorted perception. How much of this was real? *All*, he told himself. He didn't dare assume otherwise.

After two or three minutes of perfect immobility he screwed up his face like a man in a monocle and turned back to the hole.

The shadowy form seemed to be lying on its back, the face a patch of black tilted slightly in his direction. A scarf or a bonnet covered the forehead and the hair; the mouth and eyes seemed to be open, although he couldn't be sure. In the poor light, the face resembled one of those gimmick drawings of Christ with eyes that open and shut.

A cool draft ruffled his sleeve, and the lamp flared to a brief incandescence. He looked in the eyes of Margot.

He heard the noise again, but before he could turn, the door slammed shut behind him.

IV *Friday, August 15*

44

At ten minutes after 6:00 A.M. Boon decided to get up.
Cramped on Mondragon's split Naugahyde sofa, he'd
managed maybe an hour of sleep in installments. All night
long Anna hadn't left his mind. He kept reliving the night
of his thirty-second birthday, two years ago, changing the
ending to assuage his guilt. That afternoon she'd made
one of her rare telephone calls to make sure he was coming home on time. And for a change, he was. But just as
he'd pulled in, the dispatcher had put out an 010, and the
next time he'd seen his wife it was midnight. The surprise
party had gone home; most of a leg of lamb was wrapped
in foil in the refrigerator next to a piece of his favorite
eleven-layer chocolate cake, the one that took a day to
make.

He didn't need those memories.

But they wouldn't stop.

He rubbed his poached eyes and sat up, exhaling bad
air like a man blowing up a balloon. The effort made him
feel simple-minded and silly. Jesus, he said to himself, my
mouth tastes like a bull's asshole. What hit me? Somebody
get that truck's license number! Then he remembered.

He had gone to bed at home, but a call from the duty
lieutenant had brought him back to the office. An anonymous citizen had spotted a body in black robes in the bed
of a speeding pickup, but he had neglected to provide a

description of the vehicle. Boon had cruised the streets for a while and then sacked out on Mondragon's couch while cops from every precinct in town checked side streets and parking lots. The tip was probably worthless. Like most anonymous tips.

He was glad he'd come in, sleepless night or not. How could he ever forgive himself if they broke the case while he was snoring at home? The search for the judge had spread into nearby alleys and parks with tracking dogs and floodlights. If they found one body, they'd find them all; he would bet his stripes on that.

Was Anna stretched out in a seedy flophouse room, her ivory skin fouled by a pervert's bites like so many bodies he had seen? Was she floating in driftwood under a pier, her body rising and falling on the tide, the shrimp gnawing at her fingertips? He'd seen that, too. On the job and in the night, in dreams.

He sat forward on the old couch and put his elbows on his knees and his chin on his knuckles. He remembered all the times he had told himself that he didn't love her, that he lacked the capacity for love, that they would have to make it on some other basis: a marriage of convenience, maybe, the two of them joining their bodies every so often to relieve the pressure. He wondered what had been going through his thick head.

He missed her unreasonably, felt almost sick when he realized that there was going to be another great loss in his life, something else to spend the years forgetting. What would he do to heal this time? Join another police department? The Foreign Legion? Take up Polish vodka? How many losses was he supposed to suffer? There hadn't been that many people to love in the first place.

Now look, dummy, he said to himself as he surveyed the empty office, knock off the self-pity; if she's gone, she's gone; you'll survive this time just like the first time. That's what you are, Boon: a survivor; a nickel a bushel. Spend your time sympathizing with *her*, not yourself. You never gave that woman a goddamn thing. Not even the pleasure of your dull company. You *chose* to leave her alone for four years.

Fucking creep.

He grabbed his earlobe so hard he winced. Where were they? *Where were they?* If he could only get a handle on the case . . .

What did Annaliese and a retard and an artist's wife and a lady judge have in common? And a snitch who liked to dress in old women's clothes? Had they just been in the wrong building at the wrong time? Was some fool hanging around the halls and snatching innocent people? *How could he get away with it in a building full of cops?*

Using a blind van, maybe. Every lawman hated windowless vans, the Tiger tanks of crime. The candy man in Houston killed twenty-seven boys with his van and his strangler's hands, and nobody even knew they were gone till the bodies started turning up.

He shuffled down the hall to the room marked "Men" and kicked the door open. As usual, it banged against the wall on the inside; years of pounding had worn a hole exactly the size of the knob in the plasterboard.

He braced both hands against the washbowl and raised his head to the discolored mirror. Who's that? he asked himself, struggling to open both eyes. *What's* that? His reddish blond mustache drooped at both ends. His straggly yellow hair looked as though someone had combed it with a rake.

He shaved lightly with his old Remington electric, glad that his stubble was almost the same color as his skin and didn't have to be scraped to the bone. *If I have one life, let me live it as a blonde.* Anna liked to kid him with that line.

He washed his face and combed his hair and looked at the mirror and shrugged. Hardly worth the trouble. Would she even recognize him?

He took out his spare toothbrush and worked over his

teeth. It felt good; they were the only part of his body that didn't feel sensitive. He jammed his shaving kit into his pocket, fired up a Swisher, and walked back to his desk.

By the time the streets started to hum at seven he had called Tally Wickham's home number a half dozen times without answer. She's probably out playing, he decided. He remembered the definition of a bachelor: a guy who comes to work every day from a different direction. Did it apply to bachelorettes? This was a poor time for her to be out getting her ashes hauled. He should have told her yesterday.

She moped up to his desk in full uniform at eight forty-five, just as he was dialing again. "Oh," he said, "thanks for dropping by. Where ya been?"

"Working," she said, patting her open mouth with her hand. He took a closer look: the green of her eyes was tinged with red; for once those smart-ass flecks of light were gone.

"Close your eyes, you're bleeding to death," he said. "I expected you a long time ago. We got men kicking in doors all over town. I thought you were so concerned about that Schulte kid—"

"I *am* concerned," she said. "I've been—"

His phone interrupted her. He pronounced a listless "Boonhomicide" as a voice exploded in his ear: "*Johnny Boon!*" It was Foxy, the duty lieutenant, the one who always sounded as if he were auctioning tobacco. "Hey, the captain's on his way in from home! Told me tell you and your partner to stand by for a trip to the hall. Got that? The mayor's gonna be there, the commissioner, coupla councilmen—"

"Whatta they need *us* for?" He was in a hell of a shape for a command performance. And his partner didn't look much better.

"What—do—they—need—YOU—for?" Foxy said as though talking to an immigrant. "The case! It's all over page one. Mystery at the J-Building, judge vanishes, cops baffled, that kinda bull. The mayor wants a fill-in, and you're elected."

"Christ."

"Be ready, John, will ya? And listen, do me a personal favor. Don't tell the commissioner to stuff it this time. Okay, John? Just this once?"

"Don't worry your little head." The world was full of frightened sucks. And most of them had rank.

Wickham flopped into his spare chair and threw her long legs in front of her like a pitcher cooling out between innings. "We're wanted at the hall," he told her.

"Oh, Lord," she said through another yawn. "I've been working all night. Room by room."

"You been—?"

"Going through the building."

"Twenty guys did that already. Found a lotta nothing."

"That's what I found, too. But I don't believe it."

"Huh?"

"We overlooked something. A closet. A space between the walls. *Something.* It's happening here. It's got to be."

"Based on your years of experience?"

"Based on simple logic," she said, stretching her arms and rotating her head like a zoo monkey. "There's one dead and three missing—"

"Four."

"Margot Gamble, Sammy Schulte, Judge Holder. Who's the fourth?"

He realized that he hadn't reported Anna, hadn't wanted to look foolish if she turned out to be on another drunk. Besides, it was a family matter. The Wickham broad had a way of horning in on your private life. When he decided to confide in somebody, it wouldn't be a female rook. "Three," he agreed.

"One body turned up inside the building, and the others were last seen in or near, correct? And the judge disappeared in the middle of the afternoon. Who could carry off a judge in her robes without attracting attention? Spiderman?"

"I was wondering that myself," he said, wishing he hadn't agreed with her again. The best way to handle overeager young cops was to keep them off-balance, and the best way to keep them off-balance was to disagree with every word they said. He would try not to repeat his mistake.

"You know what I did about four o'clock this morning?" she said, some of the liveliness returning to her voice. "I tried to figure out where we hadn't searched. And I thought: the elevators! I found that janitor—Ugo?— and we looked down the shafts. I was *sure* we'd see bodies at the bottom."

She pulled a round golden box from her purse and began batting at her face, sending up perfumy puffs. "Yeah?" he said, trying not to sound too interested. "What'd you two Junior G-men find?"

"Orange peels. Paper scraps. Cigarette butts. Anything small enough to fit in the crack between the elevator and the landing. What a letdown."

"Worked all night, huh?" he asked. In spite of himself, he had to admire her energy. He knew cops who could get in nine hours' rest on an eight-hour watch. "Didn't sleep?"

"Sure. I took a ten-minute break in somebody's office, and when I woke up, it was an hour later. On a wooden chair, too." She stretched her arms like a cat preening in the sun.

"Well, pay attention," he said in his best supervisorial tone. "We gotta do PR at the mayor's office."

"When?"

"Eleven o'clock. Be back here at ten thirty, dressed like you had an honor guard post." He hoped she was getting the point: *he* was the senior partner; *he* gave the orders.

She jumped up. "I was on my way to the basement," she said. "Do I have time to just take a look?"

"You can't get down there."

"I *know* that." She had an aggravating way of acting one step ahead all the time. "I saw Ugo up and around awhile back," she went on. "He'll know a way. He was nice about the elevators."

"Forget it. The basement's nailed shut. You know that. There's boards across the doorways, steel slabs on the windows. There's—"

"Who nailed it shut?"

"The building commissioner. If they left one opening, every wino in town'd get in. Sure as hell, somebody'd be squashed when the demo teams blow the walls. Happened when they demolished the Luttinen Building. Not that there was any state funerals."

"In other words, nobody's checked the basement?" She looked incredulous.

"Only your mice and your roaches." He flashed the kind of expression reserved for slow children. "You wanna waste your time, go ahead. Us, uh, older officers, we got a word for that."

"Oh? What's the word?"

This woman never let anything drop. "I can't say it," he blurted out, shuffling some papers.

"Since when did you get so prissy?"

Okay, she had it coming. "It's, uh, jacking off."

"How *descriptive*."

"Just don't be long," he said quickly. She also had a way of making him feel like a foulmouthed bum when, in fact, he went out of his way to use clean language in front of females. Not like some of the garbagemouths still trying to prove that the PD was a men's club. "You're not gonna get in anyway," he said, feeling sleazy. "Not without a sledge and a crowbar. Whole building's gonna be sealed off like that, floor by floor. When the last floor's ready—*boom!*"

"Not a second too soon," she said, tilting her head to peer into her compact again. He asked himself why it was

always the best-looking ones that spent the most time on
the product. He watched as she spread a thin gel over her
lips, rolled them together sideways with a little chirp, and
tilted the compact up into the light. Apparently she was
satisfied; the gold case closed with a snap.

"Better get going," he said sternly, pointing up at the
slightly skewed wall clock.

"I know you think it's silly to go down there," she said,
sounding apologetic. "But I've just got—"

"A feeling," he interrupted. "You oughta take some
emergency treatment, cure all those feelings you get."

"You ought to take some emergency treatment for
grumpiness," she said, standing up and bouncing toward
the door. She was gone before he could extricate his voice
from a yawn.

It's just as well I dummied up, he consoled himself.
I'd of only made her sore. Can't keep up with her motor-
mouth anyway, might as well stop trying. But he could
feel a trace of a smile on his irritated face. Worked all
night, huh? Turning into a regular mule. Maybe there's
hope. . . .

45

Tally found the maintenance man buffing his work shoes
in his cubbyhole next to the elevators and told him she
wanted to visit the basement.

He looked up, smiled, raised a pair of darkly stained
palms, and said, "No understand."

She had learned in dealing with him during the night
that all instructions had to be explicit; he barely seemed
to comprehend English, despite the fact that he'd worked
in the building for longer than anyone could remember.

He looked at her with the smile that never seemed to leave his pinched face, but something in his gray eyes gave her the impression of pain. Well, you never know, she said to herself. The simplest people have personal problems that seem like the end of the world.

"Basement," she said, pointing straight down. "*Sous-sol.*" Maybe the French word would sound like the Italian.

"Yes," he said, showing the gaps in his teeth. "Base-ment!" He made it into a four-syllable word. "Yes. *No!* Basement izza shut now."

"I *know,*" she said. "Ugo, we're still checking the build-ing, and I just thought—"

"Basement shut," he repeated. He looked toward the open door, as though he had somewhere to go. Well, damn it, I'm in a hurry, too, she told herself, and I don't intend to spend the whole morning arguing with the opposite sex about that basement. There has to be a way to get down there. If I have to, I'll rappel down the damned elevator shaft.

"You don't un-der-stand," she said, carefully separating her syllables. She hated to sound patronizing, but the base-ment *had* to be searched. The police brass who had left it off the list had made a fundamental error. The "little glass house" doctrine, taught to every student cop at the academy, covered the situation perfectly: if you're ordered to search a block of houses for a runaway killer, search *every* house. If you choose to skip the "little glass house" in the middle of the block because he *couldn't* be there, that's precisely where he'll be.

"Peo-ple are miss-ing," she told the maintenance man. "Remember? I told you last night? A lit-tle boy? A . . . *bambino?*" She held her palm about four feet off the floor to illustrate. "And a woman, uh *señorita,* uh, *sig-norina?*" What was the word? "A *signora?* A judge, a *jugo,* I mean *juga.*" Wrong again. *Jugo* was Spanish for *juice.* She had just told him a juice was missing. Why couldn't the man understand simple English?

She had a flash that he was faking. Silly idea. She was turning as paranoid as that artist. "A woman in black?" she floundered on. "*Negra?*" She held her hands out from her body and fluttered them to indicate billowing robes.

His dumb smile was as fixed as the mask of comedy on a theater marquee. She looked at her watch: 9:45. She was due back on the fifth floor shined up and ready to go at 10:30. Well, she was shined up enough for a meeting with politicians. Now if Geppetto here would just cooperate . . .

Ah, a sign of life!

He extended his hand toward the hall and beckoned for her to follow. They walked a dozen steps and came to one of the boarded-up doors to the basement. "See?" he said.

"Yes, Ugo, I told you, I *know* the doors are sealed. But isn't there one that we can . . . *avanti?*" She doubted if she was even close to the word for *enter*, but with the janitor one pressed on regardless.

He shook his head briskly, still smiling.

"What about the elevators?"

She caught a change in his body language, arms slipping across his chest and face clouding over, but as dulled as her senses were from lack of sleep, she wasn't sure that her interpretations made any more sense than her attempts at Italian. "No understanda," he insisted, but he had to be lying. Even if he had just cleared customs at Ellis Island, he would know what elevators were. Elevators played a big role in a maintenance man's life. Why was he faking ignorance? What could be in it for him?

"The elevator," she repeated, moving her hands up and down and studying his face. "Lift. *Ascenseur.*"

"Oh," he said, regaining his Giaconda smile. "*Ascensore!* It'sa no work."

"I just came down in one."

"No work for basement. Izza—*blocka.*" She decided he was mentally impaired. The sickly smile and the language problems reminded her of poor missing Sammy Schulte and gave her a compassion for the poor man. He *was* trying.

"I'm sorry, Ugo," she said softly, touching his arm. "You mean . . . *blocked?*"

"Yes. *Blocka.*"

"What means *blocked*—I mean, what does *blocked* mean?"

He took a deep breath as though talking were hard work. "Izza turn offa for basement. No work. I'ma tella chiefa last night."

"Chiefa?"

"Police chiefa."

"Oh." So Denny Burns had had the same idea about the basement. "He went down?" she asked.

"No. *Impossibile.*"

"There's no back stairs, no fire stairs?"

He shifted to the mask of tragedy, a long clown's face, lower lip puffed out as though he were heartbroken that he couldn't help. She realized that she had pushed as hard as she could, short of throttling him with a Kellite.

"Okay, Ugo," she said, "I'm going to the building office for permission to break down one of the doors. Don't go 'way. I may need help."

He frowned. "Breaka . . . door?" he said. His gray eyes were almost closed.

"Yes, breaka door!" She hadn't meant to mock him, but she was bored with arguing the obvious. "This building hasn't been searched till the basement's been searched!" She knew she was acting like a Boon, bullying the defenseless, throwing her badge around, and almost certainly for nothing—what did she expect to find in a basement that had been hermetically sealed for months?—but a mule didn't canvass *most* of her assigned area; she canvassed it all.

He stepped backward as though she had pulled a knife. She had a strong feeling that he had understood every word of her rapid-fire delivery, and something about it had touched a vulnerable spot. "No helpa you," he said.

He took a wide detour around her toward his maintenance room, and she stomped off toward the building office at the far end of the corridor. She had just put her hand on the polished brass knob when she heard someone rushing up behind her. It was the janitor, sweaty face wreathed in a smile. "Izza locky," he said.

"Lucky?"

"Elev—eleva—*ascensore.*" He pointed down with a trembling finger.

"You mean . . . we can go?" She didn't understand. Why all the hassle first? His face offered no clue. It had been a language problem, she decided. A failure to communicate. With men, most hassles were.

The nearest of the three elevators was standing open when they reached it; he beckoned her inside with a pleased expression and an old-world sweep of his hand.

He opened a panel next to the self-service buttons and deftly unscrewed two bolts with a heavily taped screwdriver. He pulled the panel out an inch or two and inserted the long blade into the opening.

A bald man in tennis shorts and a green Izod shirt started to enter, but the janitor waved him away. "*Speciale,*" he said, winking at her as though they were co-conspirators. He looked thoroughly pleased with himself. She smiled back. In his little life of scrubbing and mopping and fixing, how many triumphs could there be?

She heard a crack like an electrical arc. The doors closed, and the cage lowered in an erratic rhythm, as though the old elevator were as balky as its operator. Or maybe the well-worn machinery had to readjust itself to the unfamiliar descent. She still couldn't believe how easy it had turned out to be after all that chatter. *Men. . . . !*

The door opened on a shadowed hall.

She started to step out, then shook her head at her own forgetfulness. Only the palest light trickled in from thin slits in boarded windows above. How was she supposed to search this *terra incognita* without a flash?

A ray pierced the gloom from behind her. She turned and saw Ugo's beaming face in the glow of his flashlight. "Thanks," she said, and made a mental note: people who gallop off in all directions should make sure they're on a trained horse.

She took the flashlight from his hand and surveyed the scene. There were three corridors, one to the left cluttered with junk and debris and battered old furniture, the other two clean. She took a hard right and strolled to the first door. Closed and boarded. So was the next door, and the next . . .

She finally found an unlocked door and stepped into a room that smelled as though it had housed wet dogs. She directed the light on the frosted door panel and saw the word *Pound*. It *had* housed wet dogs.

After a few more minutes she couldn't escape the conclusion that the two of them were wasting their time, "jacking off" in Boon's delicate phrase. The place had the moldy smell of long disuse. There were no signs that anyone had been here in years, let alone in the last few days.

"Let's try someplace else," she said.

"Shoo," the janitor answered. She figured he meant "sure." It was his first comment since the start of the search.

Back at the elevator foyer she motioned for him to follow and headed up the middle corridor. There was another series of sealed doors and empty rooms. Dust lay so thick it muffled their steps. There were no footprints, no traces of activity.

After she broke through her second wall-to-wall cobweb, she admitted to herself that she didn't need to be attacked by a pack of killer rats to get the message: the old pros were right; this basement was ready for the executioner's ax. She felt foolish. Boon would enjoy his I-told-you-so.

She reversed direction, the janitor padding noiselessly in her trail as she courteously aimed the flashlight straight down to help him see.

The littered hall remained. No matter how foolish she felt, it had to be searched. But her watch said 10:20; she'd have to put it off till later.

She stepped toward the open elevator. Time to leave for the command performance at City Hall . . .

"Offa Wiggum?"

God, she was so tired she was hearing voices.

"Offa *Wiggum!*" The sound came from her left. She aimed the flashlight down the littered corridor and snared a peach-colored department-store mannikin the size of a boy. Someone had dressed it in short brown pants, knee-length black stockings, high shoes from an early Norman Rockwell print, and a white peasant shirt without a collar.

"What's *that?*" she asked the janitor.

The statue stumbled toward her in a crooked lope, arms flopping, head rolling, a wide grin on its face.

"Offa Wiggum!" it called to her. "OFFA WIGGUM!"

She recognized Sammy Schulte. She whirled and said, "What's *he*—?"

The janitor caught her off-balance and rammed her backward into the elevator. The flashlight skittered from her hand as her head slammed into something hard.

She slumped half-conscious into a sitting position and felt a vague tug at her belt. Oh, my God, she said to herself, he's undressing me. And there's nobody here to help, and it's pitch-dark or . . . I'm blind.

"*Strega, strega,*" he mumbled as he leaned over her dazed body. Why was he talking about a liqueur?

Her thoughts were cut off by a yank at her waist. He had lifted her .38.

She tried to talk, but nothing came out. She raised her arms imploringly, but her heavy hands fell like barbells as the elevator doors sealed with a soft thump.

She blacked out, revived once to the sound of her own

moans, and blacked out again. After what seemed like hours she became aware that the elevator was moving . . . down. To *where?* There must be a subbasement or an elevator pit.

The cage jolted to a stop.

She had reached bottom.

46

He knew from sad experience that one uniform quickly followed another. Whenever a single brown-shirted soldier had come to a bad end on the mountain, a whole company of Nazi-Fascisti would arrive the next day, beating and torturing and killing. Any minute now they would crash through the doors of his underground fortress, and it would be up to him to defend his family. In other times that would have been Babbo's responsibility, but . . . where was he? The Virgin must come and explain his father's absence.

In his small hand, the first pistol he had ever touched felt as cold as death. Guns like this had finished the massacre on the mountain—*pop! pop! pop!* He could still hear the sound, like caps. These lumps of metal were of the devil, and now his family's safety depended on one. When the Nazi-Fascisti came this time, Ugo Ruggiero would be ready.

He double-checked the lock on the flimsy door that opened to the up stairway. He had turned off the power to the only elevator that ran to the basement and ripped out the fuse bars after the witch's cage had touched bottom. Another threat! Last night the *malocchio* pretending to be a clown, and today . . . the *strega.*

He wondered if she would have power against the gas.

He should have shot her with her own gun, but he was too afraid of the weapon to use it. If Maximiliano was endangered, or Mamma or his dear Nonna or Aunt Livia or any of them, he would aim for the body and squeeze till the gun was empty.

"Come, Maxmein," he said, taking the boy by the hand. They stepped around the broken glass and debris that he had set out to make the passageway look unused.

"This time you must not leave your room until Ugo tells you," he instructed his brother. "Soon will be the feast of *ferragosto*. But only for *good* boys."

Maxmein mouthed the same words he had said when he was under the witch's power: "Offa Wiggum, Offa Wiggum."

The Virgin could end a spell with a wave of her finger. He could have blocked the diabolical power himself if he had only remembered the ancient trick of holding his balls and making the sign of the cross. But how was he to know a *strega* would arrive disguised as a *poliziotta*?

He kissed the forehead under the white helmet. "Play, Maxmein," he said as he went out. "Brother Ugo will be back soon." He pushed hard till he heard the lock click. The boy would be safe.

As he hurried along the corridor, he wondered what could possibly be delaying Babbo. It was late morning, almost time for the feast, and soon everything would be ready: tables heaped with food, loaf-shaped ovens radiating heat, *demigiane* of Negretto wine decanting in the cool hallways . . .

A *ferragosto* without Babbo? Unthinkable!

Maybe his father was at the *tabacchi*, drinking with his friends. Once or twice a year the old man would throw back too many glasses of *grappa* and rest under the counter for a few hours. But never on a holy day.

Ugo entered a high-ceilinged room, reached behind him on his belt, and selected a key. He opened a drawer on the second shelf and removed the tank. This was the last one;

what would he do if he needed another? The Virgin would provide. He lifted the cold steel to his shoulder and nudged the long drawer shut with his foot.

Back at the elevator he used another key to open the doors. He shone his flashlight down the shaft to the top of the immobilized car. The bird of evil was still in her cage. She must not be allowed to fly.

He worked with nervous hands, thinking of his father. *Perhaps he came while I was gone and the* strega *harmed him!* No. Even if she had managed to open the doors of the elevator, she could never get out of the pit; she would be blocked by the bare walls inches in front of her eyes. That was the way to contain a witch.

Had the *gigant'* harmed Babbo then? Impossible. He had been locked up since last night.

Then perhaps something happened to Babbo earlier. . . . Was he . . . Could he be . . . dead? Ugo almost dropped the tank.

If his father was dead, then let the soldiers come and shoot them all. Without its leader, the family Ruggiero was not a family anyway. What was a lion without its head?

He must hurry. Any minute now the Nazi-Fascisti with the lightning bolts on their collars would start marching up the mountain again.

He opened the valve on the cylindrical tank and dropped it down the shaft.

47

"God *damn* it, John, we're—we're not getting ready to see some stewbum," the dragon sputtered. "We're going to see the mayor! How long's she been gone?"

"Too long," Boon said.

The dragon had been spitting and snapping like an overgrilled hot dog; he looked like one, too, in his reddish brown three-piece pinstripe and his egg-roll-colored silk tie. Hottest dresser in the home for the aged. Boon knew why the old man stood behind his desk instead of sitting; he was protecting his razor creases. What some men won't do to impress a piss-ant politician that can't find his dick in the dark with two hands. . . .

"Why'd you let her go in the first place?" Mondragon asked.

" 'Let her go'? Cap, nobody lets that broad go or not go. *She* decides. You disagree with her, she whips out her diploma."

The captain punched the intercom. "Car ready?" he asked.

"Still ready," Amy's voice answered calmly.

"Tell him to warm up the engine."

"Yes, sir, I'll tell him again."

Boon looked at his watch. The appointment was in fifteen minutes, and City Hall was eight blocks away. "Maybe I better run down and take a look," he said. "She's been gone an awful long time."

"I'll go with you," the old man said, coming around his desk. "We leave here in five minutes, with or without her."

On the way down in the elevator Boon thought he heard someone cry out.

"You hear that?" he asked, cocking his head.

"Hear what?"

The elevator slowed and stopped at the first floor, and just as the doors wheezed open, the voice came louder, "Please . . . somebody . . . *out of here.* . . *!*"

He sighed. There were people like that. "It's her," he said. "She's got herself stuck in the elevator."

"Who?" the captain said, stepping into the lobby.

"Wickham."

Boon looked up at the three half-circular dials that located each elevator. The arrow on the right pointed to "7." The middle elevator was at the lobby; they had just come down in it. The needle on the left pointed to "B." "Hey," he said, "I thought it couldn't go below the first floor anymore."

"It can't," the dragon said.

Boon pointed to the telltale dial as a weak moan came up the shaft.

The old man nudged Boon aside and stuck his heavy face against the crack where the doors sealed. "Are you STUCK?"

A scream died away as a moan.

Boon tried to pull the doors apart, but he couldn't apply enough pressure with his fingertips. "Gimme a hand, Cap," he said.

The doors held.

"Wait!" Boon said. He ran to the entrance to the police garage, fifty feet down the hall. He held up his arms as a green-and-white with a big *T* for "traffic" rolled slowly toward him.

The car stopped short and rocked on its springs. A black face peered from the driver's window. "Officer in trouble!" Boon said. "Open your trunk."

He reached under the cover for a pry bar or a tire iron and found both. This green-and-white was well stocked.

"Follow me," he ordered the uniformed man. "Wait! Bring your flash. You got two of those, too?"

"Yop," the traffic cop said. He was a lean man who looked combat-ready, and Boon was glad to have him along. Mondragon hadn't worked a hot call in years; the old man might faint dead away.

Boon led the way to the elevators. A small pack of strangers crowded the dragon, and Boon used his command voice: "Back off! All of you! Police business. *I said, * BACK OFF!"

He feinted at them like a herd dog, and the gawkers

retreated under his favorite mural. "Keep 'em back," he ordered the traffic cop as he rammed the pry bar between the No. 1 elevator's doors.

The steel tip sank three or four inches into the crack. He hauled with all his 170 pounds, but nothing moved.

"Here," Mondragon said. He outweighed Boon by at least 50 pounds. He stuck the tire iron in the slot and snapped something inside. Then he levered the doors open three or four inches.

Boon tried to look down. There was a glint of metal at the bottom of the shaft.

He called to the traffic cop, "Gimme a light! *Quick!*"

The flashlight showed the roof of the elevator about twenty feet down.

"Hey, we don't have two basements, do we?" he asked.

"No," Mondragon's voice came back. "But there's an elevator pit below basement level."

"For what?"

"Search me. Drainage, equipment housing. There's four big springs down there, catch it if it falls."

Boon looked again. "The elevator's in the pit, all right," he said. He checked the cables to see if any had broken. They looked taut. Tally was safe. Mad as a hooked eel, probably, but safe. "Don't worry!" he called down the shaft. "We're on our way."

He thought he heard a weak reply. He tilted his head and flapped his hand behind him for silence.

"What is it?" the dragon asked.

"*Quiet!*"

Then he heard the hiss.

He pointed the light down again, squinted, moved the beam back and forth on the top of the cake till he pinpointed what looked like an acetylene tank lying on its side.

Gas!

How the hell. . . ?

He studied the walls of the shaft for indentations, a

ladder down the side, anything that he could use for handholds. But the concrete was smooth.

Maybe he could slide the cables like a fireman. . . .

Use your head, he told himself. The cables are smeared with heavy grease. Even if you make the jump, you'll slide straight into a pit full of gas. Then the dragon'll have two cops to save. Or bury . . .

He whirled and said, "We gotta get downstairs."

"I'll find the janitor," Mondragon said. He sprinted to the maintenance door like a kid and banged with both fists. "Open up! *Open up!*"

Boon ran to the old basement door past the luncheonette. "Cap!" he shouted over his shoulder. "This leads down."

The two men ripped and slashed at the thick boards across the doorway. Boon wondered why it had been necessary to hammer the nails three inches deep, like a work of master cabinetry. There were all kinds of carpenters; imagine taking pains like that in a building that was condemned.

Mondragon worked on his knees, his creases shot, snorting like his nickname. The two of them heaved together and yanked off the last board with an outcry like professional wrestlers. The whole job had taken minutes. Boon hoped it was soon enough.

He looked for a knob, but the door was smooth. There was a Yale snap lock about a foot above the hole where the knob had been removed. "Stand away!" he shouted.

He pulled his .38, crouched to get a flat line on the lock, and fired.

The smell of gunpowder filled the air, and a small indentation appeared in the door. "Shit!" he said. A week ago he'd removed his 200-grain hot loads for an inspection and forgotten to replace them. This regulation ammo wouldn't pierce a hot fudge sundae.

"Let's use these," Mondragon said, waving the pry bar and the tire iron. They tried to insert them high and low, but the door and the jamb were flush, and they succeeded only in splintering the old wood. Boon tried to knock the pin off the top hinge, but it was welded in place by paint and rust.

"Gimme room," he said. "Gotta light another round." His partner's life was on the line, and that gave him the right to give orders, but he would probably have given them anyway. The dragon was too good a cop to complain.

Boon went back into his stance. In his peripheral vision he saw some gawkers, slipping closer. He braced both hands on the revolver and cinched up against the trigger. If the slug hit at a right angle to the door, there'd be no ricochet, but if somebody got nicked—he'd worry about that later.

The revolver went off with a sound like a .22. Regulation shit! All it did was enlarge the dent. Christ, they'd be here all day. What the hell kind of gas was it? And who the hell put it there?

He jerked on the trigger and jerked again till the lock was shattered. He reached through the hole and pulled the door open.

A steep flight of stairs descended to black. He headed down.

48

Tally found herself in a sitting position. She felt no pain, but she couldn't move. She wondered if her back were broken. No, she could move from the waist. But not much . . .

Her ribs.

She remembered slamming into something hard. She had bumped her head and bruised her back. Nobody ever died of a sore back.

I'm paying my dues, she said to herself, and I'm not even a real cop. Fair or unfair? Fair, she decided. Because I *am* a real cop. In more ways than I'm not . . .

The elevator was dark. She opened her mouth to call for help, but she wasn't sure if she made any sound. She knew she was disoriented and maybe in shock and thinking in circles.

She wondered if Boon had paid his dues.

She'd heard that he'd been shot twice.

Her father? Hospitalized for six months after a high-speed collision on a chase.

Mondragon? Knifed in the riots.

Now it was her turn.

Who did she have to thank for the honor? Who'd want to hurt a harmless Ph.D. candidate?

She couldn't remember. It was . . . whoever had thrown her into this dungeon.

Who? What was wrong with her memory?

She was pondering the question when she realized that an air conditioner or a fan was running. Funny she hadn't noticed before. The sound was faintly sibilant.

Maybe the fire department was here with its big portable fans.

But this felt as though something were *un*venting the air, as though a load of invisible sand were sifting silently on her chest, pushing her down, down. . . .

Why was she breathing so hard?

She clenched her left hand and pounded weakly on the wall.

Something hissed above her head. Lordie Lord, a snake?

Some dues! Her head slumped forward; she felt drunk. Why couldn't she just be shot? Was it fair that other cops got shot and clubbed and she had to face a killer snake in a black pit? *Fair's fair!*

She wondered why she was becoming incoherent, let loose a long, pealing giggle, and stopped to gasp. She saw words issuing from her mouth like comic-strip balloons. She had died and come back, come back, come back, as . . . a *Sousaphone!* No, a *Tallyphone! A Bell Tally-phone* . . .

"Look," a childish voice said, "I can do a *tummmmm-bersault!*"

That's enough, Tally, enough showing off now. Her father's voice. *Time to go home, young lady. The other kids left hours ago.* . . .

She heard herself singing, "The king of France and forty thousand men. . . ." How did it go? ". . . Couldn't put Humpty together again?" *No!* What *was* the rest? "The Jabberwock, with eyes of flame, came sizzling through the bulgy wood. . . ."

An original composition by . . . Allison?

Allison who?

Allison Wonderland!

The janitor did it.

Her mouth stretched for breath, strained and opened so that her words came out the wide end of a megaphone that danced and jittered toward her lips. She heard herself say, "For all the bears that ever there was . . . that ever there was . . . that ever there was . . ."

Her body slid sideways to the floor, and the words died away.

49

Gamble didn't know how long he had scraped and hacked at the hard wooden door, but he was sure it was nearly around the clock. He worked in a controlled panic, wondering how long he could keep running on empty. The concrete floor beneath his feet was covered with shavings; his Swiss army knife had perished blade by blade, and now he was using a claw chisel made for stone. His fingers were streaked with blood that oozed from a big open blister where the base of the chisel rubbed his palm.

The sight he had viewed through the peephole was vivid in his mind, but he would not allow himself to stop and look again. All that mattered now was to get out of this cell and into Margot's.

Besides, he had yielded to his curiosity two or six or nine hours ago and she had been in the same position: on her back, face and bare feet visible, trunk and legs hidden under black cloth. Even her slender feet had been pointed at the same angle as the first time he'd looked.

Was she dead? He refused to think about it. He dug the three points of the claw chisel into the wood and nudged it ahead with his fist. Another sliver curled up and slipped to the floor. A few more curls, and he would punch through. Then he would enlarge the hole so he could reach the outside knob.

He had changed the angle of his strokes when he heard a noise in the distance. He lifted the chisel off the wood and listened. A man's voice.

He just resumed work when it came again, this time closer.

Men were headed toward the cells. A rescue team? Cops? Was that good or bad? He was too tired to decide.

He stood watch at the tiny wired window as the cellblock door opened and a small man walked into the corridor. The man held a flashlight in one hand and a gun in the other, and he was saying something that sounded like "bobbo, bobbo!" in a forlorn voice.

Gamble slumped to the floor and shut his eyes.

Would the man see the shavings?

A light turned his closed eyelids a thin vermilion. He held his breath, and the beam stayed on his face.

Any second now, he warned himself, he'll see what I've been doing. What will he do to me? Shoot? *Then shoot straight!*

The reddish light faded to gray, then black and the footsteps moved off.

He heard a voice in Margot's cell. It was high-pitched and exuberant, as though the low mood of a few seconds before had turned into the purest joy. He picked out a few words: *vino, festa, pane.* Spanish. Or Italian. He thought he heard "mama," but he couldn't be sure.

He prayed under his breath. *Say something, Margot. Lord, make her answer him!*

The cell was silent.

He crawled to the rear and raised his eye to the peephole.

The man was leaning over the pallet that hung from the wall, his back to Gamble. He wore freshly pressed chino work pants and a clean white shirt, and his short brown hair was pasted tightly to his head. He seemed to be manipulating her body with his hands.

Gamble's stomach contracted. He clamped one of his hands against his mouth. Whatever was happening, he couldn't help his wife.

The man turned to one side and adjusted the wick on the kerosene lamp. The light came up, and Gamble saw that Margot had been dressed in a peasant blouse that was now pulled up to her neck. The straps on her slip had been cut and the slip pulled down her body. She was bared from shoulders to waist.

He filled his mouth with knuckles.

A gun lay on the table, four or five feet from the peephole. It looked like a police revolver. There was no way for him to reach it.

The man reached under the table and produced a large-mouth bottle of clear fluid. As he did, he turned full face toward the peephole, and Gamble saw that it was the same smiling little man who had sworn three nights ago that he hadn't seen Margot enter the building.

What was he doing?

The janitor turned back toward Margot's still form.

With a slow, deliberate movement, he reached inside his belt and removed a long knife with a thin blade. He stropped it on his pants and held it aloft, where it caught the light from the little lamp.

Gamble had started to scream, "No!" when a series of loud crashes reverberated throughout the cellblock. It sounded as though someone were trying to knock down a door or a wall.

The janitor whirled and grabbed the gun. He stepped through the door of the cell, then turned and carefully rearranged the blouse to cover Margot's nakedness. He reholstered the knife and walked out with the gun shaking in one hand and the flashlight in the other.

His footsteps echoed and died away.

There's no more time, Gamble said to himself. I've got to get her before that lunatic comes back.

He pushed the blade of the claw chisel into the scored wood and shoved with all his strength, butted the bloody meat of his palm against the rounded end of the tool until his hand felt numbed and the only way he could tell he was injured was by the blood dripping off his fingertips to the floor as though he had sliced an artery.

At last the blade pushed through.

He twisted and scraped to enlarge the hole, gulping for air as he worked, trying not to cry out in rage and frustration and helplessness. Sweat and blood drenched his clothes.

He shoved at the widened hole, but his hand wouldn't clear. *Goddamn hammy hands!* He hacked at the edges and felt the splinters like needles as he pushed his whole arm through.

He slapped at the panel till he hit metal. He gave a hard twist, but the knob wouldn't turn. He twisted the other way and heard the pins retract in the lock.

He was free.

Margot's door stood open. Didn't the janitor worry that she would escape? Or was she . . . ?

He had no time for questions of life or death. He only knew that he had to get her out, retrace the way he had come, through the long corridor, the morgue, the room with the stacked desks, out the broken door marked AIR RAID SHELTER in broken letters, and up to the street for help. The corridors would be black, but he was learning the management of darkness. The worst he could do was slam into a couple of walls, butt up against a few dead ends. Small matters.

Her body looked thinner than usual, waiflike, as he bent to lift her. Her cheeks were sunken, the facial bones more prominent than ever. She must be dehydrated and empty.

He rolled her on her stomach and raised her to his shoulder. She had weighed 110 before and looked lighter now, but the weight almost toppled him. He started down the corridor, lurching from wall to wall under the load.

He had nearly reached the abandoned morgue when she slipped off. He broke her fall with an outstretched thigh and transferred her heavily to the other shoulder.

The light was fading now that he was getting farther from the lamp in her cell; he wondered if a candle was still burning in the morgue at the altar of the bottled heart. After a short distance the corridor turned black, and he kicked at the wall every few feet so he wouldn't pass the opening.

There!

With his first step into the morgue he sent a tall stack of empty cans to the floor in a crash of tinny metal.

Company would arrive any second. And he couldn't run.

"I'm sorry, honey," he said as he gripped her by the hands and dragged her to the opposite wall. He tried three handles before he found an empty drawer. He laid her body gently on the nylon webbing that crisscrossed the bottom of the tray and slid the drawer closed.

He blotted his bloody hand against the remains of his shirt so he wouldn't leave a trail and walked to the far side of the room. He slumped in the lee of a dissecting table.

The door banged open, and a can rolled halfway across the stone floor.

The same voice spoke again. He picked out a word that was being repeated, first in threatening tones, then in tones of supplication: "*Morto.*" Italian? Whatever the language, the meaning was clear.

Dead.

His position was painful as he squatted on his heels, unable to move for fear his shoe would squeak against the floor. His left hand brushed another empty can; his right was flattened on the cold floor for balance.

The monologue had stopped, but now the voice resumed in soft, loving tones. The strange words sounded so unthreatening, so prosaic, that Gamble dared raise his eyes above the level of the slab and look across the room.

The janitor was visible in shadowy profile. He appeared to be talking to the jugged heart, chatting away as though it were a living organism with sense and understanding. In one hand he held the gun; in the other, a flashlight. Gamble lowered his head.

After a few minutes the talking stopped, and rays of light climbed the walls.

He crouched lower.

The light flicked off, and then he heard a huff and realized the man had blown out the candle.

Had he been seen? Or heard? Was the lunatic going to finish him off in the dark?

The light stabbed the dissecting table just over his head, then died again.

Soft footfalls . . .

Close . . .

Closer . . .

His fingers circled the empty can. If it scraped against the floor, he was dead.

The footsteps reached the opposite side of the table. Any second the light would stab in his face.

He rotated his upper body till he was facing the door to the corridor and lofted the can through the air with a short stroke of his wrist.

It rattled against the far wall and fell loudly to the floor.

The light whirled around the walls to the door. The man shouted something unintelligible and ran. Gamble heard him wrench the door open so hard that it slammed, then run into the hall screaming, "*Strega, strega!*" at the top of his lungs. The hysterical voice died away after a few minutes. *Now,* Gamble said to himself, *I've got to move Margot. . . .*

He tiptoed toward the door and peeked out.

The hall was silent.

Had the janitor sneaked back? Was he waiting outside?

He rolled a can slowly through the open door.

No response.

The madman must be occupied.

He walked to the rear wall and slid open the drawer. Margot was breathing in short gasps. The question he had not dared ask had been answered, and he was almost too weak to exult.

He tried to sling her across his shoulder in a fireman's carry, but the two of them slipped to the cold floor. He felt faint and revived himself by jamming his head between his knees. He thought of leaving her and going for help. But the janitor might come back.

He arranged her head in his lap and stroked her long black hair. "Help," he whispered, dimly aware that his body was slumping atop hers. "Oh, God, please, somebody . . . somebody help us."

He revived again, shaking his head like a spaniel. He

breathed deeply, trying to store up oxygen. Some of his strength and spirit returned. He would do it! *By God, he would do it!* He took another deep breath, knelt, and raised his wife to his shoulder, then pushed himself up inch by inch, trembling like a weight lifter.

He staggered around unseen obstacles. He wished he had more Dexedrines, but they had gone the way of his batteries and his food. He would have to do it on will. No, not on will. On love and need and fear and shame.

But mostly love.

He headed for the door to the room with the stacked desks. It was a safe route, the only one he knew. If he could carry her into the underground, the janitor would never find them.

The door was shut. He reached down with his bloody right hand and tried the knob.

It was locked.

50

Boon was stopped by another boarded door at the bottom of the staircase to the basement. This is slow work, he thought as he raised his foot. Tally'll be dead by the time I get into this goddamn basement. He kicked hard, but the door held.

"Get out of the way!" Mondragon ordered.

Boon turned in surprise as the captain's thick hand grabbed his shoulder and moved him aside. Before he could put up an argument, the old man sat heavily on the third stair, planted the soles of his wing tip shoes against the door, and shoved.

"Use your—*leg muscles*," the old man said, cords standing out on his thick neck. "That's the . . . SECRET!" The door burst open with a crash.

The hissing came from straight ahead.

"Go up and get masks," Boon said. "Aidmen. All the backup you can find. I'm going in."

"Not into that gas," the dragon said in a nasal voice. He was holding his nose.

"*Go up!*" Boon said. He doubled his handkerchief and held it over his face. He was walking toward the elevator banks when a light hit him in the eyes like a fist.

"No move!" a voice called out.

He reacted instinctively. "Get that outa my face!" He tried to duck and raised a forearm over his eyes.

"No move! *I shoot!*"

Boon saw Ugo, the janitor, standing thirty or forty feet down the long corridor. A nasty little snubnose trembled in his hand.

"What—?"

"You no talk. *I* talk!"

"Take it easy," Boon said softly.

"I tella you—*no talk!*" The janitor shut one eye like a child playing with a cap pistol, leaned backward, and straightened his shooting arm.

"Take it easy," Boon said in a voice barely strong enough to carry over the sound of the gas. "I'm not here to hurt you."

His own gun was in his belt. He started to work his hands around to it, but the janitor jabbed him in the eyes with the flash and said, "Raise! Raise or—*dead!*"

Boon raised. "Whatta you want, Ugo?"

The janitor didn't respond. His dark gray eyes were as wide as racquet balls, and he seemed to be keeping up a stream of talk under his breath. He darted a glance toward the elevator and said, "*Strega.* Witch."

"What?"

"I make *dead.*"

Boon realized the man intended to hold him at gunpoint till the gas had finished off Tally. How long would it take? Minutes? Seconds? He moved into the light beam in short shuffling steps. "Okay, buddy," he said, "just stay cool. Nobody's gonna hurt you. Remember me? I'm Johnny Boon. From upstairs? Put that thing down, Ugo. I'll get you whatever you want."

The muzzle of the gun lowered a few degrees till it pointed at Boon's stomach. The flashlight wobbled up and down his body and returned to his face. A gush of strange words filled the hollow corridor: "*Nazi-Fascisti! Nazi-Fascisti! Non sono partigiano, non sono comunista . . . !*"

All Boon could remember from the street was *amigo*, so he said it in the same voice a trainer would use on a nervous dog.

Ugo didn't react. The pistol shook in his right hand as though it was alive. Dangerous. Even if he doesn't want to fire, Boon said to himself, he might squeeze one off by mistake. Those accidental slugs can whack you out just like the intentional ones.

"*Amigo amigo mi amigo,*" Boon chanted softly. He had narrowed the distance between them, but the pace was too slow. In the bottom of that elevator pit a policewoman was being gassed. The manual counseled time and patience in dealing with mentals, but the manual didn't cover this situation.

"You and me, we always been friends," Boon said, insinuating his body forward. As he stepped into point-blank range, he twisted his upper body to reduce the size of the target.

The janitor babbled in the strange tongue, almost as though he were addressing an audience. To Boon, he didn't look or sound like a man who would kill, but fools were hard to read; fools smiled over dead humans and cried over dead birds.

"Let's talk about this," Boon said in the warmest voice he could muster. "Whatever you want, I'm gonna get it for ya. Whatever you're afraid of, I'm not gonna let it hurt you. That's my job. Okay? *Comprendo?*"

Ugo twitched, but he didn't respond.

"I'm coming nice and slow. You get me? *Slow and easy.* And you're gonna lay that gun in my hand. Okay, friend?"

He continued his shuffle. The janitor stepped backward. "No. *No!* STOP!" The wide eyes opened wider.

Boon stopped. Mustn't spook the guy. Keep smiling, *keep smiling!* He remembered how time seemed to stretch out in situations like this; seconds lengthened into minutes; the mind moved to a special rhythm of its own. Every cop knew the feeling.

He tried not to think of Anna, but she wouldn't leave his thoughts. Good-bye, babes, he mumbled to himself, I shoulda said I loved you. He raised his palms to shield his face, then lowered them and resumed his approach. At this range it didn't much matter where he got it.

The hiss sounded weaker. The janitor frowned and said, "I shoot you."

"No, *amigo,*" Boon said evenly. "You won't shoot a friend."

He fought an impulse to spring across the last few feet and close with this nut. Or go for his own gun. The worst shame was to strike out with the bat on your shoulder.

He realized the idea was self-defeating, just as foolish as jumping for the elevator cable would have been. The situation didn't call for gymnastics. Confrontations seldom did. Gymnastics were for phony heroes.

He stopped, then took one more short step. "*No!*" the janitor called out. They were four or five feet apart.

"*Amigo.*"

"You stoppa *now!*"

"Hand it over, Ugo." He held out his palm.

The janitor sighted down the barrel.

He'll fire now, Boon said to himself. Now or never. I'll know in a second—or maybe I won't. God damn it, I never bugged out on a cop in trouble before.

His mind flashed the words JOHN DOE BOON, DE-
CEASED. He imagined himself dead, saw how his death
would smooth the edges of his reputation. That was the
way it always worked with cops. Good old Johnny Boon.
Son of a bitch never backed down. Right to the end . . .
A dead Johnny Boon would be respectable, even admir-
able. A dead Johnny Boon would be . . . somebody.

But dead lasts an awful long time. . . .

He sensed a change in the air.

The hissing was barely audible. Oh, Jesus, Tally got the
full dose. She's gone. . . .

He started to take the last few steps and suddenly
stopped. Something was approaching from down the
corridor. He saw it over the janitor's shoulder: a light
bobbing and jerking in the darkness like a miner's head
lamp. He thought it was his backup, entering from a side
door. He hoped to God they didn't open fire.

"No move!" the janitor said, glittering eyes fixed on
Boon.

"No move," Boon repeated, holding his hands high.

The light came closer, and he made out the bulk of a
large man, clothes hanging like rags, one foot bare.
Jesus, it was that crazy artist. What the hell—?

He was carrying something in his arms. As Boon
watched, Gamble stopped and let his load slip silently to
the floor.

It was a body, shrouded in black.

The big man resumed his slow march like an oversized scarecrow brought to life. In his outstretched hand
he held a kerosene lamp three or four inches high. His
pale face was cut in three or four places. He looked as
though he had just stepped from a grave.

The janitor would hear him any second. The gas had
almost stopped.

The artist bumped into the wall, righted himself, and
staggered on like a movie monster. A drop of blood fell

from one of his hands. Oh, Jesus, Boon thought, he's not stopping. He's too *close*. He's a dead man now for sure.

The janitor spun and screamed, "*Gigant'!*"

Gamble broke the kerosene lamp over his head.

Boon heard a click. Another click. The fool was trying to fire his piece.

Boon fired his.

Ugo's eyes crossed beneath his flaming hair. Gun and flashlight slid across the floor as he fell on his side. He looked past Boon with a crazy fire-struck grin and said, "Babbo." Blood welled from a hole in his chest.

Boon beat out the flames with his hands. He grabbed the gun and broke it open. Empty. "Sorry, pal," he said gently. "You shoulda told me."

The janitor murmured, "Babbo babbo babbo. . . ." A bloody bubble popped from his mouth.

Boon looked up and stared at Gamble. The artist stared back, his eyes glazed, his mouth working as if he were trying to speak. He looked like somebody about to collapse. "Thanks," Boon said, and rushed toward the elevator pit.

It was a short drop to the top of the elevator cage. He landed on the steel X that crossed over the top. The spent tank lay off to the side. Something was scribbled in bold letters on a tag wired to the valve. Boon squinted and read "JUSTICE BLDG. LUNCHEONETTE." The side of the tank said "CO_2."

Carbon dioxide!

He tried to remember.

CO_2 isn't poisonous. It's heavier than air. It can suffocate.

Tally's drowning . . . or drowned.

He kicked through the flimsy ceiling and crashed to the floor of the elevator. She was sprawled on her side.

"Somebody gimme a hand!" he hollered upward.

A face in a gas mask peered down the shaft. He raised her body over his head in a dead lift. She was surprisingly light.

A uniformed cop straddled the crossbar and pulled her through. Boon accepted a hand up.

Tally lay on the floor, out cold. "Gimme your jacket!" he ordered one of the cops. He stretched it across her body. "Another one!" he said, and a suit coat flew down. He raised his head and saw Mondragon. He arranged the old man's coat and laid it under her head.

He grabbed for a pulse. He felt a rapid heartbeat and realized it was his thumb. Slow down, stupid, he told himself. Quit acting like a nervous rook.

More cops rushed into the room behind their black Kellites. "Where's the aidmen?" Boon asked.

"On the way," a muffled voice said.

He leaned over and touched her disheveled brown hair. *I'm sorry, Tally.* This seemed to be his new role: apologizing to women. Well, I *am* sorry. Never shoulda let you come down here by yourself. . . .

He put his ear over her mouth, but he couldn't hear breathing. He licked the palm of his hand and cupped it over her nose, but no air came out to cool his skin.

He tilted her head to clear the air passages. He pinched her nostrils shut and leaned over her mouth and blew.

Her chest swelled under him. He waited five or six seconds and blew in another lungful, then another, and another.

Come on, Tally, he begged, you can do it. He tried to remember if he'd smoked a Swisher lately; God, she'd flat refuse to revive if she got one whiff. He realized that the hyperventilation was making him light-headed.

He lifted his head and looked at her chest. No motion. He had gone back to work when someone pulled him by the shoulder and said, "Give me room!"

The aidman pounced on her body. "Can you do anything?" Boon asked, aware that he sounded like a scared kid. "Is she—?"

The paramedic tore open her gray police shirt and laid his stethoscope pad between her breasts. Then he turned slowly and looked up at Boon.

"You did the job," he said.

Another aidman crouched and jabbed her arm. She breathed in spasms and jerks. In a few seconds she shuddered the length of her body; her eyes widened and shut and widened again.

"Who?" she said weakly.

"Don't talk," he said. The same instruction he'd been giving her for three days.

Her head turned. Her mouth fell open. Spit appeared on her lips, and both her nostrils began to run. She looked beautiful.

He dried her face with dainty pats of his handkerchief. She blinked up at him; the gold flecks were back in her eyes.

"What kept you?" she asked.

51

Ferragosto evening. The sun has just slid behind the peak of Monte Sole. *The Virgin has kept every promise, and Babbo is back!*

Ugo walks the tilted path with his father, his Mamma, dear Nonna, little Maxmein, Aunt Livia, Uncle Duilio in his silly hat made of a handkerchief with knots at the corners. The feast is over; other families are strolling the flanks of the mountain in serpentine files, holding up flaming torches, the children running and jumping and singing songs about the boy of Pordoia and the mortar that stuck in the mud and the pig that ate the truffles and grew too rich to sell.

But the Ruggieros are far ahead, almost to the peak, chattering and laughing and touching, so happy to be together that they sometimes stop and embrace and clap one another on the back. Higher and higher they climb, into rarefied air, into charged incandescent air, until at last a single brilliant shaft angles down from the clouds and bathes them in celestial light.

Babbo takes Ugo's hand and leads the way. At the rear come the women, each of them holding aloft her own left-over *specialità*, as the family Ruggiero ascends.

52

Boon went with the search party, flashlights bobbing against the old walls. He found himself wishing he were still facing the janitor. At least he knew how to handle that situation. What would he say if he rounded a bend and there was Annaliese? How would he react? Stupid thinking. If he found her alive, what difference would it make how he reacted?

Halfway down a junk-filled corridor he heard a small voice behind a locked door and kicked it in. His flashlight picked out a boy in short pants and a white protective helmet. He was sitting in a corner, saying, "Offa Wiggum? Offa Wiggum. . . ?"

"Sammy?" Boon asked.

"Sam-u-el," the child corrected. Big brown eyes blinked behind oversize horn-rims. "Offa Wiggum?"

Boon didn't understand. He took the child by both hands. "Hey, man, good to see ya."

An aidman led the boy toward the door. "His mother's name's Betty Schulte, with a *c*," Boon said. "Call her right away."

The next few rooms were empty, but the door to the old morgue was open wide. On a counter he found a burned-out candle and a bottle with something floating inside. He looked closer. A . . . liver? No, a heart. *God, let it be Candy's. . . .*

A uniformed cop stuck his face in the door and said, "Hey, Sarge, c'mere."

Boon followed to the old office of the jail. The cop played his light across a table covered with food: Hostess pies in their wrappers, Tastykakes and Ding Dongs, Twinkies and Sara Lee brownies, trays piled high with cold cuts and cheeses, a small ham in clear jelly, sausages and hot dogs hanging from a makeshift wire rack, four or five kinds of sliced bread laid out in rows, beaded bottles of Petri white and Virginia Dare and a gallon jug of Mountain Red, and at one end of the table the head of a young pig, the eyes poked out, a stubby candle inside the mouth casting shadowgraphs of teeth against the wall.

"Sergeant Boon?" another voice called out. "We need a supervisor."

Followed by three or four officers, he walked down the corridor. A potbellied cop gestured toward the old holding cells around the corner and whispered in an awed voice, "We found . . . people."

Boon began to shake. He clasped moist palms and tried not to bend at his jellied knees. He prayed to himself: God let it be her. Oh, God, please, *please,* let it be my Anna. There isn't anything I won't do from here on in, God, you just name it. . . .

There were four holding cells, two of them locked. A tall cop was trying the keys on his belt and having no luck. Boon shone a flashlight through the view window. A angry-looking female stared back at him.

She wasn't Anna.

"Get pry bars," he said.

"Wait!" the cop with the keys said. He pulled the door open, and a heavy woman in black robes stumbled out as though pursued.

"Judge Holder?" Boon asked.

"That's right," the heavyset woman answered in a squealy voice. "What in the name of God's going on here?"

"I wish I could tell ya," Boon answered. He signaled to one of the uniformed men to lead her upstairs and turned to the other locked door.

The cop with the keys opened it, and Boon took a hesitant step into the darkness. "*Anna?*" he whispered.

A weak voice answered, "Is it . . . John?"

He stumbled toward the sound. As he reached the cot that hung from the wall, a hand came out and encircled his. "Babes," he said. "You okay?"

"So . . . tired," she answered.

He dropped to his knees and rubbed the back of her hand.

"I, uh . . . missed ya," he said.

53

Gamble opened his eyes on a field of muted white. With a few random watercolor disks, it could have been a Miro. He lay motionless, his body coming to life ache by ache. He tried to imagine where he could be. It was as though someone had photographed him lying on his rock ledge in the dark, and he had wandered into the negative: white now where it had been black before.

He smelled alcohol, the clean antiseptic scent of bandages, unperfumed soap. A light breeze wafted across his face, bringing the faintest odor of the city. He heard a trio of faint bongs and knew he was in a hospital or a department store.

He turned his head lazily and saw Margot in the next bed, eyes closed, face relaxed. Her long black hair had been tied in the back with a green ribbon.

He strained to watch her bed sheet, then relaxed as he saw that her breathing was regular. He started to get up and cross to her but decided not to disturb her sleep. He raised his hands; the right one was swathed in bandages.

He dropped back on the pillow. The last he remembered, he had been carrying her down a basement corridor. Was the danger over? Yes. Margot was back. Her loss had been the only danger.

He lay motionless, trying to fill in the gaps. He wished he were completely at peace, but he wasn't. Not quite. She was safe, yes, but by one drunken act he had erected a wall between them. It might be insignificant, and it might be insurmountable, but it would always be there. . . .

He dozed, awoke to the rustle of sheets, turned, and saw that she was staring at him with her deep brown eyes. He gave her a quizzical look, and she nodded and smiled. His long arm flopped across the space between them, and she reached out and touched his bandage and said weakly, "Oh, angel, what happened?"

He told her about the chisels and the three-inch wall and the cops who wouldn't search for a missing person, and she told him how the janitor had lured her into the elevator and the next thing she knew she was being locked in a cell.

They talked for an hour, and he felt himself growing stronger, flourishing in their old symbiosis, but he carefully avoided any mention of Ciel or Brooks. He was deep in an explanation of what had drawn him to the underground when he looked across and saw that her eyes had fallen shut. "And they lived happily ever after," he whispered, half in hope. She exhaled so hard that her lower lip wobbled.

There would be a better time for confession. The physical hurts would heal; he had no idea how she would react to the other. But if he didn't tell her, it would remain a secret between him and Ciel. And that was another form of betrayal.

"Margot," he whispered, "I love you." He could have sworn she smiled.

54

Tally heard a voice from miles away: "You awake?" A man. Someone she knew. She decided she was still dreaming. What would *he* be doing here?

She tried to remember the last time she'd been conscious. A few hours ago, before she'd dozed off again, Carl Mondragon had sat at her bedside, holding her hand, and told her what had happened. Or had that been a dream, too?

"Police work chews you up and spits you out." Had Carl really said that? Or was it her father, years ago?

Whoever said it, she decided, it's the truest truth. May it please the court, I offer into evidence Sgt. J. Boon. His job has masticated him into something less than human. And yet he offered his life to save mine. Carl said he didn't hesitate a second. . . .

She opened her tired eyes. "Oh," she said. "You. What time is it?"

"Five to eight," Boon answered.

"Is it . . . Friday?" she asked.

"All day," he said. "How ya feeling?"

She took a deep breath, and the tape that bound her bruised ribs squeezed back. The pain was still there, but it was dulled. She was full of dope; she hoped it wouldn't make her say anything stupid. "I feel okay," she answered. Not too bad for a starter.

"Don't talk. The nurse said you should just listen. I

told her, 'That'll be a first.' "

She felt the laugh in her rib cage. "Please," she begged him. "No funnies."

"The nurse told me that, too. She said don't make that poor woman laugh, she's had enough humor for one day."

A definition popped into her mind. Sadist: someone who refuses to beat a masochist. Or makes a rib patient laugh. "Carl was here," she said. "He told me what happened. Sorta." She turned and looked at him. "I think he must've left a few things out." His pale blue eyes with the dark centers only confused her more.

"Name ten."

"The janitor. Was he really . . . cutting out hearts?" She pulled the sheet up to her chin.

"That was the plan, near's we can tell."

She shuddered.

"Course, my snitch made it easy for him, kicking off in the elevator. Doc Madona cut up that bottled heart and diagnosed, uh, mild cardial infraction, I think he called it. Candy musta been fighting the gas, and his heart gave out."

"The janitor, he, he took the heart from . . . *a dead body*?" The more she learned, the sicker it got. Maybe she should ask for a moratorium till she felt better. Or maybe she should be taking notes on her Minitex. No, she had enough tapes. And one tape she wished to God she didn't have.

A nurse swept into the room ahead of a flying gray ponytail. "How're we feeling tonight?" she asked.

"We're fine," Boon said.

"Remember now," the nurse said, puffing the pillow and heading back out the door without slowing down, "you're not to get excited. Understand?" She was gone.

Tally's head swam with Boon's latest information, but she had to know more. "Do you honestly think he would've cut up the others?" Tally asked.

"Looks that way. Gamble's wife—"

"Gamble?"

"The artist. She was in a drug coma when he hauled her out. Looked like someone had prepped her for surgery."

"Gamble hauled her out?"

"Yeah. You were a mile ahead of me, Tally, but he was a mile ahead of everybody."

"Sammy's okay?"

"His mom and uncle came for him right away. George said it was all our fault. Said we shoulda seen what was happening. Said—can I repeat it?"

She smiled. The proper Victorian again. "Repeat it," she told him. "If I go into shock, push this buzzer."

"George takes me aside and says, 'Alla you cops got shit for brains.' I says, 'Hey, man, if it wasn't for Officer Wickham, everybody'd be dead by now.' He stops and thinks, and then he says, 'A stopped clock's right twice a day.' "

She started to laugh, and the adhesive bit into her sides. "You promised not to be funny."

"Blame Uncle George."

"How about . . . your wife?"

"Anna? She's fine. We talked for two hours. Longest since . . . Longest we *ever* talked."

"That makes me feel good."

He frowned. "I been meaning to ask you. Why were you holding empty?"

She knew he'd get around to that. "Oh, I'd *never* carry a loaded gun," she said.

He whistled under his breath. "You're a cop!"

"I don't care."

"Did you ever stop to think that's a dangerous habit for a police officer?"

"Did you ever stop to think it saved your life?"

His face showed that he hadn't. "How'd the hell'd you pass inspection?" he asked.

"I kept clean rounds in my locker."

"What about snap inspections?"

She was going back to Stanford in a month; she could afford to give away her secrets. "I always excused myself to go to the bathroom. Picked up my bullets on the way. Same way you men exchange your hot loads and dum-dums."

He smiled slyly. The real J. Boon—an elemental force of nature, like a typhoon. Stashing extra bullets was something he could understand.

"The paper ran your picture," he said proudly. "You're a hero."

"A *hero*? I'm the wrong sex."

"A hero*ine* then?" He pronounced it "hero-een," like a first grader. He had so many childish characteristics. He reminded her of a baby elephant, blundering through the brush, crushing other forms of life. Steinbeck's Lenny. Except that Lenny didn't pack a badge and gun . . .

She deliberately closed her eyes and tried to think. *Damn you, Boon, for making me owe you! For all you knew, one whiff of that gas could kill. And yet you walked into that crazy man's gun and jumped in the elevator pit to save me. Why?*

She knew the answer. *Because that's what cops do.* Who else would take on work like that? Dr. Spock? Henry Kissinger? Ever since she'd set foot in the Justice Building she'd had to make her peace with necessary evils: strip cells, body searches, Mace, CS spray, guns and slap-jacks and blackjacks and truncheons, the everyday tools of the cop. Was Johnny Boon a necessary evil, too?

She turned and studied his face. He was nodding; he probably couldn't wait to finish up this courtesy call and light up one of his foul little cigars.

"Boon?" she said.

He yawned and smiled at her through the grillwork of his fingers. *What would her father have done about that taped confession?*

"Oh," he said. "You're awake?"

"Sure. Are you?" *He'd have turned it in.*

"Yeah. I was just thinking about my wife and stuff." He acted as though he wanted to say more.

"Your wife and stuff?"

He sighed, got up and walked to the window, and spoke with his back to the bed. "One Christmas me and my brother Richie asked for a beagle." His voice was unexpectedly gentle. "We got a duck instead. We put it on a leash and took turns walking it all day long, and it . . . it died."

"Of what?" she asked, trying to understand.

"Of not being a beagle, I guess."

Lordie Lord, what was the man talking about now?

"I should of learned from that. Maybe a person can change, but he never oughta try to change anything else. Animals, I mean." He turned. His face was flushed. "I mean, uh, ducks . . . uh, *people*. That make any sense?"

"*Quack*," she said without thinking. It must be the dope.

He stood up. "You need rest," he said.

"Wait." She took her purse off the night table and rooted around in the bottom. "Here," she said.

He turned the little package over in his hand. "What's this?"

"A minitape."

"Of who?"

"You."

"Me? *You taped me*? Saying what?" His eyes opened wide.

"Never mind. It was strictly by accident. Think of it as . . . a memento. Something to remind you of what you sound like. Sometimes."

He looked more nervous than angry. "You're full of surprises," he said, edging toward the door. "I gotta go say good-night to Anna."

She beckoned him with her finger. "Come . . . here," she said weakly.

He bent over her face, and she kissed his stubbly

cheek. "Good-bye, Boon."

He popped up like a jack-in-the-box, eyes rolling. Halfway out the door he called over his shoulder, "So long, uh . . . partner."

55

Gamble awoke from a deep sleep and tried to figure where he was. The night light flickered over a shiny porcelain sink. He was in the hospital with Margot. The ordeal was over. Most of it.

Every cell in his body felt as though it had been laundered. He had no idea how long he had slept, but he knew it hadn't been a catnap. He lifted his watch from the night table: 11:35.

"A hundred and sixty-four cents for your thoughts?"

"*What?*" He almost jumped. Margot lay in shadow on her side, her fine black hair arrayed like a halo. "How long have you been watching me?" he asked.

"About an hour," she said. "I've been thinking about . . . us. How *lucky* . . ."

Down on the bay, a ferry whistle sounded, then repeated. He turned away as he remembered what he hadn't told her. Would she still think they were lucky when she knew? "Where're you getting the energy?" he asked, fidgeting.

"From hospital food, can you believe it? That's all that was wrong with me. Hunger. I've been a glutton. And you've been Sleeping Beauty. Ten hours nonstop."

He couldn't figure out a way to deliver the news gradually. "Margot, honey, I've got to tell you something."

"I know it already," she said. "You love me. Love my liver. Love my big toes. Love my . . . certain other areas. Oh, Sev, I feel so *horny.*" She whispered the word.

"Baby, that's not it. I mean . . ." He decided to spit it out, quick and dirty. "The night you went to your mother's?" he said, looking at the ceiling.

"Yes?" She echoed his serious tone.

"And I had the hot bath with Brooks and uh . . . Ciel—?"

"Oh, *that's* it," she interrupted. "You and Ciel."

She didn't sound surprised or annoyed. Had Ciel talked? Denied him the right to make his own confession?

"Because if you *are,*" Margot went on, "then *don't.* I worked it out in my mind, and I'd just as soon not be reminded."

"Worked what out?"

"I knew something was weird as soon as I came back from Mother's," Margot said. "Because . . . I asked you what you did while I was gone and you kept avoiding the subject. Then Ciel took me to lunch, and *she* was different, too."

So Ciel had talked. He might have known.

"She was kind of squirmy. I've known her a long time, Sev. She's an open book, just like you. So I asked a few questions."

"When was this?"

"Two days after . . . the night."

"You've known since then?"

She nodded. "I was pretty sure. Then you talked in your sleep and gave it all away. I thought a lot, and I . . . I had two choices. Leave or stay. I decided to stay, Sev. Simple as that."

He pushed up on one elbow and stared across at her. "I wish I understood."

"Someday you will. When you learn to quit being so hard on yourself. When you realize you're—what's the expression?—a good and decent man? One dumb drunken mistake can't change that."

He felt childishly transparent. "Why didn't you say

something? Why didn't you throw a lamp, kick me in the balls, anything?"

"Because I love you."

His throat ached. He was brushing one of his bandaged hands across his eyes when he felt the sheet lift off his naked side and her cool body crawl in alongside.

"Sev, make me one promise, will you?"

"Anything," he said, trying to regain his composure.

"The next time you get lonely and I'm away, would you just . . . see a movie?"

He laughed to keep from crying and reached for her. As he did, she slid out of bed and stood up. He wondered if this was the way she was going to punish him. He wouldn't blame her.

He watched as she walked unsteadily to the door and snapped the lock. As she turned around, her white cotton gown slipped slowly to the floor.

56

It was midnight. Boon had stayed with Anna till the nurse threw him out, but he still had things to do before he went to bed.

His monkey suit hung in the closet under clear plastic, every crease sharp, shoulders stuffed with tissue, the chevrons and service stripes and commendation ribbons all sewn in place by Anna with invisible stitches.

He laid the uniform across the kitchen table, reached high in the cupboard for the Brasso, borrowed a rag from Anna's supply, and rubbed till the buttons shone.

He unsnapped his badge and his cap piece and dumped them in a shallow saucepan, added lukewarm water, and sprinkled in some Drano. While he was waiting for the tarnish to disappear, he rubbed the brim of his cap with a cotton rag, added a thin coating of Kiwi neutral, buffed the brim to a mirror shine with spit, and finished off with a light spray of Endust from Anna's pantry.

He pulled out his battered old patrol shoes, laid on a coat of Kiwi black, brushed it off, and repeated the operation twice. He shined the shoes with a long cotton rag and daubed on a double coat of sole dressing.

He arranged his Sam Browne belt, gun holster, cuff case, and ID pouch on a sheet of newspaper and rubbed them lightly with neat's-foot oil. He shined his handcuffs, sprayed Endust on his plastic nameplate, rubbed the black residue off the rims of every bullet on his belt, drowned his shield and cap piece in cold water, and made them sparkle in the kitchen light with a new flannel rag.

Then he started to dress.

Just after midnight he walked into the detective bureau, looking over both shoulders. For as long as he could remember, he had tried to avoid good-byes; they were like that long ending of Shostakovich's Fourth: too intense, too painful, on and on and on till you wished it would just quit. There'd been too many good-byes.

He pulled out his file drawer and slammed it shut. He'd be a week writing status reports. It would have to wait till after his trip with Anna.

His phone rang. He picked it up and said, "Boonhomicide," without thinking.

"Dispatch office," a voice said. "I saw your light. A guy in the drunk tank just copped to the Hayden Harrier killing."

"Hayden *who?*"

"The old man at the beach. One slug in the temple?"

"Oh, yeah."

"I thought you might want to take the confession."

"Maybe later," Boon said. He put the phone down. Somebody else could clean it up. Funny how important that case had seemed a few days ago.

He slipped a fingernail into one of his albums and flipped it open. Page after page . . . Sure is an awful lot of fools, he said to himself. God must love killers and muggers and crooks, he made so many of them. Well, there's one less tonight. Too bad I had to shoot him. He was just a crazy.

He slid his resignation papers under the captain's door and walked past the chalkboard with the words *Time Out* and *Expected*. He rode the No. 2 elevator, cocked his ear for a hiss, hurried past the mural with the blimp and the trains and the boats, and shoved open the big brass doors. Halfway down the outside steps he turned and looked back and mumbled, "So long, Richie." He didn't know why.

Jack Olsen is the author of twenty books, published in eleven countries and nine languages, including such noted works of nonfiction as SILENCE ON MONTE SOLE, NIGHT OF THE GRIZZLIES, THE BRIDGE AT CHAPPAQUIDDICK, THE GIRLS IN THE OFFICE *and* THE MAN WITH THE CANDY—*the story of the Houston mass murders—and the novels* ALPHABET JACKSON, MASSY'S GAME, THE SECRET OF FIRE FIVE *and* NIGHT WATCH. *His shorter works appear in many anthologies. An award-winning journalist for newspapers in Washington, New Orleans and Chicago, he was a chief correspondent for* TIME *magazine and senior editor of* SPORTS ILLUSTRATED. *He now makes his home on an island in Puget Sound, Washington.*